The Spirit of Protestantism

THE SPIRIT OF PROTESTANTISM

by *ROBERT McAFEE BROWN*

Jesus Christ is the same yesterday and today and forever.
Hebrews 13:8

But we have this treasure in earthen vessels to show that the transcendent power belongs to God and not to us.
2 Corinthians 4:7

New York OXFORD UNIVERSITY PRESS 1961

Library of Congress Catalogue Card Number: 61-8367

Third Printing, April 1963

Printed in the United States of America

FOR MY CHILDREN,

Peter (11) and Mark (8), who helped me rearrange the pages that Alison (3) had examined one morning after we had all been awakened at a very early hour by Thomas (6 months).

Foreword

This book has been written with five kinds of readers in mind:

1. *Perplexed Protestants.* I am aware that there are many Protestants who are either genuinely perplexed about their Protestant heritage, or have worked through enough perplexities so that they are ready to venture further. To such Protestants this book is offered as a next step.

2. *Wistful pagans.* This is a descriptive and not an abusive term. It describes the many people who would *like* to believe if they could, and who are willing to listen to one who affirms a faith they cannot yet share. Such readers will not, of course, be converted by a book, and after reading this one they will still be able to find many reasons not to believe, for there is no attempt here to "sell" Protestantism by exaggerating its virtues, ignoring its vices, or slanting the facts to produce the most desirable effect. Protestant faults get at least equal time with Protestant virtues in the pages that follow — this is the way the Reformation continues. Furthermore, readers unconvinced by what they read here will not have proof that Protestantism is unconvincing. They will merely have proof that the author of this book has been an unworthy servant, and they can be sure that Protestantism has outlasted many such.

3. *Concerned Roman Catholics.* This does not mean Roman Catholics who are concerned because their faith is wavering, but those who are concerned about the present Protestant-Catholic impasse, and who want to take the first step beyond that impasse, which is to learn something about the faith of their Protestant friends. They will of course find dissent from Roman Catholic belief in this book, or it would not be a Protestant book, but they must be assured that comments about Roman Catholicism are not introduced to score points. There is a type of Protestant insecurity that manifests

itself by the vigor of its attacks on "Romanism," and remains more concerned to demonstrate how wrong Roman Catholics are than how right Protestants are. But I am sure that it is truer to the spirit of Protestantism to turn our polemical barbs in upon ourselves before we essay to cast them at others, and the Protestant capacity for self-criticism, based on loyalty to Jesus Christ, is one of the things I hope Roman Catholic readers will discover as they read.

4. *Inquiring college students.* This book was originally conceived because there appeared to be no comparable Protestant counterpart to Karl Adam's *The Spirit of Catholicism;* namely, a book that tried to describe the faith unashamedly from the *inside* in such a way that it might also communicate to those on the *outside*. I warn the student reader in advance that he will not find here the objective, dispassionate, arm's length treatment he has been taught to admire in academic pursuits. To deal with God's concern for men in such terms would be most *un*academic, since it would be describing something by means of the wrong categories of description. So I shall not worry if the student discerns that I believe in the things I write about; I shall worry only if he fails to discern this.

5. *Beleaguered Protestant ministers.* No Protestant minister will need to have the adjective explained to him. His problem is how, in the midst of the inordinate demands of parish life, he can carve out even a little time for study. This book will not tell him much that he did not learn in seminary, but it may provide him with a point of departure from which he can venture forth to do further reading and reflecting about the faith it is his responsibility to proclaim.[1]

How can one have the audacity to claim that there is such a thing as "the spirit of Protestantism"?

[1] A footnote about footnotes is appropriate here. Save for this one instance, all footnotes will be found at the back of the book. They have been put there (a) because otherwise they would clutter the reading of persons who are not interested in footnotes, (b) because it is convenient to have all bibliographical data assembled in one place for persons who are interested in bibliographical data, and (c) because the publisher insisted that they go there.

The footnotes are included not only to document direct quotations in the text, but even more to provide reading helps for those who wish to pursue any given topic at greater length. They are occasionally employed also to indicate other places in the present volume where a given theme is pursued at greater length.

Surely the patent facts of Protestant discord and division suggest a more modest title, perhaps "the spirit of Protestant*isms,*" or "the spirit*s* of Protestantism."

Even if there *were* a spirit of Protestantism, no Protestant could write about it in the definitive way, for example, that Karl Adam writes about the spirit of Catholicism. Catholicism is "there." It has recognizable boundaries. It has discernible practices. It has infallible dogmas. There is no excuse for a Roman Catholic author to misrepresent the Roman Catholic faith, although few of them can represent it as magnificently as Karl Adam has done.

But Protestantism is not "there"; it is all over the place. It does not have recognizable boundaries; it is extremely difficult to know when an individual or a church has ceased to be Protestant, and whether all who claim the title either deserve or honor it. Protestantism does not have discernible practices; at least, the ones that can be discerned are so inconsistent that it is difficult if not impossible to find a unifying principle of interpretation. Nor does Protestantism have infallible dogmas; at most it has a body of shared convictions, but it also has sharp differences about convictions that are not shared.

How, then, can one have the audacity to write about "the spirit of Protestantism"?

There are two things that can be said in justification of the attempt. The *first* of these is that Protestantism does, in fact, have "a large body of shared convictions." If this seems unapparent to the outsider, he can only be invited to step within and discover that it is so. Although the divergences among Protestant groups are significant (notably in their differing interpretations of the sacraments and the ministry), the convergences among them are nonetheless significant. This means that while Anglicans and Baptists, for example, will certainly not agree with all that is said in the following pages, they should be able to agree with a lot that is said. Many convictions are shared by almost all Protestants, and these can be described at the same time that the differences are being described.

But the matter cannot be left there. The *second* thing that must be said is this: the spirit of Protestantism cannot be conveyed by an outsider's description of what *they* believe; it can only be conveyed by an insider's confession of what *we* believe. The convictions attributed to Protestants in this book are convictions that I hold to be true, and I would serve them ill if I tried to disassociate myself from them. Therefore this book is, whatever else it may be, a personal confession of faith, and when words like "Protestants" or "Protestantism" are used as the subjects of sentences, the reader is at liberty if he so desires to translate these into statements by the author that read, "This is what I believe."

But not just "what *I* believe." For these convictions are not my own creation. They are gifts I have received. Others have received them too, and we are bound together by the fact that we share these common gifts. None of us understands them fully. But all of us believe that one way to understand them more fully is to talk about them — however haltingly — so that the error within our truth may be purged, and the truth within our error may be purified.

No Protestant theologian has a right to be too impressed with his own theologizing. There is something comic, if not downright absurd, about the claim that a human creature can penetrate the veil of holiness surrounding the transcendent God, or describe with accuracy the events that took place when God penetrated that veil himself in the incarnation of his Son.

Rule One for every theologian ought therefore to be, "Don't take yourself too seriously." This is very different from saying, "Don't take your faith seriously." It means that all our attempts to express our faith — excepting liturgy and prayer, and perhaps occasionally even then — must include an echo of laughter. This will sometimes be the laughter of self-mockery at the notion that our fleshly words can encompass the Word made flesh. But it can also be the laughter of delight and pure joy that through the disclosure of his Word in Jesus Christ God has seen fit to allow his creatures the audacity of forming words about him. If anything comes of the words it will not be by the power of the words themselves, but by the grace of the Word made flesh to whom they point.

Authentic religious language is not the language of books and arguments but the language of liturgy and prayer. Singing one of Luther's hymns is usually a deeper means of grace than reading *The Bondage of the Will*. Praying one of Calvin's prayers usually brings one closer to the throne of God than reading his *Letter to Cardinal Sadolet*. Protestantism, when all is said and done, is more adequately represented by its hymns and prayers than by its textbooks. And so the reader will not grasp the spirit of Protestantism by reading this or any other book. But if a book can help him learn to sing and pray, it will not have been in vain.

ROBERT MCAFEE BROWN

St. Andrews, Scotland
June 1960

Acknowledgments

Portions of Chapters 1, 5, 7, 8, and 9 were originally given as lectures at Montview Boulevard Presbyterian Church, Denver, Colorado, and I must express special thanks to the "lay theologians" of Montview Church who acted as indispensable midwives at the birth of what gradually grew into the present book. These lectures were later given as part of a Lenten series at Madison Avenue Presbyterian Church, New York City, and at two Auburn Seminary Extension Institutes in upstate New York. Chapter 13 is drawn in part from my contribution to Scharper (ed.), *American Catholics: A Protestant-Jewish View,* and I am grateful to Sheed & Ward for permission to make such generous use of their copyright material. Chapter 14 is a radical condensation of material first presented in a series of lectures to the Society of Inquiry at New Brunswick Seminary, New Brunswick, New Jersey. I have frequently made use of ideas and expressions contained in my chapter on "Classical Protestantism" in Johnson (ed.), *Patterns of Faith in America Today,* Harper & Brothers, a series of lectures first delivered at Jewish Theological Seminary, New York City.

I am also indebted to the following publishers for permission to quote from works published over their imprint:

A Handbook of Christian Theology, copyright 1958 by Meridian Books. A Living Age Books Original, published by Meridian Books, Inc. Reprinted by permission of Meridian Books, Inc.

W. H. Auden, *The Collected Poetry of W. H. Auden,* Random House, Inc.

Karl Barth, *Church Dogmatics,* I, 2, Charles Scribner's Sons.

Barth-Hamel, *How To Serve God in a Marxist Land,* Association Press.

John F. Clarkson, S.J., and others, *The Church Teaches: Documents of the Church in English Translation,* B. Herder Book Co.

Suzanne de Dietrich, *God's Unfolding Purpose,* copyright 1960 by W. L. Jenkins. The Westminster Press.

Vergilius Ferm, ed., *The Protestant Credo,* The Philosophical Library.

Clifford Howell, S.J., *Of Sacraments and Sacrifice,* The Liturgical Press.

"Community Church" from *Times Three* by Phyllis McGinley, copyright 1946 by Phyllis McGinley, originally printed in *The New Yorker,* and reprinted by permission of The Viking Press, Inc.

C. C. Morrison, in *Presbyterian Life,* March 2, 1957.

C. C. Morrison, *The Unfinished Reformation,* Harper and Brothers.

Lesslie Newbigin, *The Household of God,* Friendship Press, Inc.

H. Richard Niebuhr, "Issues Between Catholics and Protestants at Mid-Century," *Religion in Life,* Spring 1954.

Albert Outler, *The Christian Tradition and the Unity We Seek,* Oxford University Press, Inc.

J. K. S. Reid, *The Authority of Scripture,* Harper and Brothers.

Philip Scharper, "What A Catholic Believes," *Harper's Magazine,* March 1959.

William Temple, *Nature, Man and God,* Macmillan and Company Ltd., and St. Martin's Press, Inc.

Paul Tillich, *The Protestant Era,* The University of Chicago Press, copyright 1948 by the University of Chicago.

Oliver Tomkins, *The Wholeness of the Church,* Student Christian Movement Press, Ltd.

Charles Williams, *The Figure of Beatrice,* Faber and Faber, permission granted by David Higham Associates, Ltd.

All Biblical quotations, unless otherwise noted, are from the Revised Standard Version of the Bible, copyrighted 1946 and 1952 by the Division of Christian Education, National Council of Churches, and are used by permission of the publisher, Thomas Nelson and Sons.

The actual writing of the following pages was completed during a sabbatical leave from Union Theological Seminary, and was made possible by a fellowship grant from the American Association of Theological Schools.

I am grateful for the suggestions given to me by a number of my friends on whom I inflicted various drafts of the work as it was in progress. I also appreciate the labors of certain anonymous "readers" provided by Oxford University Press, whose healthy lack of critical inhibition may have set back the publication date of the book by a year, but who saved me from at least some of the more egregious errors I would otherwise have perpetrated.

I owe a special debt of thanks to Wilbur D. Ruggles of Oxford University Press for originally suggesting the theme of the book, and to both Mr. Ruggles and Miss Marion Hausner for seeing it through the various stages of production with both competence and compassion.

"Time would fail me" if I began to list those who have taught me what is contained in these pages. But I cannot refrain from an expression of special gratitude to three among that number, George W. Webber, Robert W. Lynn, and the late Alexander Miller, who, by their devotion to the church, their theological honesty, and their critical discernment, have over the years given me a more ample understanding of the spirit of Protestantism than I have found in any book or can hope to communicate in this one.

R. M. B.

Contents

PART TWO

CENTRAL PROTESTANT AFFIRMATIONS

PART ONE

Approaching Protestantism: Some Basic Preliminaries

1. The Misunderstandings of Protestantism (what Protestantism is not)

"What is your wife really like? All I know about her is that she has red hair, enjoys science fiction, and dislikes children." If a man says this to me, I have a difficult assignment on my hands. My first task must be to clear up certain misunderstandings. I must convince him that my wife does *not* have red hair, does *not* enjoy science fiction, and does *not* dislike children, before I can begin, however imperfectly, to tell him what she is "really like."

"What is Protestantism really like? All I know about it is that it is negative, and that it means believing whatever you please." If a man says this to me, I have another difficult assignment on my hands. And my first task, once again, must be to clear up certain misunderstandings. I must convince him that Protestantism is *not* negative, and that it does *not* mean believing whatever you please, before I can begin, however imperfectly, to tell him what it is "really like."

So it is not sheer perversity to begin a book about what Protestantism *is,* with some attention to what it is *not*. Since few words have been more widely misunderstood, or more variously defined, than "Protestantism," it will be clear gain if we can exclude some of the more fanciful misunderstandings at the very start.

Four false images

ONE: PROTESTANTISM AS PROTEST AGAINST

To a good many Protestants, and to most non-Protestants, this is the sum of the matter: Protestants are people who protest against things. They protest against the Pope, or against religious authoritarianism, or against card-playing, or against an ambassador to the Vatican. They may not be sure of what they are *for,* but they are very sure of what they are *against.* Mr. T. S. Eliot has given a classic statement of this image: "The life of Protestantism," he writes, "depends on the survival of that against which it protests." [1]

Now to modern ears the word "protest" does carry this negative implication. A baseball game is finished "under protest" because one of the managers thinks the umpire is wrong and so protests against his decision. And it must be acknowledged that *part* of the Protestant witness has this negative quality. Part of the impetus for the Protestant Reformation of the sixteenth century was borne out of the fact that, as Roman Catholic historians are quite prepared to admit, things were in a sorry state in late medieval Christendom, and many practices and beliefs needed to be opposed, protested against, as strongly as possible.[2]

But when all that has been acknowledged and documented, it is still erroneous to describe Protestantism as protest against, and there are at least three reasons why the image is inadequate. *First,* the very word itself has a different meaning, a positive meaning. The verb "to protest" comes from the Latin *pro-testari,* and means not only "to testify," but, more importantly, "to testify *on behalf of* something." Webster's Dictionary gives as a synonym, "to affirm." The Oxford English Dictionary defines it, "to declare formally in public, testify, to make a solemn declaration." The notion of a "protest against error" is only a subsidiary meaning. Thus the actual word itself is charged with positive rather than negative connotations. "To protest," then, in the true meaning of the word, is to make certain affirmations, to give testimony on behalf of certain things.

Second, the image of Protestantism as protest against fails to do justice to the intent of the Protestant Reformers. If the Reformers were *against* certain things, it was only because they were primarily *for* certain other things. The very term "Protestant" was first used at the Imperial Diet of Speyer (1529) by a minority group of Lutherans who disagreed with the majority decision to curtail their rights, and who therefore "protested." But if we read their statement carefully, we discover that they were making rousingly positive assertions. If they rejected churchmanship under the papacy, it was only because they believed that true churchmanship must be exercised under Scripture:

> There is, we affirm, no sure preaching or doctrine but that which abides by the Word of God. According to God's command no other doctrine should be preached. Each text of the holy and divine scriptures should be elucidated and explained by other texts. This Holy Book is in all things necessary for the Christian; it shines clearly in its own light, and is found to enlighten the darkness. We are determined by God's grace and aid to abide by God's Word alone, the Holy Gospel contained in the Biblical books of the Old and New Testaments. This Word alone should be preached, and nothing that is contrary to it. It is the only Truth. It is the sure rule of all Christian doctrine and conduct. It can never fail us or deceive us. Whoso builds and abides on this foundation shall stand against all the gates of hell, while all merely human additions and vanities set up against it must fall before the presence of God.[3]

Third, no faith, Protestantism least of all, lives by its denials. The denials, unless they are simply neurotic, are by-products of the affirmations. To believe in salvation by grace, for example, means opposing salvation by works, just as today, by the same logic, to believe in racial integration means opposing segregation. The important thing is that the negative consequence grows out of the positive affirmation, and not vice versa. Contemporary Protestants actually distort and destroy their faith when they emphasize its negative rather than its positive assertions.

TWO: PROTESTANTISM AS DILUTED CATHOLICISM

This is a favorite image of aggressive Roman Catholics and wistful Protestants. Roman Catholics, according to this view, believe a great many things which, when taken together, constitute the fullness of the Christian faith, while Protestants believe fewer things and thus possess only part of the Christian faith. Roman Catholics, for example, believe in "all seven sacraments," while Protestants believe in only two.

Now it is quite natural that Roman Catholics should interpret Protestantism in this way. Since for them the Roman Catholic faith is by definition the "full" faith, Protestantism will inevitably appear to lack certain elements of that fullness. And many Protestants often express a certain wistfulness when the dramatic splendor and fullness of Roman Catholicism is contrasted to their own apparent barrenness and simplicity. "Surely," they feel, "we lack something; our faith is simply a faith from which a great deal has been subtracted."

But Protestants who feel this way are reasoning from premises that deny their Protestant heritage. The image rests on a confusion over the meaning of the "fullness" of the faith, particularly as this is related to the words "catholic" and "Roman Catholic." The "fullness" of the faith cannot be defined quantitatively. That is to say, having seven sacraments is not *per se* better than having two. In that case, having twelve would be better still. There is always the possibility that the observance of two sacraments represents the norm, and that the observance of more than two represents a departure from the norm. From the one perspective, having *only* two sacraments seems like an unwarranted diminution, whereas from the other perspective having *more* than two sacraments seems like an unwarranted addition.

Here is a place, in other words, where there is a fundamental and apparently irreconcilable difference of opinion. The image of Protestantism as "diluted Catholicism" is comprehensible from the perspective of the Roman Catholic, the Eastern Orthodox, and perhaps the Anglo-Catholic. But the Protestant who adopts it as a valid description has already abandoned his Protestant stance.

Much the same confusion surrounds the use of the words "catholic" and "Roman Catholic." The Roman Catholic feels quite confident that the words can be used interchangeably, since for him "catholicity" or "wholeness" is found only in that branch of Christendom which acknowledges the bishop of Rome as the vicar of Christ. But Protestants cannot accept this understanding of catholicity, and feel that at certain basic points Roman Catholicism departs from the catholic faith rather than exemplifies it. The equation of "catholic" and "Roman Catholic" must therefore be rejected by Protestants, and with it the notion of Protestantism as diluted Catholicism.[4]

THREE: PROTESTANTISM AS "BELIEVING CERTAIN THINGS"

Protestants with a conservative theological orientation often imply that to be a Protestant is to assent to a group of carefully defined doctrines. High on the list will be a claim about the Bible, usually couched in terms of the doctrine of plenary inspiration (i.e. a belief that the words of the Bible were written down by men whom God inspired in such a way that their writings cannot contain error). Based on this infallible Biblical witness, will be doctrines describing the virgin birth of Christ, the miracles he performed on earth, the saving power of his death, his physical resurrection from the tomb, and his return in glory at the last day. Frequently appended is a description of the everlasting hell fire that awaits those who refuse to believe the doctrines as formulated.

Sometimes the priorities vary. Certain Baptists might deny salvation to those who did not make "believer's baptism" a cardinal tenet. Certain Lutherans might demand explicit recognition that the fullness of the faith is found only within their own brand of Lutheranism. Certain Reformed groups might make belief in double predestination mandatory.

Two kinds of things must be said in assessing this image of Protestantism. On the one hand, there is clarity and precision here, particularly in contrast to the vagueness of much Protestant thought. The Protestants just described have the virtue of knowing where they stand and why. They claim to be the possessors of authentic tidings about God, and they proceed to the necessary task of working out doctrines and statements expressing those tidings.

But having granted that, we must go on to question the adequacy of the image, for it blurs a fundamental distinction — the distinction between *what God does,* and *statements about* what God does.[5] To believe, for example, in "the substitutionary doctrine of the atonement," may be a very different thing from believing that Christ died for me. "Believing the doctrine" almost inevitably becomes a substitute for committing one's life to the God whom the doctrine is trying to describe. Doctrinal statements are not themselves the truth. They are merely attempts to point to the one who said, "I am . . . the Truth." Thus statements of doctrine, and even the words of the Bible must not be confused with the events they are describing. God does not give us doctrines. He gives us himself in Jesus Christ, and the doctrines are no more than our way of attempting to think through what that gift means. We must, to be sure, think it through as well as we possibly can, but what we think must not become the object of our faith. It is only an attempt to express our faith.

FOUR: PROTESTANTISM AS "THE RIGHT OF PRIVATE JUDGMENT"

This familiar phrase describes the most widely accepted image of Protestantism. Protestants who believe the image to be a proper one often defend it in these terms: Until the time of the Reformation, men had to believe what the church told them to believe. There was no freedom of thought. But fortunately Luther and the other Reformers broke the medieval chains and freed men to think for themselves. As a result, Christians no longer have to believe what the church tells them. They can believe what their own private judgment tells them, and nothing must be allowed to violate the integrity of that judgment. If Protestants do not like the beliefs and practices of one denomination, they are free to join another denomination. If they find none with which they can agree, they can start a new denomination, or belong to no denomination at all.

Now whatever we may think about the adequacy of this viewpoint, it is certainly the image that Protestants have communicated to non-Protestants. A Roman Catholic, for example, could scarcely come to any other conclusion, for this is exactly what Protestantism "looks like" to him. Father Clifford Howell, S.J., mirrors this image perfectly, and the accuracy of his description may be measured by the degree to which many Protestants would accept it as adequate:

> The fundamental principle of Protestantism is what is called "the principle of private judgment." Protestants say a man has a right to decide for himself what he will believe; he can choose this or that religion just as he thinks fit. They object to the Catholic Church "dictating" what is true or false, what is right or wrong. That is why they reject the Catholic Church — they "protest" against it . . . They say they will believe, they will behave, and they will worship as they think fit,

not as somebody tells them. *The "principle of private judgment" is the very essence of Protestantism.*[6]

But on at least three counts this image of Protestantism must be rejected as a false image. *First,* it is a serious misunderstanding of the intention of the Reformers to describe them as striking blows for "the right of private judgment." They did not appeal to a new faith of their own, and would have been shocked by such a suggestion. Quite the contrary, as we saw in the quotation on p. 5, they appealed to an old faith they had not invented at all, the faith they rediscovered in their study of Holy Scripture. If they had talked about "the right of private judgment," which they did not, they would have asserted that it was medieval Christendom that had inaugurated the era of "private judgment" by introducing new doctrines not found in Scripture.[7]

So much can be proven by reading the Reformers. But this does not necessarily establish the inadequacy of "the right of private judgment." For many Protestants will respond, "That's the whole trouble. The Reformers remained medievalists at heart. We must finish the task they couldn't complete, by making the right of private judgment the cornerstone of our faith today."

So a *second* thing must be said, and it is this: the important thing in the Christian faith is not what we decide about God, but what God decides about us. If what we decide about God is the decisive matter, then all things are permitted. If it is my "private judgment" that God has red hair and dislikes children (whatever he may feel about science fiction), then that is the end of the matter, for one opinion is just as good as another opinion in this particular court. There is no higher court of appeal. But the Christian gospel has a "given-ness" about it that clearly defies this kind of treatment. It offers no assurance that God will accommodate himself to the ways we choose to define him. The right of private judgment, then, refashions God on our terms, rather than recognizing that the important thing is for God to refashion us on his terms.

In the *third* place, the right of private judgment is closely linked to the expression of religious individualism. It is hard to relate the notion of private judgment and the notion of community. This is not to say that differences of opinion cannot exist within a church, but rather to say that when differences of opinion are accepted as *normative,* and one opinion is quite as valid as another, the survival of the community becomes more and more problematic and perhaps even undesirable. Christian faith must then be defined in individualistic rather than corporate terms. If to some this seems a desirable definition of Christian faith, they must at least acknowledge that it is a novel one. To whatever degree, therefore, the right of private judgment is exalted, the concept of the church is imperiled, and Protestantism proceeds further down a self-appointed path to death by anarchy.

Having made these harsh judgments about private judgment, it is only fair that we ask what truth lies imbedded in the phrase. For no matter how mixed up it may be with error, there is a real truth here, and it can be stated thus: while the right of private judgment does not mean that I can make up my own gospel, it does mean that I must make my own decision about the gospel that is proclaimed to me. No one else can make that decision for me. "The right of private judgment" also means "the need for personal decision," and in these terms few things could be more characteristic of the spirit of Protestantism. For part of the urgency of the Protestant message has always been the insistence that I must decide — for or against. I must be *involved* in the truth or falsity of the Christian claim.[8] This personal dimension of faith has a particularly Protestant significance.

Now it must be quite clear that the judgment or decision we make is not a judgment about something that is our own creation, or we would merely be repeating the wrong notion of "the right of private judgment." We decide about something that comes *to* us, rather than about something that comes *from* us. "Did we in our own strength confide," Luther sings, and Protestants sing with him, "our striving would be losing." Rather than trusting the strength in ourselves, Luther continues, we trust the strength that comes from God in Jesus Christ, who is "the Right Man on our side, the Man of God's own choosing." [9]

He makes the same point just as vigorously elsewhere:

> And this is the reason that our doctrine is [most sure and] certain, because it carrieth us out of ourselves, that we should not lean to our own strength, our own conscience, our own feeling, our own person,

and our own works; but to that which is without us, that is to say the promise and truth of God which cannot deceive us.[10]

If Luther's point is clearly understood, but only if it is clearly understood, we may say one thing more about the truth in the notion of private judgment. There is a tension between recognizing that "we should not lean to our own strength . . . but to . . . God," and recognizing that "the need for personal decision" is forced upon us. But it is in this tension that the *creativity* of Protestant faith and life is to be found. There can be a venturesomeness in Protestant life and thought that often seems to the non-Protestant Christian to get out of bounds. But it is in this area that new advances, new insights, new understandings of the faith grow. Very often the man who first appears as a heretic turns out to be the one who was recalling Christendom to a long-neglected truth. He may have shouted a little too loudly, as the only way of getting a hearing, but had he not shouted, had he not rocked the boat a little, his fellow Christians might not have become aware that they were heading for dangerous shoals. Protestantism has an obligation to suffer fools gladly lest it stifle the message of one who is a "fool for Christ."

The truth in the false images

We do not define Protestantism simply by denying false images. No more do we define it by assuming that the opposite of a false image will be a true one. But we can get help, even this early in our investigation, by drawing together those elements of truth that can be found even in the false images themselves.

We can assert, therefore, that (1) Protestantism is primarily affirmative, and is negative only in the sense that to affirm one thing is necessarily to deny something else; (2) Protestantism is an interpretation of the wholeness of the Christian faith, rather than a diluted form of it; (3) Protestantism has a genuine content that can be described, but the descriptive statements must always point beyond themselves and must never become the object of faith; (4) Protestantism is man's decision concerning the faith given him by God, rather than man's creation of a faith of his own.

The historian Philip Schaff offers us further help in his description of the Reformation as "a deeper plunge into the meaning of the Gospel than even St. Augustine had made." [11]

"A deeper plunge into the meaning of the gospel . . ." This is an excellent counterbalance to the various misunderstandings of Protestantism. For Protestantism exists to serve that gospel, which is the good news that "in Christ, God was reconciling the world unto himself" (2 Cor. 5:19). He was not content to remain aloof from us, in some far-off heaven, but shared our lot, right up to the very nail prints. In so doing he changed our lot, for by his coming he demonstrated that although we could not get to him, he could come to us, and that he thought we were worth all that was involved in living a life of suffering love and dying an ignominious death. In so doing he conquered the twin enemies of sin and death which hold us in bondage, and emerged as King and Victor, Lord of life and death.

He did all this — for us. For our part, we are asked to trust him, and to be part of the people who live as his witnesses, serving him in the world he created and redeemed, with the promise that our relationship with him will never end.

Anything else we affirm must serve the cause of that gospel.

2. The Catholicity of Protestantism (reform or revolt?)

"When we don't know where we are," a Cambridge don once remarked, "it is sometimes a good idea to take a backward look and discover where we once were. I sometimes have the feeling," he concluded, "that in Cambridge we haven't known where we are for the last 200 years."

Whether or not this is a correct assessment of Cambridge, it is certainly a correct assessment of the importance of the "backward look." We cannot understand twentieth-century Protestantism simply by reference to the twentieth century, and we have already seen that many of the misunderstandings of Protestantism spring from misunderstandings of the Protestant Reformation. We must therefore look back to see where we came from, and why. Only after we have done this, can we look intelligently at twentieth-century Protestantism.

The sixteenth-century movements usually referred to as "the Protestant Reformation" are not easy to assess. Few historical periods have been subjected to such diverse interpretations. Some historians have asserted that the whole period was dominated by nationalistic or economic concerns: the German princes did not want to pay for the support of an Italian Pope, so they backed Luther in order to free the German church from Italian domination. Others have claimed that people in northern Europe simply wanted a cheaper religion, and were willing to trade an expensive church for an inexpensive Bible. Voltaire disposed of the English Reformation by remarking that "England separated from the Pope because King Henry fell in love." Guizot described the Reformation as "a great effort to emancipate the human reason," while Heine commented that when Luther deposed the Pope, Robespierre decapitated the king, and Immanuel Kant disposed of God, it was all one insurrection of man against the same tyrant under different names.[1]

Was the Reformation a "revolt"?

For our purposes, the interpretation that comes closest to a Protestant interpretation, and yet paradoxically is farthest from it, is the interpretation given by most Roman Catholic, Anglo-Catholic, and Eastern Orthodox churchmen, that the Reformation was a "revolt" — a religious revolt against the church. This is close to the Protestant interpretation in the sense that it assesses the Reformation as a *religious* movement rather than as an economic, cultural, or nationalistic movement. How far this is from the Protestant interpretation will be clear only after examination.

The Roman Catholic philosopher, Jacques Maritain, has referred to "that immense disaster for humanity, the Protestant Reformation." [2] What leads a man to this conclusion? The pre-suppositions would seem to be these: Jesus Christ willed that there should be one church and that it should have one head. He himself is the one head of the one church, but he made provision for Peter to be his vicar on earth, and for subsequent vicars to be appointed after Peter in unbroken succession. To give allegiance to the vicar of Christ (now called the Pope) thus means to give allegiance to Christ himself, and assure that his church will remain undivided. Those who do not give allegiance to the vicar of Christ are disloyal sons who revolt against Christ and his church, splitting it into factions and creating new groups that falsely claim the name of "church." When abuses creep into the life of the church, the way to correct them is not to separate and start new churches, but to work within the church for its purification. Rather than "revolting" (as the so-called "reformers" did), the true Christian will reform from within (as the delegates to the Council of Trent did). In this way, abuses will be cleared up without scandal and division. "Luther was not a good listener," the Roman Catholic historian Lortz has remarked,[3] meaning that he asserted his own will instead of "listening" to the voice of the church. Because of the Protestant revolt, therefore, we have hundreds of competing sects, no single one of which can trace its lineage back to Jesus Christ. These divisions in Christendom have been responsible for the disruption of western civilization.[4] Thus the Reformation is indeed an "immense disaster for humanity."

So much for a view of the Reformation as a "revolt" against the church.[5] The view is wholly consistent if the initial premise is accepted that the Pope is indeed the vicar of Christ. If to repudiate the Pope is in fact to repudiate Christ, then the Reformers and all Protestants (indeed, all non-Roman Catholics) are "revolters" of the most revolting sort, and Roman Catholic polemics against these betrayers of Christ are quite justified. Protestants might remember, when they feel that Roman Catholic polemics are too heated, that the intent is not to be nasty to Protestants but to speak what Roman Catholics feel to be the truth. Where they see the truth betrayed, they must speak vigorously. Roman Catholics in their turn might remember, when they feel that Protestant polemics are too heated, that the intent is not to be nasty to Roman Catholics, but to speak what Protestants feel to be the truth. Where they see the truth betrayed, they too must speak vigorously. Both groups might remember more frequently than they do that the intent of the Christian is not only to speak the truth, but to speak the truth in love.

A Protestant view of the Reformation

What does the Protestant believe about the Reformation?

The Protestant, agreeing with Philip Schaff that the Reformation was "a deeper plunge into the meaning of the gospel," feels that ultimate loyalty must be given to that gospel, the subject and object of which is Jesus Christ. The Protestant feels that he belongs to the church of Jesus Christ, which is a fellowship of those who give allegiance to him, called into being by Christ himself. The Protestant believes that *his fidelity to the church must be measured by the degree of the church's fidelity to the gospel.* If the church departs from that gospel, then the church is an unfaithful witness and must be called to account in the name of the faith it has forsaken.

The church is always in danger of being an unfaithful witness.

In no period of its history has it been immune to temptation. Throughout the Middle Ages, for example, there persisted what James H. Nichols has called "the evangelical undertow." [6] Man after man, group after group, rose up to declare that the church was betraying the gospel and that the church must be purified and "re-formed." In almost every case, these witnesses were repudiated, defamed, excommunicated, and even killed by the church they loved and were trying to serve. By the sixteenth century, the situation had come to such a pitch that the church could no longer stifle the voices crying for reform and renewal.

What were the voices saying? Anyone who is familiar with the Bible will wonder why all the shouting was necessary. For what we find the Reformers preaching is not some "new" gospel, created by them, but the "old" gospel, received by them, which they had rediscovered in the Old and New Testaments. Their central concern was to give that Biblical faith a chance for a real hearing, since, as they felt, it had been stifled and distorted by the church for many centuries. Far from "revolting" against the church, they were trying to re-form it, to recall it to the faith that had brought it into being many centuries before.[7]

We can describe their concern in three distinct but overlapping ways.

1. The message of the Reformers stressed *continuity with the past* — not, of course, continuity with every element of the past, but continuity with those elements of the past that gave expression to the gospel that had brought the church into being. The Reformers felt that they were working within and on behalf of the church of Jesus Christ. The church, they believed, was on a most unpromising detour that might never return to the main road. Or, as P. T. Forsyth put it in even stronger terms, the church was like a train that had gone into a long, dark tunnel; when it emerged from the tunnel it had somehow become a different train, going on a different track in a different direction. Thus, to be loyal to the church meant to call a halt, to ask God to restore the church to what it had been, rather than to tolerate what it had become.

All this means that in the minds of the Reformers there was no thought of repudiating the church. There was only the thought of being faithful to the church by calling it back to the gospel it was created to proclaim. All the Reformers, for example, put great stress on the creeds of the early church; Bullinger's Second Helvetic Confession goes so far as to define heresy as departure from them. Calvin's *Institutes* is full of references to the early church fathers, particular attention being given to Augustine, and the sequence of his chapters is patterned after the Apostles' Creed. The Reformers, then, had a fundamental concern to maintain continuity with all that had been creative in the church's witness, and to repudiate only what had been falsely imported into that witness.

2. But it is not enough to speak of continuity with the past. For the Reformers had to decide *which* elements of the past gave expression to the gospel that had brought the church into being. They had a clear criterion in this matter: *faithfulness to the gospel found in Scripture*. When they had to determine which beliefs and practices were essential to the true proclamation of the gospel, and which were man-made inventions, their touchstone was the Word of God. They took the early church fathers seriously, because the early church fathers had taken Scripture seriously. They concentrated on Augustine, because Augustine had concentrated on the Bible. They emphasized the teachings of the early creeds, because the early creeds had emphasized the teachings of the Old and New Testaments. Calvin made it a rule that nothing should be allowed in the church that did not have Scriptural warrant.

Luther's understanding of the Christian faith was revolutionized by his direct exposure to Scripture. It was as he studied Psalms, Galatians, and above all Romans, that he came to see that the God of the Bible was a different God from the God of the medieval church. And so Luther was faced with a hard choice: either the medieval church was right, or Scripture was right. But not both. Luther took his stand on the conviction that Scripture was right, which meant that the medieval church was wrong. Which meant, in turn, that if Luther was to be faithful to Scripture, and to the church as it ought to be, he must speak his dissatisfaction with the church as it was, and call upon it to reform. In these terms Luther was a very *good* listener, for he listened to the voice of Scripture, and therein heard the gospel.

Not, of course, that adopting the Biblical criterion didn't raise problems. It did. And it still raises problems for Protestants, problems more grievous today than they were in the sixteenth century.[8] But the problems can be held in temporary abeyance, if the point is clear that for the Reformers, the faith they proclaimed was not "new" but "old" — as old as the Scriptures through which they heard it.

3. All this means that the concern of the Reformers was *a concern for catholicity*. "The Reformation," Philip Schaff wrote over a hundred years ago, "is the greatest act of the Catholic Church itself, the full ripe fruit of all its better tendencies." [9]

This contention will startle Protestants for whom the word "catholic" is a term of abuse, and it will startle Roman Catholics who assume that the word is their own and no one else's. We must therefore try to clarify what this important word means.

a. To say "I am a man of catholic tastes" is to describe an open, cosmopolitan temperament, able to appreciate both Rembrandt and Picasso, both Haydn and Schoenberg. This rather sophisticated use of the word is the least significant for our present purposes.

b. To say "I am a member of the Roman Catholic Church" is to indicate allegiance to a particular segment of Christendom (the segment that acknowledges the bishop of Rome as the vicar of Christ, as distinguished from other segments such as the Old Catholic Church). Most of our difficulty with the word "catholic" arises because of the implicit but incorrect assumption that "catholic" and "Roman Catholic" are interchangeable terms.[10]

c. To say "I believe in . . . the holy catholic church" and mean what the writers of the creed meant, is to affirm belief in a universal church, in time and also beyond time, spread throughout the world, rather than a parochial church, restricted and limited.[11]

d. To say "Since I profess the catholic faith, I do not believe that there are four persons in the Trinity" is to assert that there is a content to faith and that right belief must exclude wrong belief.

e. To say, as St. Ignatius said, "Where Jesus Christ is, there is the catholic church" is to describe the center of the content of the catholic faith as the presence of the living Christ.

No one of these statements is fully satisfactory, but (c), (d), and (e) at least point toward a proper meaning of "catholicity," for they suggest that it means universality and wholeness, that it implies a content, and that the content is the living Christ. Perhaps the single word that comes closest to our present needs is the word "wholeness." The catholic faith is faith in its wholeness or totality. The catholic church is the church that proclaims the whole faith. And on these terms, the Reformers had no difficulty in affirming their belief in "the holy catholic church" and their allegiance to it. For them the issue of the Reformation was precisely the issue of catholicity. They contended, as we have seen, that medieval Christendom had surrendered the notion of catholicity to a limited and distorted understanding of the Christian faith. And the Reformers, in trying to recapture the wholeness and universality of the faith, were simply trying to be true "catholics."

Thus it will be clear how far from the mark the Protestant must judge the assertion that "Calvin demanded of his followers a clean break with historic Christendom," [12] or the contention that "the Protestant churches began in the sixteenth century when their founders, rejecting certain doctrines of the faith, broke away from Catholic unity." [13]

It is no part of the spirit of Protestantism to be anti-Catholic. Protestants who still fear the word today should recall that the Reformers used it without qualms. In the description of the church, for example, in the Westminster Confession of Faith, the word "protestant" does not occur, while the word "catholic" is used four times. Indeed, the true Protestant considers himself a member of the catholic church of Jesus Christ, reformed; the universal church that was reconstituted so as to be faithful to its Lord; the church that was rescued at the time of the Reformation from many corruptions by the renewing power of the Holy Spirit; the church that must continue to be rescued in every day and age from the new corruptions that constantly threaten it. Members of this holy catholic church, reformed, look to the future sure of only one thing — that the church must be faithful to Jesus Christ. When anything stands in the way of fidelity to him, whether it be medieval indulgence or Renaissance Pope, Protestant pride or maltreated Scripture, it must be judged and purged by the redeeming activity of the Holy Spirit, who is a consuming fire.

On avoiding idolatry of the past

There is a danger in this. It is a subtle danger, and therefore a powerful one, for if it is not recognized it undoes all that the Reformers tried to do. This is the danger of assuming that everything the Reformers said or did was right, and that our contemporary religious problems can therefore be solved in sixteenth-century terms. If this seems an unlikely temptation, let the reader reflect on the way many Lutherans bristle when something unflattering is said about Martin Luther, or the way many Episcopalians appear mortally offended if it is suggested that the love affairs of Henry VIII had anything to do with the establishment of the Church of England, or the way many Presbyterians accept as gospel all the conclusions of John Calvin — often, in our day by paying him the dubious compliment of trying to prove that he "didn't really mean" what he quite obviously said.

The danger, in other words, is that Protestants will be content to look *at* the Reformers. But true Protestants can never be content to look *at* the Reformers. All they can properly do is to look *through* the Reformers, using them as a helpful means of looking at something else more clearly, namely that which the Reformers themselves looked at — the redemptive work of God in Jesus Christ.

What Protestants can learn from the sixteenth-century Reformation is that *the catholic faith is recoverable.* It can break out of the strongest chains that men put around it. It has done so in the past, and the sins of men in the church are such that it will need to do so again and again in the future. In every age, therefore, members of the catholic church, reformed, must pray for the coming of the Holy Spirit, that he will be pleased to reform and renew the church with his cleansing vigor and indwelling power.

APPENDIX: *What happened "back then"*

Although the above comments are meant to stand on their own, they have most significance when seen against the historical panorama of the Reformation events themselves. The following capsule account is offered in the hope that it will make further study of the Reformation seem worthwhile to the reader. It also tries to provide a minimal historical background for this and subsequent chapters.[14]

The "reformation" of the Christian community began at Caesarea-Philippi with Jesus' rebuke to Peter, "Get behind me, Satan! You are a hindrance to me; for you are not on the side of God, but of men" (Matt. 16:23). Since then, there has not been a moment in the church's life when it has not stood in need of reformation, redirection, and renewal at the hand of God. At the hand of God — for reformation is not something men do, it is something God does through men of his own choosing, and very often in the history of the church he has chosen the humble to confound the wise.

Long before the sixteenth century, God raised up men to speak his word *in* the church, *to* the church, and *against* the church, but always *for the sake of* the church. Such a voice was St. Francis (1182–1226); such voices were Peter Waldo (?–1218), John Wycliffe (?–1384), Jan Hus (1369–1413), William Tyndale (?–1536), and a host of others whom we call the "pre-reformers." In most cases, their voices were silenced by the church that was straying further and further from the gospel, and was consequently less and less able to bear the white light of truth upon it. Not even the combined voices of a series of ecumenical councils (between 1215 and 1512) could bring about real reform.

Finally, however, "the time was ripe," and the movements for reform that had been stifled for hundreds of years came to maturity in person of a German Augustinian monk, Martin Luther (1483–1546). In 1517 Luther posted a series of ninety-five "theses," i.e. propositions, he wished to debate, concerning the indulgence traffic in which the church was involved, and by means of which the journey of souls through purgatory could be hastened by the payment of a sum of money. Nobody turned up to debate with Luther, but the theses were printed and circulated throughout Europe. They were like a tinderbox set off in the midst of a powder keg, and Luther soon found himself at the forefront of a vast revolution and reform in the life of the church, assisted notably by Philip Melanchthon (1497–1560). Luther was excommunicated by the Pope, and spent the rest of his life with a price upon his head, but he nevertheless spearheaded the reform of the German church. At the Treaty of Augsburg (1555) shortly after Luther's death, the expedient of *cuius regio eius religio* was adopted, meaning that the people of a given province would adopt the religion of their prince. To this day the division in Germany of Protestants and Roman Catholics is largely along geographical lines.

In Switzerland, a reform movement almost coincident with that of Luther was inaugurated under Ulrich Zwingli (1484–1531) and carried on after Zwingli's death by his friend Heinrich Bullinger (1504–75). But Geneva became the center of Swiss Protestant activity, and the center of Geneva's Swiss Protestant activity was John Calvin (1509–64). Calvin, a convert in his student days, had hoped to make his contribution to the Reformation by a life of quiet study, but when Calvin was traveling through Geneva, the reformer William Farel drafted him, much against his will, to stay and help with the practical problems of running the city. Calvin was later banished and spent several happier years in Strasbourg, working with Martin Bucer (1491–1551), but Geneva, finding that it could not get along without Calvin, begged him to return. He spent the rest of his life there, preaching, teaching, and writing, and produced the most comprehensive statement of the Reformed faith, *The Institutes of the Christian Religion* (final edition, 1559).

Calvin had come from France, and Calvinism returned to France under Protestants who became known as Huguenots. They were among the most persecuted groups of Protestants on the Continent. The Reformed faith (as Calvinism is also called) likewise spread to the Netherlands, to Hungary and to Scotland.

The Reformation extended its impact to England when Henry VIII (reigned 1509–47), after a series of complicated maneuvers with the papacy, finally broke with Rome in 1534. When Edward VI (reigned 1547–53) was succeeded by Mary (reigned 1553–58), the country again became Roman Catholic, but during the reign of Elizabeth (reigned 1558–1603) the breach with Rome became final, and the Church of England, or the Anglican Church, has remained the "established church" ever since. In Scotland, the forces of reform were led by John Knox (1505?–72) who had lived in Geneva, which he called "the most perfect school of Christ since the apostles." Scotland became Protestant in 1560, though the story is a stormy one since Mary Queen of Scots (reigned 1542–67) remained a Roman Catholic all her life.

The spread of the Reformation across Europe finally forced the Roman Catholic authorities to act, and the Council of Trent (1545–63) was called to state precisely the Roman Catholic faith that had been challenged by the Reformers. It had originally been hoped that this council could heal a divided Christendom. Actually, it widened the gap more than ever, for it solidified in Roman Catholic doctrine many things that the Reformers had insisted were un-Biblical, and anathematized many of the Reformers' affirmations. The Council of Trent was one of the activities of what is called the Roman Catholic or Counter-Reformation. A particularly unfortunate instrument of the Counter-Reformation was the Inquisition, which condemned Protestants for heresy and delivered them to the state for torture (as a means of inducing them to repudiate their heresies) or execution (if they still remained impenitent).

Protestantism spread to America in the early seventeenth century as persecuted minorities (usually persecuted by their fellow Protestants) crossed the sea to achieve freedom of worship. The new world was predominantly Protestant (save for a Roman Catholic settlement in Maryland) until a later wave of immigration brought many Roman Catholics to America.

The nineteenth century witnessed tremendous missionary expansion as Protestants went literally to the ends of the earth to preach the gospel to every creature. The seeds then planted have come to creative flower in the twentieth century in the contribution which the so-called "younger churches" now make to world Christianity through the ecumenical movement, which, as we shall see in the next chapter, is the most significant reforming activity of Christendom at the present time.

3. The Varieties of Protestantism (a swift catalog of family quarrels, family reunions, and the patience of God)

Protestants often sing,

> We are not divided,
> All one body we,
> One in hope, in doctrine,
> One in charity.

A more honest version would go,

> We are all divided,
> Not one body we,
> One lacks faith, another hope,
> And all lack charity.

As we turn from the sixteenth century and try to describe the present-day Protestant scene in this chapter, we cannot disguise the fact that there are skeletons as well as treasures in the Protestant closet. The skeleton most difficult to hide is contemporary Protestantism's divided character, and we must have the honesty to start with it.

The denominational families

The first Christians knew nothing of "denominations." They had their various factions, to be sure, as Paul's Corinthian correspondence makes lamentably clear, but for a brief time at least "they were not divided, all one body they." The subsequent history of Christendom, however, has been marked (and marred) by the tendency of Christians to take issue with one another, separate from one another, and form rival Christian communities. There was a considerable amount of this in the early centuries, more than is usually recognized,[1] and a very serious rupture between East and West in A.D. 1054, which is still perpetuated in the division between Eastern Orthodoxy and the rest of Christendom. The Protestant Reformation of the sixteenth century produced another such rupture, as we saw in the previous chapter.

The tragic thing about this is that Christians do not divide for petty reasons. New Christian groups always feel that they are either conserving an ancient truth, or combating a modern error, or doing both. At the time of division they may have been doing God's will. But whether denominational divisions that may have been historically justified in the past can still be justified today is another question entirely — a burning one for the Protestant conscience.

There are difficulties in any attempt to "schematize" the divisions into which modern Protestantism has fallen. Even at the risk of over-simplification, however, the attempt must be made, and the following five main denominational families are suggested.[2]

1. The *Lutherans* [3] are the oldest Protestant group with a self-conscious identity. The Lutheran churches came into being as a result of Luther's reforming activity in the early sixteenth century in Germany, when Luther and his followers put fidelity to the gospel above fidelity to medieval ecclesiasticism. Lutheran churches have always put central emphasis upon Scripture as the source of the gospel, and have understood the gospel particularly in terms of belief in justification by faith alone. This means that Lutheranism gives a high priority to right doctrine; so important is doctrine, indeed, that a number of different Lutheran groups exist, each feeling that the others compromise the truth at some important point. Lutheranism managed to conserve more of the elements of pre-Reformation liturgy than most other Continental Protestant groups, and is thus characterized by a rich liturgical worship. In virtue of its doctrine of the separation of the "two realms" (e.g. the church and the magistrate), Lutheranism has historically inclined to an attitude of political quietism, an attitude now being rethought as a result of the church's necessary resistance to nazism.

2. Churches in the *Reformed* or *Presbyterian* tradition have

arisen from the reformation activity in countries other than Germany, notably Switzerland, France, Holland, Hungary, and Scotland.[4] The spiritual father of the Reformed family is John Calvin (1509–64), a French convert who spent most of his Protestant life in Geneva, preaching and teaching, and taking an active part in the political life of the city. Like Lutheranism, the Reformed faith is motivated and informed by central attention to Scripture. Scripture witnesses to Jesus Christ, whose reality is conveyed to believers by Scripture, sermon, and sacrament. One of the greatest contributions of the Reformed family has been its stress on Biblical preaching and its concerted emphasis on the sovereign grace of God. Reformed doctrine has also emphasized church order as one of the marks of the church, and the offices of pastor, teacher, elder, and deacon derive from an attempt to conform to New Testament practice. The name "presbyterian" signifies the form of government of many Reformed churches. *Presbuteros* is the Greek word for "elder," and Presbyterian churches are governed by elders, elected to serve in local churches and in larger representative bodies from local churches, known as presbyteries.

3. A third denominational family includes those within the *Anglican* or *Episcopal* tradition.[5] Many of these describe themselves as Protestants or Evangelicals. The Anglo-Catholic wing, however, disavows the Protestant label, and agrees with Roman Catholicism on almost all points of doctrine save papal infallibility. This diversity of theological belief within Episcopalianism, while the despair of those who try to describe it simply, is one of the sources of its greatness, for the church has managed to conserve within its diversity many of the best features of historical Catholicism and Protestantism. For this reason many of its communicants feel that it can serve as the "bridge church," or the *via media,* between other groups in Christendom.

As the name Anglican implies, the historical roots of the church are to be found in the English Reformation, where the reforms were less radical than those on the Continent — a fact that makes Anglicans particularly conscious of their continuity with the past. As the name "Episcopal" implies, the church is governed by bishops (*episkopos* is the Greek word for "bishop"), and episcopal ordination is a distinguishing mark of its ministry. Another distinguishing characteristic of the Episcopal family is *The Book of Common Prayer,* one of the liturgical treasures of Christendom, which is used at all services of worship, and from which other Protestant groups unblushingly borrow liturgical materials.

4. Another Protestant family, more diverse than any of those mentioned so far, can be identified as the family of *free churches.*[6] The free churches were usually formed, as the name would suggest, in the face of oppression by established churches from whose domination the free churchmen wished to be released, so that they could preach and worship as they felt they should. The story of the free churches is a story of faith bought at the price of suffering and persecution. The theological convictions of free churchmen were often nurtured in the Calvinist wing of Christendom known as Puritanism.[7] Originally the Puritans were members of the Church of England who wanted to "purify" worship of Romanizing tendencies, and who put Biblical truth above human creeds and traditions. But this Calvinist-Puritan impulse became much broader than the Church of England, and has led in many directions.

Among the many free church groups, the following are particularly worthy of mention:

The *Congregationalists* and *Baptists* [8] share an understanding of the church as a "gathered community," i.e. a voluntary association of believers. The name of each group indicates the emphasis it has particularly stressed. In *Congregationalism,* the government of the churches is vested in the "congregational meeting," where all members may discuss and vote on the policies to be pursued by the individual church. Contemporary Congregationalism has greater doctrinal latitude than was true in the seventeenth century, and creeds are usually considered as testimonies to faith rather than tests of faith. The *Baptists* have practiced "believer's baptism" rather than infant baptism, i.e. baptism administered to those of mature years who have made public profession of faith, in accordance with what is felt to have been the New Testament practice. Baptists have considerable variety on other points of doctrine, and today the different Baptist groups comprise the largest denominational family in the United States. Historically, Baptists have had a special concern for religious liberty and the separation of church and state.

The Society of Friends or *Quakers* [9] are difficult to fit into a Protestant scheme, and are often classified as a "sect group," since they lack such normal characteristics of a church as sacraments, ordained ministers, or creedal affirmations. They stem, however, from left-wing Puritanism, having pushed the Puritan anti-sacramental emphasis to the extent of denying any sacraments at all. The spiritual father of Quakerism is the Englishman George Fox (1624–90), whose religious doubts and dissatisfactions with established religion were resolved by a series of mystical experiences which led him to rely on the "Inner Light," or the "Seed of God within," rather than on external forms. In line with this emphasis there is no formal order of worship at Quaker meetings. Members of the group sit silently, waiting for the leading of the Spirit before getting up to speak. Quakerism has exercised influence on other Protestant groups all out of proportion to its small numbers, particularly through the expression of an acute social conscience and a consistent pacifist testimony.

The *Methodists* [10] owe their historical identity to the spiritual leadership of John Wesley (1703–91), an Anglican clergyman whose "heart was strangely warmed" upon hearing a reading from Luther's Preface to Paul's Letter to the Romans, and who subsequently engaged in widespread evangelism throughout England. Wesley's converts and followers organized groups of their own within the Church of England. When Methodist activity spread to America and there was need for more ministers, Wesley finally took the bold step of ordaining them himself. From this time on, Methodism was distinct from the Church of England, although Wesley himself never left the church. Methodism stresses the doctrine of sanctification and the experience of salvation. "Christian perfection" is the goal of Methodist living, and Methodism places particular stress on personal religion and social responsibility.

The Christian Churches (*Disciples of Christ*) [11] were founded in America in the nineteenth century by Thomas Campbell (1763–1854) and his son Alexander Campbell (1788–1886), for which reason its members are sometimes called "Campbellites." The driving force behind the history of the Disciples has been a desire for Christian unity based on the example of the early church, stressing the authority of the Bible, the practice of believer's baptism, and weekly celebration of the Lord's Supper. Doctrinally the church has remained flexible ("no creed but Christ") and its members have been active in the struggle for church unity.

5. Problems of description and classification are difficult enough with the free churches, but they are even more difficult when we turn to a final and heterogeneous family, the *sects*.[12] The sects have been done a particular injustice by Protestant historians, who usually see them as no more than aberrations from the "central stream" of the Reformation.

During the Reformation period many of the sect groups were called "Anabaptists," a term of derision meaning "re-baptizers." The term was not strictly accurate; the Anabaptists did not feel that they were "re-baptizing" at all, for they did not consider that infant baptism had been a true baptism. The sectarians believed that the state was corrupt, and that the church should be separated from the world. For this reason, the name "separatist" was often applied to the sect groups. As a result, the sects often formed small communities, usually striving for economic self-sufficiency in order to be relieved of compromise with the evil world outside. Pacifism was a strong plank in most sectarian platforms. Very often the sect groups believed that the millennium was about to be inaugurated and that they must prepare the evil world for this imminent catastrophe. They tried to pattern their life on that of the primitive church in the New Testament, particularly as found in the book of Acts. But they also felt a strong dependence upon the Holy Spirit, who was believed to give direct guidance to members of the sect groups. Confusion between the voice of the Spirit and the desires of the sectarians was often a source of difficulty. Some of these groups became more solidly organized than others, and many of them, such as the Mennonites and Hutterites, survive to the present day.

But not all of the sect groups of the present day trace their roots back to the Reformation. Many of them are of quite recent origin. An emotional type of religious conversion is usually normative for membership in these groups, and those converted expect the imminent return of Christ in judgment. They make repeated use of a few Biblical passages to support their position and believe intensely in the present and direct guidance of the Holy Spirit. As a rule they have little social concern, putting their emphasis on keeping "unspotted from the world." Most of the contemporary sect groups proliferate rapidly, each new faction trying to recapture the "purity" which has been lost by its contaminated forebears. Other sects, however, gain stability, and with the passage of time tend to become virtually indistinguishable from other "denominations."

This curious conglomeration of denominational families (each with its own inner divisions) must seem confusing to the outsider. He can be sure that it is depressing to the insider, who recognizes that all this is a far cry from the one body of Christ. We have already pointed out that even if there were historically valid reasons for the formation of these groups, such reasons do not necessarily validate continued denominational separation. In the light of this, we must examine two further facts: (a) theological differences do not usually follow denominational boundaries, and (b) responsible members of almost all denominations are working to heal the divisions that are the shame rather than the glory of Protestantism.

The theological families

Most Protestants belong to one of the first four denominational families just described, and the differences that separate them from one another are less than the similarities that unite them. It is a hopeful sign that there are often greater affinities between members of different denominations than exist within a given denomination itself. We can distinguish four kinds of theological families within Protestantism, whose convictions cut across denominational affiliations in a remarkable way.

1. The modern phenomenon of *fundamentalism* [13] claims the allegiance of a certain group of Protestants. It accounts for most of the members of the sect groups and includes a number of Baptists, Presbyterians, and Lutherans. "Fundamentalism" is a recent term, derived from an attempt early in the twentieth century to rally Protestants around a number of so-called "fundamentals" of the faith, similar to those described on p. 7 above. The cornerstone of the fundamentalist edifice is the belief that the Bible is

infallible and inspired in all its parts. Fundamentalists may differ at other points, but they will rally indefectibly in their appeal to an infallible Scripture.

Fundamentalism is not typical of Protestantism as a whole. Indeed, a few years ago many Protestants would have considered it dead and almost buried. But there has been a strong resurgence of fundamentalist conviction, some of it fostered by the uncertainties of modern life and the realization that fundamentalists, whatever their other strengths and failings, offer definite and clear-cut answers to perplexing questions.[14]

2. A second theological family is more difficult to locate. It offers an attitude rather than a series of dogmas, and can be called the attitude of *liberalism*.[15] Liberalism is in part a reaction against Biblical fundamentalism and extreme theological conservatism, but it recognizes positively that twentieth-century Christians live in a twentieth-century world, and must speak to that world. Phyllis McGinley characterizes the liberal thus:

Community Church

The Reverend Dr. Harcourt, folk agree,
  Nodding their heads in solid satisfaction,
Is just the man for this community.
  Tall, young, urbane, but capable of action,
He pleases where he serves. He marshals out
  The younger crowd, lacks trace of clerical unction,
Cheers the Kiwanis and the Eagle Scout,
  Is popular at every public function,

And in the pulpit eloquently speaks
  On diverse matters with both wit and clarity;
Art, Education, God, the early Greeks,
  Psychiatry, Saint Paul, true Christian charity,
Vestry repairs that shortly must begin —
  All things but Sin. He seldom mentions Sin.[16]

This is satire, and not quite fair, but it has the value of indicating the liberal's genuine concern to speak to the modern world in which he lives ("Art, Education . . . Psychiatry"), even though in the process he may ride lightly over certain other things ("He seldom mentions Sin").

The liberal feels that he must be open to truth from whatever quarter, and that he must respect the findings of those engaged in a historical study of the Biblical documents. He believes that he can maintain loyalty to the Bible, so long as it is not a loyalty that makes the Bible the exclusive vehicle of revelation. He takes social responsibility very seriously, believing that the teachings of the prophets and of Jesus offer a real guide for the transformation of the world. The "social gospel" is not an idle phrase on liberal lips; it is a recognition that God is concerned with every aspect of his world, and not simply the status of individual souls. The structures of society, which can warp those souls, are God's concern and therefore also the Christian's concern. Thus the impact of the gospel must drive the church into the struggle for social justice, whether this means the city court, the state legislature, or the federal government.

In many quarters today it is popular to deride liberalism as naïve or sentimental. But it should be pointed out that liberalism's strongest critics have been liberalism's most gifted children, who might never have been drawn into the orbit of Christian faith had it not been for the emancipating atmosphere of liberalism in the face of sterile orthodoxy. Many things can, indeed, be said in retrospect about the shortcomings of certain kinds of liberal theology, and H. Richard Niebuhr has said most of them in his famous characterization: "A God without wrath brought men without sin into a kingdom without judgment through the ministrations of a Christ without a cross." [17] But when liberalism is true to itself, it does not solidify into an unchanging structure of thought, but retains an adaptability that makes it possible for its adherents to grow and change.

3. That the sands on the theological beach have been shifting is due not only to the pressure of worlds events but also to a new theological current as well. This particular current eludes descriptive labels even more tenaciously than the liberal sands upon which it beats, but the most widely used label is *neo-orthodoxy*.[18] As the name suggests, it is orthodoxy, but orthodoxy-with-a-difference. It stands on *this* side of the Biblical-critical movement inaugurated by the liberals, and it makes unhesitating use of the insights of Biblical study.

Indeed, its main emphasis is surely a new appreciation of the Bible and its relevance to man's situation. In Reinhold Niebuhr's words, "The Bible must be taken seriously but not literally." This attempt to look at the world through Biblical eyes has meant that the great Biblical themes of sin and grace, judgment and mercy, crucifixion and resurrection, have been central in the thinking of members of this family.

We may see this at work in the dual emphasis on sin and grace. It has been seen that the reality of human sin furnishes a way of understanding the Europe of the 'thirties, the world of the 'forties, the America of the 'fifties, and the heart of man at all times. But with the recognition of the reality of man's sin goes the complementary recognition of the reality of God's grace. A convenient symbol of the interrelationship of these two themes is the sequence of Reinhold Niebuhr's Gifford Lectures: Volume 1 on "The Nature of Man" is a devastating description of human sin, while Volume 2 on "The Destiny of Man" is a hopeful account of the adequacy of God's grace to deal with the fact of man's sin. Similarly, the theme of Karl Barth's theology has been described as "the triumph of grace."

The recovery of such themes has meant a wide use of the language of paradox — a trait that has not endeared neo-orthodoxy to those who want simple answers. But if it be acknowledged that the center of the Christian faith involves the affirmation that God became man, i.e. the paradox of the incarnation, then it is clear that "simple answers" must be suspect. To the question, "Is Christ human or divine?" for example, the only answer that will suffice is that he is both. This may not satisfy the tidy logician, but it is the only thing that can satisfy the Christian, for he cannot rest content with an answer that affirms either half of the paradox to the exclusion of the other. An analogy suggested by D. M. Baillie helps to explain why this is so.[19] A cartographer has to depict a round sphere on a flat plane. The best he can do is to draw the earth as a flat circle and also as a flat rectangle (Mercator's projection). Neither map is fully accurate by itself, nor will the two maps agree at every point, but *by examining them together* we get a better idea of the structure of the earth than we can get with only one. Similarly, the Christian, in talking about God, is using modes of speech applicable to one plane of existence to describe someone who cannot be contained solely within that plane of existence. He must therefore make statements that initially seem contradictory ("Christ is human *and* divine") if he is to do even minimal justice to the reality he is trying to describe.

Recent Protestant theology has also had an existential character. This does not mean that it has adhered to the existentialist philosophy of a Sartre or a Heidegger, but that its articulation has been characterized by the faith of the participant rather than the attitude of the spectator. Søren Kierkegaard (1809–55) put the difference between these approaches clearly when he distinguished between the questions, "What is Christianity?" and "How can I become a Christian?" The first question is the question of the spectator: he can pursue it quite apart from its meaning for his own life and destiny. The second question is an existential question, which means that the life and destiny of the questioner are involved in the answer given.

4. The dividing line between "liberal" and "neo-orthodox" has become increasingly difficult to trace. Many "liberals," for example, could accept most if not all that has been said above about the "neo-orthodox." Protestantism, in other words, is engaging in an interior dialogue, out of which is emerging a theological position that leaves the above positions dated, as far as being adequate descriptions of contemporary Protestantism. We may describe this emerging position as an *ecumenical theology*.[20] "Ecumenical," coming from the Greek *oikoumene* meaning "the inhabited world," is a word increasingly used in Protestant circles to describe the activity of the church of Christ throughout the world. Ecumenical theology reflects the interchange that is going on between Indian Lutherans, American Congregationalists, Scottish Presbyterians, Italian Waldensians, Ceylonese Methodists, and many more. It represents an understanding of Protestant faith which, because of this interchange, is losing some of the insularity and angularity that characterized various expressions of it in the past. It will be the aim of the present book to think within this emerging ecumenical framework.

The ecumenical family [21]

The word "ecumenism" is here to stay, and Protestants have no choice but to take it into their vocabularies. What does it mean?

As we have just seen, it comes from *oikoumene,* meaning "the inhabited world." It used to refer chiefly to the activity of the whole church in earlier times: an "ecumenical council" was a council in which the whole church was represented, just as an "ecumenical creed" was a product of the thinking of all Christendom. In the nineteenth century the word acquired the additional nuance of referring to attempts at unity between various branches of Christendom, and in our own day it is used, as Visser 't Hooft has said, to express *"a consciousness of belonging to the world-wide Christian fellowship and a desire for unity with other churches."* [22]

It is this reality that William Temple correctly described as "the great new fact of our time." It is the new fact that gives hope in the face of the discouraging picture of Protestant disunity. Until about 1900 it could be urged with little fear of contradiction that Protestantism had been a divisive force in Christendom. Premature attempts at reunion only multiplied the number of dissident groups. (One New England town tried to unite its two churches. A survivor of the crusade for union reported, "We used to have two churches. Then we united the two churches, so now we have three.")

But divisiveness is not native to Protestantism as such. The Reformers' concerns, as Professor John T. McNeill has convincingly shown in *Unitive Protestantism,* were what we today would call ecumenical concerns. Commenting on this fact, Charles Clayton Morrison writes:

> The ecumenical awakening in our time is . . . not an experience alien to Protestantism. It is the resurgence in Protestantism of the ecumenical awakening of the sixteenth century. As the Reformers discovered the true church behind the façade of the hierarchical institution, we are discovering it behind the façade of the denominational system . . . The ecumenical movement in our time is thus an awakening of Protestantism to the fact that it is the inheritor of an unfinished Reformation. It is motivated by the same insight which inspired the Reformers.[23]

Today this aspect of the Protestant heritage is being explored and made real in a way that would have seemed impossible half a century ago. In 1925, the Methodist, Congregational, and two-thirds of the Presbyterian congregations in Canada formed the United Church of Canada. In 1947, Presbyterians, Congregationalists, Methodists, and Episcopalians joined together to form the Church of South India, an event that Henry Sloane Coffin described as the most important event in Protestant history since the Reformation.[24] Plans are under discussion for similar mergers in North India, and for a United Church in Ceylon.

Much of this impetus to reunion has come from the "younger churches," the products of the Protestant missionary enterprise. The notion of Christian groups in competition with one another has been a luxury that the frontier situation could not afford. Some of the impetus has come from a recognition of the pitiful image which a divided Christendom presents to the outside world. The major impetus, however, comes from a recognition that *Christians are already one in Christ,* and must, in obedience to him, make their unity manifest.[25]

As long ago as 1910, Protestant Christians from diverse backgrounds began meeting together to discuss problems of missions, evangelism, the social order and the unity of the church. The milestones on this road have been conferences at Edinburgh (1910), Stockholm (1925), Lausanne (1927), Jerusalem (1928), Oxford and Edinburgh (1937), Madras (1938), Amsterdam (1948), Lund (1952), Evanston (1954), and Oberlin (1957). Out of these conferences came an awareness of the need for a means by which ecumenically minded Protestants could work together more effectively. The result was the formation of the World Council of Churches at the Amsterdam Conference in 1948. Ecumenical concern receives concrete expression through the World Council. The Council is not a "super-church," nor does it force its members to unite with one another. "Rather," says Visser 't Hooft, the General Secretary of the World Council, "it is a fellowship of churches which acknowledge Jesus Christ as God and Savior and which desire to enter into constructive relations with each other. It is a platform for serious conversation about the issues of unity, a means for cooperation in matters of common concern, an organ of common witness when it is given to the churches to speak together to the world." [26]

The road leading the churches to what Dr. 't Hooft calls "the fulfillment of their calling to unity in Christ" is a hard road to walk, for it involves the willingness of denominations to sacrifice their hard-won identity. Denominations do not do this easily. But just as crucifixion was the price that the Head of the church had to pay in order that resurrection might occur, so in the life of his church there will be need of many deaths if new life is to spring forth. The price is high. That increasing numbers of Protestants seem ready to pay it is a hopeful sign.

The varieties of Protestantism

If there is any sure proof of the patience of God, it is in the fact that he has endured the varieties of Protestantism for four centuries. If there is any sure sign of the humility of God, it is in the fact that he has been willing to make use of the feeble instrument of organized Protestantism. If there is any sure indication of the power of God, it is in the fact that through the Protestant churches Jesus Christ has become a reality in countless lives. If there is any sure pointer to the compassion of God, it is in the fact that he deigns to make use of the humblest offerings of his divided flock.

It is such facts as these that enable Protestants to look ahead in hope, no matter how demonic may seem to be the ways men thwart God's will. For it is by his finger that the demons are cast out.

APPENDIX: *Eastern Orthodoxy*

In this book, Roman Catholicism is the main non-Protestant branch of Christendom to receive attention. This is due to the fact that the historical destinies of Protestantism and Roman Catholicism have been inextricably intertwined in the western world. But there is another large segment of Christendom, Eastern Orthodoxy, which is neither Protestant nor Roman Catholic, and with which Protestantism will have increasing relationship in the future.

It is always difficult for an "outsider" to describe a faith other than his own, and this is particularly true in the case of Eastern Orthodoxy. The following comments must therefore be supplemented by reference to such books as Bulgakov, *The Orthodox Church,* Centenary Press; French, *The Eastern Orthodox Church,* Hutchison's University Library; and Hapgood, *Service Book of the Holy Orthodox Catholic Apostolic Church.*

Orthodoxy regards itself as the true church of Jesus Christ, and considers that all other Christian bodies are in error. It feels that Christian reunion will come when Catholics and Protestants return to the Orthodox fold. Orthodoxy's membership in the World Council of Churches, therefore, does not imply its acceptance of the ecclesiology of other member churches, but is an expression of its missionary concern to be ready at all times to guide other branches of erring Christendom back to the truth.

Orthodoxy consists of a number of "autocephalous" churches, i.e. churches with their own organization, but in full communion with one another and sharing a common life of worship and doctrine. The main divisions within Orthodoxy are geographical, and its greatest strength is concentrated in such places as Greece, Russia, Bulgaria, Yugoslavia, etc.

Doctrinally, Orthodoxy considers itself bound by Scripture and tradition. Tradition is formally defined by the early ecumenical church councils, but it is also the living and dynamic activity of the Holy Spirit in the church — an activity that never ceases. In its handing on and proclamation of Scripture and tradition, Orthodoxy considers the voice of the church to be infallible. This quality is not localized in a bishop or bishops, but is held to inhere in the life of the church as a whole.

The clearest expression of the ethos and life of Orthodoxy is found in its liturgy, in which those in heaven and on earth are held to be united in their common acts of worship. The liturgy has great dramatic power and musical richness. The liturgical forms are ancient and at many points similar to the Roman Catholic mass, although the service is spoken in various ancient languages rather than in Latin. The full liturgical life of Orthodoxy includes seven sacraments, as in Roman Catholicism, and a sharp distinction is likewise made between clergy and laity. A particular emphasis in Orthodox worship is the stress on ikons (sacred pictures) which are "venerated" as channels through which divine power flows.

Closer contact with Orthodoxy in the future will probably lead Protestantism to further re-examination of its own heritage in such directions as: (a) the place of tradition in the life of the church, (b) the way in which corporate worship is an expression of Christian faith, and (c) the need to see more clearly the present, ongoing activity of the Holy Spirit in the Christian community.

4. The Spirit of Protestantism (Protestantism as constant renewal at the hand of God)

A theme has been running through the preceding chapters and will continue to run through succeeding ones. Each chapter, in fact, could be described as a variation on this theme.

How shall we describe it? A definition of the spirit of Protestantism would be too static. It would run the risk of stifling what it was meant to clarify. A description, while preferable to a definition, is still a far cry from the real thing, for words cannot capture the "spirit" of anything.

But words are the only tools a writer has. And if the reader is unmoved by them, and is willing to take risks, let him join a congregation of the faithful singing "A Mighty Fortress Is Our God," let him kneel with them in prayer, let him hear the Word of God with them as it is read and preached, let him receive with them "the body and blood of our Lord Jesus Christ," and let him go forth with them to be a Christ to his neighbor. Then, perhaps, the spirit of Protestantism will be more than a string of words upon a printed page.

But let us take a string of words as far as it can take us. Let us begin by calling the spirit of Protestantism an openness to the judging and renewing activity of the living God made known in Jesus Christ. Protestantism at its best is willing to submit to the corrective activity of God, and to hold all things of no account so long as he is honored, which also means to hold all things in honor that can be used by him. The spirit of Protestantism involves a willingness to live at risk, not only because the claim to human security is a denial of God, but because when human securities have been destroyed, God can enter in.

Not, it should be added, that this sort of thing comes very easily to the Protestant, or to Protestant institutions. Men have a deep-seated tendency to cling to the established and to look for ultimate securities of their own devising, and Protestants are no exception to this rule. But they are sometimes willing, thanks to the grace of God, to be shaken up and radically challenged, and then to submit to the painful but exhilarating process of being refashioned into something closer to the divine purpose. Before long, they need to be shaken up, challenged and refashioned again — and it is in this *constant renewal at the hand of God* that Protestants conceive the life of the church to exist. Through it all, God and his purposes remain constant. Nothing else.

Let us look at this from four perspectives.

The Lordship of Jesus Christ

The earliest Christians could proclaim their faith with the two words *kurios Christos* — "Christ is Lord." [1] This is the most positive and direct way of describing the spirit of Protestantism — it is allegiance to Jesus Christ as Lord.

Now the term "Lord" or *kurios* is a term than which there is no higher. It is reserved for God alone. To acknowledge someone as "Lord" is to acknowledge that he is supreme and that he occupies a place no one else can occupy. To acknowledge Jesus Christ as Lord is to acknowledge that he is supreme and that he occupies a place no one else can occupy. To him and to him alone is full allegiance given. There can be no other Lord if he is truly Lord. In a passage in his letter to the Philippians, after describing Jesus' humbling of himself and his obedience unto death upon a cross, Paul continues:

> Therefore God has highly exalted him and bestowed on him the name which is above every name, that at the name of Jesus every knee should bow, in heaven and on earth and under the earth, and every tongue confess that *Jesus Christ is Lord,* to the glory of God the Father.
> (Phil. 2:9–11)

Professor Albert Outler provides a telling example of what this means for the life of the church. He describes a church in Ystad,

Sweden, of fairly conventional design save that on the pillar opposite the pulpit stands a crucifix, life-size and life-like, "with human hair matted under the crown of actual thorns." Why this strange arrangement?

The story, as it turned out, goes back to a visit to Ystad, and to this Mariakyrchen, of the great warrior hero king, Charles XII, in 1716. The visit was unexpected, and the pastor was so overwhelmed by this sudden burst of glory that he put aside his prescribed text and substituted an ardent eulogy of the king and the royal family. Some few months later, the Church received a gift from King Charles. It was this second crucifix, and with it these instructions: "This is to hang on the pillar opposite the pulpit, so that all who shall stand there will be reminded of their proper subject." [2]

Andrew Melville did not succumb to the temptation of the Swedish pastor, but saw clearly that if Christ was Lord, everyone, kings included, must be in subjection to him. As he said directly to James VI of Scotland in 1596, "There are two kings and two kingdoms in Scotland; there is King James the head of the Commonwealth, and there is Christ Jesus the King of the Church, whose subject King James VI is, and of whose Kingdom he is not a king nor a lord nor a head; but a member." [3] There is no record that James felt compelled to send a crucifix to Melville to remind him of his "proper subject."

The historian Herbert Butterfield concludes his *Christianity and History* with the provocative advice, "Hold to Christ, and for the rest be totally uncommitted." [4] If properly understood, that assertion could almost be said to epitomize the spirit of Protestantism, for it affirms the Lordship of Christ and excludes the possibility of rival "lords." To be "totally committed" to anyone other than Christ, is in fact to dethrone Christ, and to enthrone some rival in his place.

"You shall have no other gods before me."

It is always our temptation to enthrone some rival in his place. And against this temptation stands the first commandment, a commandment that expresses the spirit of Protestantism from another perspective: "You shall have no other gods before me" (Ex. 20:3). To put "other gods" before the Lord is to succumb to the sin of idolatry, the worshipping of "idols" or false gods. The theme has been elaborated by Paul Tillich in what he calls "the Protestant principle."[5] This is the insistence that no partial object of loyalty may be transformed into an ultimate object of loyalty; nothing man-made, or less than divine, may be treated as though it were divine.

> [The Protestant principle] contains the divine and human protest against any absolute claim made for a relative reality, even if this claim is made by a Protestant church. The Protestant principle is the judge of every religious and cultural reality, including the religion and culture which calls itself "Protestant" . . . It is the guardian against all the attempts of the finite and conditioned to usurp the place of the unconditional in thinking and acting. It is the prophetic judgment against religious pride, ecclesiastical arrogance, and secular self-sufficiency and their destructive consequences.[6]

This sin of idolatry is the characteristic religious temptation of the twentieth century. We see it most clearly in the idolatrous claims that are made on behalf of a nation, a tendency given classic expression by Stephen Decatur: "My country right or wrong, may she be right, but right or wrong my country." To say this is to disobey the first commandment. Christians in Germany were called upon to do just this after Hitler came to power. But the first declaration of the Barmen Conference of 1934, one of the great utterances of modern church history, demonstrated an obedience to the first commandment and showed how an affirmation of the Lordship of Christ meant a denial of all other claimants:

> Jesus Christ, as He is attested to us in Holy Scripture, is the one Word of God, whom we have to hear and whom we have to trust and obey in life and in death.
>
> We condemn the false doctrine that the Church can and must recognize as God's revelation other events and powers, forms and truths apart from and alongside this one Word of God.[7]

Christ is Lord, so Hitler cannot be Lord. "Other events and powers" (Hitler, nazism, anti-Semitism) must be repudiated.

This is not a new notion in the life of Christendom, as we can discover by returning for a moment to the situation in which the first Christians affirmed *kurios Christos,* "Christ is Lord." For this apparently inoffensive theological formula was loaded with political consequences. In the first century, the inhabitants of the Roman Empire were required to confess a different faith: *kurios Caesar,* "Caesar is Lord." This meant that the Christian in making *his* affirmation was actually doing two things; he was saying "Christ is Lord," and he was also saying, "Therefore Caesar is *not* Lord." One reason for the persecution of the early Christians was the clear awareness of the Roman authorities that an affirmation of the Lordship of Christ was a denial of the Lordship of Caesar. Christians captured by the state were persecuted unless they would swear the totally unambiguous oath, *kurios Caesar, anathema Christos,* "Caesar is Lord, Christ is accursed." [8]

Ecclesia reformata sed semper reformanda (*the church reformed but always to be reformed*)

It is relatively easy for Protestants to point a prophetic finger at "secular" idolatries, to call down judgment on those who say, "My country right or wrong," "My political party right or wrong," "My corporation right or wrong," or "My labor union right or wrong." It is less easy for Protestants to remember that there is as great or even greater error in saying, "My church, right or wrong." The eye of judgment must be turned inward as well as outward; the church must recognize that *in its own life* it betrays the Lordship of Christ and breaks the commandment, "You shall have no other gods before me."

There is a clear Scriptural mandate concerning this. It goes, unambiguously and disturbingly, "The time has come for judgment to begin with the household of God" (1 Pet. 4:17). At no time is the church in greater peril than when, fighting against idolatry without, it succumbs to idolatry within. "We must fight their falsehood with our truth," Reinhold Niebuhr has admirably put it, but, as he has even more admirably continued, "we must also fight the falsehood *in* our truth." The same concern can also be put in the phrase "the Reformation must continue," or in the phrase *ecclesia reformata sed semper reformanda,* or in the words of Professor J. T. McNeill: "The Reformation was not completed in the sixteenth century; it is never completed. We may for the sake of comfort try to transform Protestantism into a closed system; but it breaks out again. It has no 'infallible' voice to silence other voices in decrees that are 'irreformable.' Protestantism cannot be static." [9]

Exactly. The notion that the Reformation is complete, or can be completed, is a denial of what "reformation" in the Protestant sense really means.

This is perhaps the ultimate issue dividing Protestantism and Roman Catholicism. The Roman Catholic could agree with much that is said in the first part of this chapter, particularly the judgment on secular idolatries. But when the judgment turns to a radical judgment *upon the church,* the Roman Catholic would have to demur. He would have to insist that the church does not need reformation in any basic sense, that by its very nature it is irreformable, and that its dogmas are infallible. The notion behind this, that the words of any human being can be unequivocally equated with the words of God, is precisely what the Protestant principle denies. Visser 't Hooft points out that Roman Catholicism can allow for the possibility of reforms *in* the church, the cleaning up of aspects in the church's life that have gotten tarnished. But it cannot allow for the possibility of reform *of* the church, the recognition that at the very basis of its being the church may need to be shaken, judged, purged, and re-made.

Protestantism affirms that the church *must* be shaken, judged, purged, and re-made. It cannot be renewed once. Its life must be a life of constant renewal, for it is an *ecclesia peccatorum,* "a church of sinners," a church that is constantly failing to fulfill its high calling. The attitude that must characterize the church, therefore, is the attitude of *repentance.* St. Augustine, who used to describe the church on earth as being without spot and wrinkle, realized toward the end of his life that the description was incorrect, and that the church could only pray, "Forgive us our sins." [10] The church is not exempt from God's judgment. The church is the place where God's judgment is most severe.

It can be objected that the Reformers themselves had no such clear understanding of the necessity of "the ongoing Reformation," and that their undoubted gifts of judging the shortcomings of others did not extend very conspicuously to judgment of their own failings and inadequacies. We must acknowledge a certain truth in the charge, but insist that the notion of "the ongoing Reformation" was implicit in their concerns even if not always explicit in their actions. Here, as at many other points, they built better than they knew, and to refuse to learn from their implicit concerns as well as from their explicit actions would be, in fact, a denial by us of the possibility of an ongoing Reformation.

It will help to illustrate the maxim *ecclesia reformata sed semper reformanda* if we give some examples of its relevance to contemporary Protestantism.

Most Protestant groups, for example, show a phenomenal resistance to institutional change. When ecclesiastical machinery has been designed to do things a certain way, the most convincing reasons can be elaborated for continuing to do it that way and no other. And by the time a church has adapted itself to a new situation, that new situation has become old, and a yet newer situation is calling, not very successfully, for recognition. This problem of resistance is more serious when it is suggested that one denomination might have something to learn from another denomination about, let us say, the essential meaning of the ministry — surely the most pressing thorn in the ecumenical flesh. Denomination A will argue that its conception of the ministry must not be "compromised" (although denomination B could surely profit by extending its conception of the ministry to include those benefits which denomination A alone possesses). But for denomination B to make any such concession would be, as its adherents say, "a betrayal of our precious heritage." And so the battle rages. The stalemate remains. The church stands still.

Another place where "the reformation must continue" in contemporary Protestantism is related to the social message of the church. It must be acknowledged that Protestantism has usually been willing to sanctify the *status quo* and has done little more than reflect the interests of the middle class. There is a thesis, chiefly propounded by R. H. Tawney and Max Weber,[11] that the rise of Protestantism and the rise of capitalism went hand in hand. And with whatever modifications might seem called for in that thesis, it is undeniable that western Protestantism has been remarkably uncritical of the economic systems in which it has lived.

Our present interest in this fact is not to find a springboard from which to launch into a judgment on western capitalism, but to find a base from which to judge the church for its complacent unconcern about whether or not western capitalism stands in need of judgment. In our own day an alliance has arisen between the Protestant theological right wing and the American economic right wing, in which it is taken as axiomatic that Christianity and *laissez-faire* economics are identical, and that the American way of life is not only beyond criticism but is a way of life that must be kept free of any kind of "governmental interference."

It is not the rightness or wrongness of these judgments that is here being questioned (although the author vigorously dissents from them). What is being questioned is the disturbing fact that even to raise the issue is to be rendered suspect in many Protestant quarters. Apparently it does not occur to the upholders of such claims that the issue could be raised in the name of the gospel; it must be assumed that the issue is being raised either by overt "socialists" or by covert "communists." It has been decided, in other words, that in the area of social concern the Reformation shall *not* continue.

Frequently, indeed, the church becomes so entrenched in this kind of thinking that it can be dislodged only by pressures from without. "Good pagans" often exhibit a greater sense of responsibility for social reform than good Christians. Protestants must have enough grace to acknowledge this and be willing to learn, from whatever source, something of their own responsibility before God. If the church does not continue to be reformed from within, we can be sure that God will reform it from without. As John Bennett writes:

> Often unwelcome pressure on the Church from outside has proved to be necessary to shake it out of quite unholy ruts. I doubt if the Church, either Catholic or Protestant, without such pressure, would ever have accepted fully and ungrudgingly the principle of religious liberty for all citizens in a country. I doubt if the Churches, apart from

the pressure upon them of the whole modern democratic revolution, would have come to see as clearly as they see now the Christian reasons for the trend toward social and economic equality in the world . . . Correction of the Church from outside is a costly process but it is often necessary, and the Christian who sees truth in these tendencies and movements which may even be hostile to the Church has a responsibility to represent that truth within the Church.[12]

Jesus Christ . . . treasure in earthen vessels

We can sum up our description of the spirit of Protestantism by reference to the two Biblical verses on the title page of this book. On the one hand, the content of the Christian gospel, the *raison d'être* of Protestantism, is a conviction that "Jesus Christ is the same yesterday and today and forever" (Heb. 13:8). He does not change. He has been, he is, he will continue to be. But, on the other hand, this fact about Jesus Christ must be related to a fact about ourselves. Jesus Christ *is* the same yesterday and today and forever, "*but* we have this treasure in earthen vessels to show that the transcendent power belongs to God and not to us" (2 Cor. 4:7).

The fact of Jesus Christ assures us that there *can* be constant renewal at the hand of God. The fact that we have this treasure in earthen vessels reminds us that there will always *need* to be constant renewal at the hand of God.

The danger inherent in Roman Catholicism is that it will equate the treasure and the earthen vessels, and that it will therefore assert that the vessels are no longer earthen. The danger inherent in sectarian Christianity is that it will assume that the treasure can be possessed apart from earthen vessels, and that therefore the vessels are no longer necessary. And while there is no assurance that Protestantism will not continually be impaled on one or another of the horns of this dilemma, there is always here a great evangelical responsibility and possibility for Protestantism. For at its best, Protestantism can recognize *both* that there is a treasure, Jesus Christ, *and* that this treasure is mediated to us through earthen vessels. Without the treasure, Protestantism is nothing. But without the recognition that its vessels are earthen, Protestantism betrays the treasure and forgets that "the transcendent power belongs to God and not to us."

The transcendent power belongs to God and not to us . . . This means that Protestants can never claim that it is they who reform the church or are the agents of its renewal. If the church is always to be reformed (*semper reformanda*), it is because the agent of the reforming activity is God himself. If the preceding pages have seemed to stress the spirit of Protestantism as *"constant renewal* at the hand of God," it must be very clear that this presupposes that it is "constant renewal *at the hand of God."*

The early church between the Ascension and Pentecost is a picture of what the church must always be — a group of people gathered together praying for, and waiting for, the coming of the Holy Spirit. The church does not "have" the Spirit, nor does it "possess" him. The church can only wait for him and live in dependence upon him. Jacques Ellul comments with insight:

> The whole history of the Church is the history of the reformation of the Church by the Spirit. That work must not cease, for Satan who attacks the Church from without does not stop, and the Spirit of God which gives life to the Church by reforming it, does not stop either . . . The permanent reformation of the Church is therefore the obedience of the Church to the Spirit; it means accepting that God leads his Church forward and changes it, that the Church does not settle down in a revelation which it treats as if it were its own property, but rather that it is constantly on the lookout to receive the new order which the Spirit brings.[13]

So Protestants will have a "style of life" that is not easy to describe but nevertheless has upon it the stamp of authenticity and integrity. It involves an assurance about God combined with modesty concerning the reports we make about God. It means trusting him utterly and at the same time never trusting any human account of him utterly. It means being committed and recognizing that statements about our commitment must always be tentative. It means the assurance of an ultimate security and the likelihood of an immediate insecurity. It means a risk, but a risk in the context of a promise.

"The new order which the Spirit brings" (to quote again the luminous phrase of M. Ellul) will be an order in which the vessels are still earthen. Our hope does not lie in the fact that the transcendent power will then belong to us. It lies in the fact that the transcendent power will never belong to us, but that it belongs to God — the God who meets our sin with his grace, and who meets our misuse of his grace with his healing and corrective power.

PART TWO

Central Protestant Affirmations

Introductory Note

We turn now to deal with some of the things that Protestants believe. We shall not attempt to produce a miniature "systematic theology." There are plenty of good books that do that.[1]

Rather, if we may call upon italics to help us out, we will deal with *central* Protestant affirmations (not all Protestant affirmations but only those that seem to be basic), we will deal with central *Protestant* affirmations (not the affirmations of other branches of Christendom save as they help us to understand the Protestant position better), and we will deal with central Protestant *affirmations* (not the things Protestants deny but the things they affirm).

Three comments are in order:

1. This attempt will run the danger of appearing to say, "Here are the ideas you must accept to be a good Protestant," with the erroneous implication that being a good Protestant means assenting to ideas. This kills the spirit of Protestantism by encasing it in stifling forms.

2. A second danger is a reaction against the first danger. In an effort to guard against claiming too much for statements, the opposite sin of vagueness may result. This will foster the illusion that Protestantism is an innocuous combination of generalities that people can take or leave just as they choose.

3. The goal, therefore, toward which this section of the book must aim (and the goal toward which the life of the Protestant must aim) is that of *tentativeness of statement combined with finality of commitment*. The Protestant does not commit his life to statements, but he uses statements to describe the One to whom his life is committed. Christian statements will always be vulnerable, because they are such a far cry from the real thing. But the real thing is never vulnerable because the real thing is not man and his stumbling statements, but the living God himself, whose reality is not dependent upon the adequacy or inadequacy of our statements about him.

5. The Centrality of Grace and the Life of Faith

Where do we start, if we wish to describe the "central Protestant affirmations"? We start with God. We start with a description of what God has done and is doing.

Where do we start, if we wish to describe "what God has done and is doing"? We start with Jesus Christ.

When we start with him we find that God is "a gracious God" and that Protestantism is the religion of grace.

The meaning of grace

"Grace" is therefore the most important word in the Protestant vocabulary. It is also the most abused. We have difficulty in answering why the rallying cry of the Reformers should have been *salvatio sola gratia* (salvation by grace alone). And yet the destiny of Protestantism is bound up with that affirmation. Grace cannot really be described, it can only be experienced. All we can do is try to describe what is experienced.[1]

1. We miss the point if we talk in abstract terms. For grace, in Christian terms, is not the least bit abstract: it is very specific. It is *the grace of our Lord Jesus Christ.* We cannot talk about grace apart from him. The prologue to the Fourth Gospel reminds us that "the law was given through Moses, but grace and truth came through Jesus Christ" (John 1:17). Paul stresses this even more than the author of the Fourth Gospel, and it is not surprising that the Reformers leaned heavily upon him. For Paul, the heart

of the gospel is "the grace of God which was given you in Christ Jesus" (1 Cor. 1:4). When he blesses the Corinthian church, he makes grace pivotal for everything else: "The grace of our Lord Jesus Christ, and the love of God, and the communion of the Holy Spirit, be with you all" (2 Cor. 13:14). Grace is defined by who Jesus Christ is, or better, by what Jesus Christ does. He is the one who transforms grace from an idea into a reality. To understand grace we must look beyond books on the spirit of Protestantism: we must look to a life lived, a death died, a grave overcome. Grace and truth came through Jesus Christ.

We cannot talk very long about the grace of God without talking about the love of God. And here again we have a problem, for love, in ordinary English, can mean a variety of things. It means one thing in a grade school play and another thing in a French movie. It means one thing when the object of our love is a cocker spaniel, and something else when the object of our love is a refugee child. It has different meanings depending on whether we are speaking of our love of art, or our love of justice, or our love of God. None of these really tells us what it means to say that *God* loves.[2] To learn about God's love we have to turn to the New Testament again and see that love in action. The New Testament words love (*agape*) and grace (*charis*) are very close to one another in meaning. It would not be fair to make them identical. But it is fair to say that if God's love (*agape*) is his love toward the loveless, love toward those who really do not deserve his love, then this is very close to what we mean by "the grace (*charis*) of our Lord Jesus Christ."

Here is how Paul describes it. In Romans 5, he is discussing ways in which love is demonstrated. "Why," he comments, "one will hardly die for a righteous man — though perhaps for a good man one will dare even to die" (Rom. 5:7). It is at least conceivable, he feels, that one of us might lay down his life for an exceptionally worthy person. "But," he continues in sheer astonishment, "God shows his love for us in that while we were yet sinners Christ died for us" (Rom. 5:8).

If we had ceased to be sinners, we might be worthy of this kind of love; but that this should happen "while we were yet sinners," while we were *un*worthy of this kind of love, is inconceivable and inexplicable. Yet this is what "the gracious God" does: rather than waiting until we are worthy, he involves himself with us while we are still unworthy. He endures the incredible humiliation of becoming what we are, in order that he may transform us into what he is: "For you know the grace of our Lord Jesus Christ," Paul says, "that though he was rich, yet for your sake he became poor, so that by his poverty you might become rich" (2 Cor. 8:9).

2. "The grace of our Lord Jesus Christ" is not a "thing," an object, an impersonal something or other. It can only be described in personal terms. Grace is not something God himself gives us, it is the way God gives us himself. Grace is *God's personal relationship to us.* But his relationship to us is unlike most of the human relationships we experience, and we must distinguish carefully between them.

Some human relationships are based on *merit:* a baseball club employs a player because he can hit .340 or is exceptionally adept with a glove. Some relationships are based on *need:* I get acquainted with a garage mechanic because he can fix my broken carburetor, or I get acquainted with a banker because he can help me stay solvent. Some relationships are based on *appeal;* a man does not love a woman because she can fix his carburetor or help him stay solvent, but because he finds her beautiful, or appealing, or exciting to be with. (He may even be so swept off his feet by her that he ends his sentences with prepositions.)

The relationship based on grace is unlike the relationship based on merit or need or appeal. God does not enter into personal relationship with his children because they are "good." They are not. Nor does he do so because he "needs" them. He does not. He is not gracious to them because they are "appealing." They are not. Quite the contrary. The Bible is emphatic in asserting that God's relationship to man is not based on the fact that man offers something to God, but on the fact that God offers everything to man. God does not love Israel because Israel is a great or a good nation. Israel, as a matter of fact, is an insignificant nation and (by all normally accepted standards of judgment) a bad nation. And yet God loves Israel . . . simply because he loves Israel. That is the kind of God he is.

It was not because you were more in number than any other people that the Lord set his love upon you and chose you, for you were the fewest of all peoples; but it is because the Lord loves you, and is keeping the oath which he swore to your fathers, that the Lord has brought you out with a mighty hand, and redeemed you from the house of bondage, from the hand of Pharaoh king of Egypt.

(Deut. 7:7–8)

The closest Old Testament equivalent of grace can help us here. In the King James version it was translated "loving-kindness." In the Revised Standard version it is more adequately translated "steadfast love." This is what the love and grace of God really are — his steadfast love, reliable, constant, trustworthy.[3] And this is what the New Testament claims has been incarnated in Jesus Christ, through whom a new relationship between God and man is established that can never be earned but can always be received.

3. We can discover two further things about "the grace of our Lord Jesus Christ" but they must always be mentioned together.

First of all, we learn that grace is *mercy* or *forgiveness*. "While we were yet sinners" was the time God visited us with his grace, and, instead of condemning us, forgave us. We get an inkling of what this means even on the human level. If I have wilfully hurt someone, and thus destroyed our relationship, what I "deserve" is to be condemned and punished. This will never heal the hurt or restore the relationship, and the hurt can be healed, the relationship restored, only when the one who has been wronged is willing to bear the pain of having been wronged, and yet forgive me. Nothing I can do will ever be enough, no matter how hard I try. Mercy and forgiveness must come from the one I have hurt. The most I can do is to accept forgiveness when it is offered, realizing that I do not really deserve it.

That is how Protestantism explains the relationship between God and man. We have wilfully "hurt" God, and thus destroyed our relationship with him. We have spurned him, sinned against his children, answered his love by our hate. And what can overcome love answered by hate? Grace, and grace alone: grace as mercy, grace as forgiveness, grace that bears the hurt in suffering love, grace, in short, made real upon a cross.

Because it is mercy and forgiveness, grace is also *power*. It is the gift of new life. The one who has been forgiven lives in a new situation. Paul reports the word from on high that came to him: "My grace is sufficient for you; for my power is made perfect in weakness" (2 Cor. 12:9). The weakness of the human frame becomes the channel of divine power, so that new energies are unleashed. The recipient of the power will need, of course, to remember its source, and Paul himself could come close to forgetting this. "I worked harder than any of them," he boasted before he caught himself and described what this actually meant, "though it was not I, but the grace of God which is with me" (1 Cor. 15:10).

Elsewhere he compresses the whole process into a single statement: "I am crucified with Christ, nevertheless I live, yet not I, but Christ liveth in me" (Gal. 2:20).[4] *I am crucified with Christ:* my sinful self, Paul realizes, must be destroyed. As I now am I cannot save myself. My old self must die. *Nevertheless I live:* crucifixion is not a final word, it is only a preliminary word. As I die to self, I am raised up to a new life by the power of God. *I live, yet not I, but Christ liveth in me:* this new life is not something I have achieved. It is Christ himself who is at work within me.

Not many people, of course, can talk that confidently. But some people experience this in fragmentary form. Sometimes they speak of "the grace of our Lord Jesus Christ." Sometimes they speak of "the power of the Holy Spirit." Sometimes they say that God is working in them to will and to work to his good pleasure. Luther said it in five words: *Christus Gottessohn ist unser Heiland* (Christ, the Son of God, is our Saviour). However anyone says it, it finally comes back to that.

> All the great Reformation watchwords [Albert Outler writes]—*sola Scriptura, sola fide, sola gratia*—have one essential meaning: *solus Christus*. This is the source and center of Christian faith—and it is only when this faith is hardened into disparate doctrinal systems, and the systems substituted for living faith, that community disintegrates. *Solus Christus* is the content of Christian theology and it is the source and center of Christian community . . . Jesus Christ is the Christian dogma. Everything else in Christian thought derives from or subserves this primordial conviction.[5]

"The grace of our Lord Jesus Christ" is not only news. It is "good news." It is the kind of news its hearers must share. That is exactly what the first Christians did, and they upset the ancient world. That is exactly what the Reformers did, and they upset the medieval world.

But they saved the church.

The surprises of grace

"Grace is insidious," wrote Péguy. "When you think it will come from the right it comes from the left. When you think it will come from the left it comes from the right." Péguy was a Roman Catholic, albeit an unconventional one. But there could scarcely be a more Protestant statement, for it underlines the fact that we have no control over grace. It is God's grace, not ours, and it comes to us on his terms. It may come to us as a gift, but we can never claim it as a right. All we can do is accept it.

That grace should have this quality of surprise is understandable when we look at what can be called the central surprise — the surprising notion that God himself should take flesh and dwell among his children. That there should have been any incarnation at all is surprising. But that the incarnation should have taken place as it did is surely more surprising. We would never have done it the way God did it. If we had been running things, the Son of God would not have been born into a lower-class Jewish carpenter's family, nor would we have allowed him to live in obscurity and die in disgrace as a common criminal. But we were not running things, and that is the surprising way God chose to do it.

His way of doing it forces a choice on us: *either* we reject the way God did it because it is too much of a surprise, too unlikely, too incredible, too shabby; *or* we accept the surprise for what it is and allow it to become normative for everything else we think and do.[6]

If we are willing to let the central surprise become normative, then, while other manifestations of grace may still seem surprising, they will not seem capricious, for at least they will be consistent with the central surprise. Having seen God at work in one unlikely spot, namely, a place of execution outside Jerusalem, we will remember that he can work in other unlikely spots as well, and that it will be in his control, rather than in ours, to determine how he shall visit us with his gracious and redeeming love.

On the face of it, nothing is more surprising, for example, than that bread and wine should speak of grace, and Protestants often refer too glibly to the sacraments as "means of grace." But in the light of the central surprise of the incarnation, where God is revealed among things mean and lowly, it is no longer surprising that things mean and lowly, such as bread and wine, should call to mind the death and resurrection of the Son of God. But — such are the further surprises of grace — we can never go on to claim that God's grace comes *only* through the sacraments or *automatically* through the sacraments. "The grace of our Lord Jesus Christ" may seem most real when we are seated at the Lord's Table in a place of worship, but we deny that the grace is *his* if we assert that it may not also be real at many other tables and in many other places.

Grace is no longer grace when it ceases to surprise us.

The meaning of faith

Our response to grace is faith. We speak of faith more frequently than we speak of grace. But faith means many things on different lips, and we must disentangle some of these if we are to capture the distinctively Protestant flavor of the word.

1. By faith, the non-believer means a desperate attempt to avoid reality. He only says in more sophisticated tones what the schoolboy said: "Faith is believing what you know ain't true."

2. The attempt to contrast "faith" and "facts" is a slight refinement of this. Facts are tangible, provable things: Julius Caesar crossed the Rubicon in 49 B.C., a table top is hard, the existence of three pieces of candy on a low table in a room with four children means trouble. Faith consists in believing intangible, unprovable things: there will never be a third World War, Christ rose from the dead, fairies dance on the lawn in the moonlight.

Faith and facts do not actually divide themselves so tidily. We accept the fact that Caesar crossed the Rubicon in 49 B.C., only if we trust the integrity of the historians and believe in the actual existence of a real Caesar. But neither of these things is "tangible" or "provable." And physicists tell us that a table top is not really hard at all, but is mostly empty space in which a few electrons are dancing around. None of this proves that Christ rose from the dead but it does render suspect the attempt to put faith and facts in mutually exclusive compartments.

3. We often use the word faith to mean "*the* faith," when we are referring to a definite body of belief such as "the Lutheran faith" or "the faith once delivered to the saints." Non-Lutherans do not always believe that these two things are synonymous, and we can examine both of them in an effort to find out. We can learn what the Lutheran faith is by reading *The Book of Concord;* we can describe the faith once delivered to the saints by reference, let us say, to the various phrases of the Apostles' Creed. From this point of view, "the Christian faith" is a body of beliefs with an identifiable content.

4. It is not a long jump from this to the notion that "having faith" means believing the content or giving *assent to the statements* that describe the content. A Christian may assent to the notion that all the words of the Bible are true; he may assent to the Westminster Confession of Faith as containing the system of doctrine taught in Holy Scripture; he may assent to whatever the Roman Catholic church pronounces to be irreformable dogma without believing which he cannot be saved. In each case, faith is assent to statements. This seems to have been the dominant understanding of faith among the late medieval schoolmen, and a rejection of it was one of the reasons for the Reformation.

5. In contrast to this, Luther and the other Reformers understood faith primarily as *trust.* To have faith in something is to commit oneself to it confidently. This kind of faith can be illustrated on different levels. Many people have faith in the democratic process; they trust it to work and commit their lives to it in the confidence that it will work. At least as many people have the same kind of faith in the ultimate triumph of Communism (Communists are often more passionate "believers" than lukewarm Christians). I have faith in a friend, meaning that I trust him to the full, sure

that he will not let me down, and surer still that he will not double-cross me. When we talk about faith in God in this framework we mean primarily not that we assent to certain statements about him, but that we have utter trust in him and rely upon his "steadfast love."

This does not mean, of course, that there is no "assent," or that there is nothing to be "believed." A faith without content (a "faith in faith") would be the most dangerous thing of all, for we could change the object of belief at a moment's whim. But this does mean that the depths of faith have not been plumbed until assent is encompassed by trust. Luther makes the contrast with characteristic gusto:

> There are two kinds of believing: first a believing about God which means that I believe that what is said of God is true. This faith is rather a form of knowledge than a faith . . . Men possessing it can say, repeating what others have said: I believe that there is a God. I believe that Christ was born, died, rose again for me. But what the real faith is, and how powerful a thing it is, of this they know nothing . . .
>
> There is, secondly, a believing in God which means that I put my trust in Him, give myself up to thinking that I can have dealings with Him, and believe without any doubt that He will be and do to me according to the things said of Him. Such faith which throws itself upon God, whether in life or in death, alone makes a Christian man.[7]

As Luther said elsewhere, *"Faith is a lively, reckless confidence in the grace of God."* We can be content to leave it at that.

We now begin to see how Protestants understand the relationship of grace and faith. But this is a difficult task at best, and we can see it more clearly by examining the well-known phrase, "justification by faith." We can understand neither Protestantism nor the Protestant emphasis on grace until we have wrestled with this phrase.

It was Martin Luther who wrestled with it most vigorously. Not, of course, that Luther "made up" the notion. He found it in Scripture. When Luther read, "The just shall live by faith" (Rom. 1:17, K.J.V.), and really saw what it meant, everything was changed.[8]

Luther's "problem" can be stated simply: he felt that before God he was in the wrong. The more he pondered, the surer he was that

God, who had far more penetrating eyes than he, must be even more aware of Luther's sin than Luther was. Since God was of purer eyes than to behold iniquity, Luther could come to only one conclusion: before God, he didn't stand a chance.

Now medieval Christendom had a solution for Luther's problem. He could become "justified," set right, that is, by doing certain things to make himself more pleasing to God. He could be justified by doing good works.[9] There were many "works" a medieval Christian could do. He could become a monk instead of remaining an ordinary Christian, for monks were felt to be living a life more pleasing in the sight of God — and so Luther did that. He could pray special prayers and mortify his flesh, fast and go on pilgrimages to show how concerned he was — and so Luther did all that. Or he could pray twice as many prayers and mortify his flesh twice as much and fast twice as long and go on twice as many pilgrimages to make doubly sure he was pleasing to God — and so Luther did all that too.

But the works didn't work.

No matter how much he did, the old questions remained: "Have I done enough? Shouldn't I have done more? Am I *really* worthy of forgiveness yet?" Luther was not sure. His last state was worse than his first.

In happier times it was customary to dismiss all this by asserting that Luther was a gloomy, sin-obsessed sixteenth-century man. But people in the twentieth century know in their own lives something of what Luther was going through. No one who tries to justify himself (whether to God or to his neighbor or to his own conscience) by "living a good life," can escape Luther's haunting questions: "Have I done enough? Shouldn't I have done more?" There always remains an unpleasant suspicion that some first-century words are still true: "We are unworthy servants: we have only done what was our duty" (Luke 17:10).

But if it is easier to accept the reality of Luther's problem than it once was, it is no easier to accept the answer he got than it ever was. This is not because the answer came in sixteenth-century terms, but because the answer is a blow to our pride on any terms. We evade it as long as we can before we submit, and Luther was no exception to this rule. He simply ran out of evasions.

What happened was this: Luther discovered that he could do nothing about his problem, and that God had done everything about it. He rediscovered, in other words, the reality of grace. God, he found, is "the gracious God," who does not demand that we become worthy before he will love us, but who loves us while we are still unworthy. We are "justified" not by what we do, but by what he has done. "By grace are ye saved through faith," Paul writes, "it is the gift of God, not of works, lest any man should boast" (Eph. 2:8).

The usual way of describing this is to refer to "justification by *faith,*" in contrast to "justification by *works.*" But this way of stating it often leads to a misunderstanding. It suggests that Protestantism has gotten rid of "works" merely by a verbal trick. If I am "justified by my faith," is there not in fact something I have to do, namely "have faith," and is not faith therefore only a new kind of work? Am I not once again responsible for my own salvation?

The question fails to recognize how all-encompassing grace is, and the response that must be made to the question will seem at first to create more problems than it solves. For the Christian answer — an answer by no means limited to Protestants — is that *faith itself is a gift of grace*. That I can believe is only possible because God himself has empowered me to believe. The Reformers taught that grace produces faith, rather than the other way around. The gospel does not say, "Trust God, and he will love you," the gospel says, "God already loves you, so trust him." Faith is not a "work" that saves us; it is our acknowledgment that we are saved. So all-encompassing is God's grace that it is responsible for the miracle of faith in us.[10] The most accurate way to describe Luther's experience, therefore, is not "justification by faith," but "salvation by grace through faith."

The surprises of faith

It is all very surprising and not at all what we would have expected. But the most surprising thing of all is that people who believe this do not draw from it the conclusions they could logically be expected to draw.

1. Since faith is a gift of grace, we would expect the response to be, "In that case, *I can't do anything about it.* God gives faith or he doesn't. Either way it's his decision, not mine."

But the recipients of faith do not talk this way. For Christian experience discovers that the assertion, "I worked . . . though it was not I but the grace of God," is neither theological nonsense nor a *non sequitur,* but a simple description of what the Christian life is like. No recipient of faith ever claims that his new status is the result of his own wisdom and self-dedication, or that his good works are something for which he can take credit. Rather, he acknowledges that he is unworthy of the gift of faith, that he cannot achieve it on his own resources, and yet that it has been given to him anyhow. On the other hand, when he disbelieves, or when he does evil works, he does not try to place the blame on God and relieve himself of responsibility. He *is* responsible, and he knows it.[11]

Furthermore, he discovers that these conclusions are not neurotic nonsense of his own invention, but that they are consistent with the recorded experience of other Christians as well. "Work out your own salvation with fear and trembling," Paul asserted, emphasizing human responsibility, and then went on without pausing for breath, emphasizing that salvation is the gift of God, "for it is God that worketh in you, both to will and to work to his good pleasure" (Phil. 2:12–13).

2. Since man is saved not because he is good but in spite of the fact that he is evil, we would expect the response to be, "In that case, *I can do anything I please.*" Non-believers always feel that Christians should interpret free grace as a sign that "anything goes." W. H. Auden comments that "Every crook will argue: 'I like committing crimes. God likes forgiving them. Really the world is admirably arranged.' "[12]

The most convincing answer to the question, "Shall we sin that grace may abound?" is Paul's emphatic negative in his letter to the Romans, "By no means!" (Rom. 6:2, 6:15, 7:7). If an expostulation does not seem an adequate rejoinder to the outsider, he must realize that it is the only appropriate rejoinder the insider can make. For the question is an "academic" question: to assume that because God loves me and forgives my sin I should therefore sin with even greater abandon, is like assuming that since my wife trusts me and will forgive me if I am unfaithful to her, I should therefore be unfaithful on every possible occasion.

What is missing from the question is the slightest inkling of what grace really means in the life of the believer. The question assumes that grace is what Dietrich Bonhoeffer scornfully called "cheap grace," grace that costs nothing either to giver or recipient. But grace is actually what Bonhoeffer called "costly grace," the grace of our Lord Jesus Christ, who had to endure a cross to make that grace real for us, and in response to whom we are called not to a life of libertinism but of discipleship.[13]

3. Since man can contribute nothing to his own salvation, we would expect the response to be, "In that case, *I don't need to do anything at all.*" This is the commonest misunderstanding of justification by faith — that it relieves the believer of the necessity of doing good works. The Reformers did, to be sure, deny the value of good works *as a means of earning salvation.* But this does not mean that they denied the value of good works. They insisted that good works were a fruit of salvation. "Good works do not make a good man," was Luther's way of putting it, "but a good man does good works." [14]

Why does a man do good works? No one has captured the true flavor of the Protestant answer more wonderfully than Luther himself:

> Well now! My God has given to me, unworthy and lost man, without any merit, absolutely for nothing and out of pure mercy, through and in Christ, the full riches of all godliness and blessedness, so that I henceforth need nothing more than to believe it is so.
>
> Well, then, for such a Father, who has so prodigally lavished upon me his blessings, I will in return freely, joyously and for nothing do what is well-pleasing to Him, and also be a Christian toward my neighbor, as Christ has been to me; and I will do nothing except only what I see to be needful, useful and blessed for him, because I indeed through my faith have enough of everything in Christ. See, thus there flows from faith love and delight in God, and from love a free, willing, joyous life to serve our neighbor for nothing. For just as our neighbor suffers want and is in need of our superabundance, so have we suffered want before God and been in need of his grace.

Therefore, as God through Christ has helped us for nothing, so ought we through the body and its works to do nothing but help our neighbor.[15]

It is clear that grace forces us to think in a new way about freedom. On the one hand, the reality of grace does not deny the reality of freedom. The fact of the matter is that *grace secures freedom.* It is when the individual has been the recipient of grace that he is freed from his false allegiance to self and to sin, and can for the first time fulfill his true destiny as a child of God.

But this means, on the other hand, that the kind of freedom the Christian has to fulfill his true destiny is not a freedom *from* having to do things and being able to leave everything to God. Rather, as Paul made clear in his letter to the Galatians, since it is "*for* freedom [that] Christ has set us free," we must "through love be servants of one another" (Gal. 5:1, 13). The first epistle of Peter states quite baldly what Christian freedom involves: "Live as free men . . . live as servants of God" (1 Pet. 2:16).

Confronted by the fact that he can do nothing to procure his salvation, the Protestant's response is not to sit back and do nothing. His response is to be a servant of God by being a servant to his neighbor. To "live as free men" and to "live as servants of God" are not two contradictory things. They are two ways of talking about the same thing.

The great "doctor of grace," St. Augustine, to whom Roman Catholics and Protestants alike stand in debt, saw as few men have seen how grace and faith and salvation and works and seeking and finding must all be understood in the light of Jesus Christ:

Walk by him the man and thou comest to God. By him thou goest, to him thou goest. Look not for any way except himself by which to come to him. For if he had not vouchsafed to be the way we should all have gone astray. Therefore he became the way by which thou shouldst come. I do not say to thee, seek the way. The way itself is come to thee; arise and walk.[16]

6. The Authority of Scripture

Protestantism asserts that a collection of writings composed between 750 B.C. and A.D. 150, give or take a few years either way, shall be the source and standard of the church's life until the end of time. The Reformers cried *sola Scriptura* — Scripture alone as the source and test of faith — and Protestants, with varying degrees of consistency and enthusiasm, have echoed that cry ever since. All the topics we have explored, and all the topics we have still to explore, must sooner or later submit to the question, "What does the Bible say about this?" [1]

How are we to understand this strange persistence of the Bible in the life of Christendom? What place should it occupy in a modern statement of the Christian faith? To answer these questions we must first get our historical bearings.

Pre-Reformation gains and losses

The centrality of Scripture (from *scriptum,* meaning "something written") was no invention of the Reformers. Before there were any Christian writings at all, the early church was reading, studying, and interpreting the Jewish Scriptures it had inherited, which now comprise our Old Testament. Early Christian preaching took as its theme the announcement that all the events foretold by the prophets in those Jewish Scriptures had come to fulfillment in the life, death, and resurrection of Jesus Christ.[2]

But it was not enough just to preach this. It had to be written down. For those who had seen and heard these things were mortal men. Witnesses to the cross who did not die in bed died in the arena, or on crosses of their own. But they left their accounts of what they had seen and heard, so that later generations could also get it firsthand.

A literature of considerable proportions accumulated, and for well over three centuries the church was occupied with weighing and sifting this literature, until finally twenty-seven writings had been accepted throughout Christendom as authoritative accounts of the *new* testament (or covenant) between God and man, revealed in Jesus Christ. These twenty-seven writings, together with the Jewish Scriptures, became "canonical." Since the word "canon" means norm or yardstick, this is a way of saying that the Scriptures were the norm or yardstick of the faith.[3]

It was not that simple, of course. For the problem remained: How were the Scriptures to be *interpreted* so as to be a proper norm for faith? By a common-sense interpretation? A literal interpretation? A sophisticated or philosophical interpretation? By the Middle Ages, four different ways of interpreting Scripture had become common. A familiar example from St. Thomas Aquinas (1225–74) illustrates the differences. He shows that the word "Jerusalem" has various meanings. In its *literal* meaning it refers to a city in Palestine. But the word can have an *allegorical* meaning, signifying the church. It can also have a *moral* meaning, representing the individual. Finally, it can have an *eschatological* meaning, standing for the heavenly kingdom still to come.[4]

Long before the Middle Ages, however, the allegorical interpretation had become a particular favorite. It meant that one could discover spiritual riches in the most unlikely places—many people still interpret the Song of Songs as an allegory of Christ's love for the church — but it also meant that with a little ingenuity one could find anything in Scripture he wanted to find. It seems to Protestants today that the resultant interpretations of Scripture got farther and farther away from the clear intent of the original writers.[5]

Along with this went an increasing appeal to the traditions of the church as having an authority equal to that of Scripture. It seems to Protestants today that the traditions also got farther and farther away from the New Testament gospel.[6]

Reformation gains and post-Reformation losses

It seemed that way to the Reformers too. They read their Bibles and found a disparity of astonishing proportions between the early church and their own church. They could not feel that the disparity represented progress. To them it was retrogression of a fatal sort. And when the conflict finally focused on the irreconcilability between what followed the words, "The church says . . ." and what followed the words, "The Bible says . . ." they opted for the latter alternative with consequences we have already traced. Their appeal was to Scripture (given by God, as they believed) over against tradition (given by men, as they believed). So great was their distrust of tradition that they appealed not only to Scripture but *only* to Scripture (*sola Scriptura*) — which did not mean that they looked at nothing else, but that when they looked at anything else (whether at Augustine's preaching about sin or at Tetzel's preaching about indulgences) they looked at it in the light of Scripture and judged it by what they found there. Augustine got high marks and Tetzel flunked.

Now sentences beginning, "The Bible says . . ." and "The church says . . ." should not lead to dissimilar conclusions. When they do, as they most certainly did in medieval Christendom, the remedy is not, the Reformers said, to disregard the Bible's message, the remedy is to readjust the church's message, as radically as may be necessary, until it conforms with the Bible's message. In making this readjustment, the Reformers re-established the crucial fact that the church must be a *listening* church, which does not mean listening to its own interior monologue, but listening to the voice it hears in Scripture — the voice it dares to call the voice of God, and in obedience to which it must be prepared to sacrifice all else.

So much for Reformation gains. But there were losses too. The Reformers to a limited extent, and their descendants to an unlimited extent, tried to *guarantee* the authenticity of what they heard in Scripture. They endowed Scripture with more and more authority, by making it less and less human. Gradually the Holy Spirit was credited with *full* responsibility for everything in Scripture, and the human writers reduced to passive instruments. The Spirit not only inspired the content and sense of Scripture but "actually supplied, inspired, and dictated the very words and each and every term individually." [7] So Quenstedt, a seventeenth-century Protestant, was content to put it. Advocates of the position finally insisted that the location of the Hebrew vowel points (not found in the original Old Testament manuscripts) had been infallibly guaranteed by the Holy Spirit.

From this position, which J. K. S. Reid characterizes as *rigor scholasticus*, there can be no retreat. There can only be increasing rigor. The concession that Scripture contained a single error, however minor, would threaten the entire edifice of belief. When it became clear and unavoidable that there *were* errors in *all* the manuscripts, these were finally attributed to copyists who had incorrectly reproduced an *original* infallible manuscript that God in his inscrutable wisdom had now withdrawn from mortal gaze.

This kind of defense is a credit to human ingenuity under pressure, but it is hardly a credit to divine revelation in action.

1. Our basic discontent with *rigor scholasticus* must be precisely its stultifying of divine revelation in action. We have already discussed our dissatisfaction with the view implicit here that God reveals information about himself and that our response consists in learning the information correctly.[8] We must concede, of course, that if this view of revelation is correct, then the view of Scripture under discussion must be maintained at any cost. For if the Holy Spirit has permitted one bit of misinformation to invade his book, he has proved himself an unreliable witness, and nothing in the book can henceforth be trusted.

2. This view embodies the Protestant counterpart of an error that Protestants attribute to Roman Catholicism. It is frequently pointed out that in place of an infallible Pope, a large segment of Protestantism substituted an infallible book, a "paper pope." What is not so frequently pointed out is that if it is wrong to assert that a man (in this case, the Pope) can speak for God beyond possibility of error, it is also wrong to assert that a group of men (in this case, the writers of Scripture) can speak for God beyond the possibility of error. If papal infallibility is wrong, so is paper infallibility.

3. The upholders of this interpretation fall prey to a heresy they condemn elsewhere. When they make the writers of Scripture passive agents of the Holy Spirit, they are denying that God uses the writers' *humanity* in the composition of Scripture. Elsewhere God does not appear to work apart from the humanity of his witnesses. He works, in fact, *through* their humanity. To deny the human element in the Bible is to commit what is known as the "docetic" heresy. This is the belief, in doctrines of the person of Christ, that Christ was not really human but only seemed to be human (*dokeo* is Greek for "seem" or "appear to be"). Christian faith has rejected this heresy, insisting that the Word was made *flesh,* with all its frailties and limitations. This carried with it the attendant risk that God incarnate might not be acknowledged as such, but that he might be, as indeed he was, rejected by men.

But believers in infallibility, while forced to acknowledge that God took a risk with the Incarnation, are not willing to let him take a second risk with Scripture. And their assertion that the truth of Scripture can be *guaranteed* by the fact that the Holy Spirit overrides all human agency, is actually their assertion that *at this one point* docetism is really correct, and that the Scriptures only "seem" to be human products.

"Critical" gains and "critical" losses

Rigor scholasticus became *rigor mortis.* No matter how valiantly they tried, Reformation Biblicists could not breathe new life into the body of Scripture, and it took the alien baptismal waters of Biblical criticism to effect a regeneration. The baptismal formula, which went "interpret the Bible like any other book" was a harsh formula but a necessary one. The right to interpret the Bible like any other book was a hard-won right. But won it was, and the procedures of literary criticism were applied to the Bible with devastating thoroughness. As this went on, both gains and losses became apparent.

On the credit side was the fact that one could now have a clearer understanding of Scripture than had ever been possible before. To know which strands of the Pentateuch were early, and which late, obviously made it possible to understand the Pentateuch better. To know the probable date of the composition of Amos, and therefore to be able to picture the historical situation to which he was preaching, was to hear more clearly what he was saying. To know that Isaiah 40–55 came from the time of the Babylonian exile and not from the time of Isaiah the prophet, was to enter into its message of hope with a new sense of assurance. And — no small achievement — to be freed from the world of floating axeheads and chariots ascending to heaven, was to be free to be a man of faith and a contemporary man at one and the same time.

But a price was paid for these gains. The old assurances were gone for good. The virgin birth, the Christmas stories, the miracles of Jesus, the ascension, the second coming, all these disappeared as certainties and were at best only probabilities. Many of Jesus' sayings were treated as interpolations placed on his lips by later writers with ecclesiastically vested interests. Once the critics had begun (and this had been the great worry of their opponents), where were they to stop? A radical principle of discrimination had been introduced into the interpretation of Scripture, and if the world of floating axeheads had dissolved, might not the reductive process go on until the world of faith itself dissolved, and nothing was left in its place?

One unforeseen thing, however, happened. It resulted from the fact that the Biblical scholars were men of integrity: if the textual evidence led them away from what they had expected to find, they were prepared to follow the evidence. Many of the New Testament critics had been sure, for example, that as they stripped away the layers of interpretation they would move from the incredible account of a risen Lord who had burst the bonds of death back to a credible account of a peasant Galilean who preached the love of God and neighbor. But as they worked back through the material, they found that the "fact" behind the "embellishments" was not a collection of aphorisms attributed to a Jewish rabbi named Jesus, but the triumphant assertion that God had raised that same Jesus from the dead and made him both Lord and Christ.

Here, at any rate, was a clear choice: *either* recapture this apostolic faith, with whatever modifications are necessary in the twentieth century, *or* dismiss it as outmoded and devise some new faith to take its place. If contemporary Protestantism has chosen the alternative of recapturing the apostolic faith, it has been able to do so only by taking with utmost seriousness the qualifying clause — with whatever modifications are necessary in the twentieth century.

Gains and losses today

Let us state the modern predicament as sharply as we can: We are confronted with the historic claim that the Bible is authoritative, and yet when we read it, we find ourselves in an unbelievable world. We read about bodies being levitated up into heaven — and we know that heaven, wherever it may be, is not located 50,000 feet or so above Palestine. We read about demons leaving demented persons and taking up habitation in herds of pigs so that the latter rush headlong over cliffs into the sea — and nothing in modern psychiatry leads us to place any credence in the tale. We discover that the whole Biblical framework seems to presuppose a "three-story universe," with heaven up in the air, hell beneath the earth, and earth a fixed point in between — and we know that this view was exploded at least as long ago as the seventeenth century.[9]

These may not have been problems for the Reformers, but they are most certainly problems for us. We cannot accept either the Reformers' view of the universe or their sixteenth-century view of the Bible. Too much has happened in between their day and ours. So we must ask ourselves: *Can we retain a Protestant emphasis on the centrality of Scripture, and still do justice to the fact that we live in the twentieth century?*

To ask the question is to assume that "the Reformation must continue." To try to answer it is to make the same assumption. We must see, therefore, what emphases in the Reformers' outlook are still valid in our day, and we can distinguish at least four things, each of which represents a slight refinement of the preceding one.[10]

1. Our whole approach must be based on *a distinction between the Word of God and the words of Scripture*. The Word of God can be none other than Jesus Christ, "the Word made flesh" (cf. John 1:14). Any other meaning of the phrase must be subservient to

this. Protestants often speak of the Bible as the Word of God, or refer to someone "preaching the Word of God," or describe the sacraments as the "enacted" Word of God, "the Word made visible," as Augustine said. These uses are legitimate only so long as it is remembered that the right of Scripture, sermon, and sacrament to be called the Word of God does not derive from themselves, but only from the fact that they all point beyond themselves, and are vehicles for the incarnate Word of God, Jesus Christ. The whole disaster of post-Reformation biblicism can be traced to an unwillingness to take this distinction seriously.

Although the Reformers themselves did not consistently make this distinction, Luther at least describes with great winsomeness what is involved, in his figure of Scripture as "the manger in which Christ lies." Scripture is not Christ, but it houses Christ. He is found within it. The purpose of Scripture is simply to witness to him. He is *rex et dominus Scripturae,* "king and lord of Scripture." The whole point of Scripture is that it should "ply Christ."

> That is the true test by which to judge all books, when we see *whether they deal with Christ or not,* since all the Scriptures show us Christ, and St. Paul will know nothing but Christ. What does not teach Christ is not apostolic even though St. Peter or Paul taught it; again, what preaches Christ would be apostolic even though Judas, Annas, Pilate, and Herod did it.[11]

Bishop Nygren gives a modern analogy of the difference between the Word of God and the words of Scripture. At the end of World War II, the "good news" of liberation from the Nazis came to the Norwegians by radio and newspaper. But their radios and newspapers were not themselves the liberation. They were simply the means by which the liberation was proclaimed and became a reality for those who heard it. Similarly, the "good news" of liberation from sin comes to us by a book. But the book is not itself the liberation. It is simply the means by which the liberation is proclaimed and becomes a reality for those who hear it.

2. If one is willing to make this initial distinction between the Word of God and the words of Scripture, he can go on to discover that *Biblical criticism serves a creative rather than a destructive purpose.* J. K. S. Reid puts it this way:

> If the authority of the Bible be located . . . not in the printed page, but in Him to whom the printed page bears witness, Jesus Christ Himself the Word incarnate, crucified, risen, and regnant, in the transmitted message rather than the transmitted letter, it will be possible to accommodate the results of criticism of the words, and yet to credit the Bible with all the authority of Him to whom it testifies.[12]

To study the meaning of the words written about the Incarnate Word can only help us to understand him better. Only the person who denies the distinction between the Word of God and the words of Scripture will be "afraid" of Biblical criticism. If he fears that tampering with the text will destroy his faith, he makes clear that the real object of his faith is the text, rather than the one to whom the text bears witness.

No Protestant who really believes in the ongoing activity of the living God will be fearful of attempts to understand more clearly the book in which that activity is recorded. He will rather feel that the very nature of God's activity demands the fullest possible examination, for reasons Suzanne de Dietrich has made plain:

> Suppose that we knew nothing of the Bible, and were told that God had revealed himself to men through a book in which those who had seen and heard him bore witness to him. We would probably imagine a book of such overwhelming and invincible logic that it could convince anybody who would read it. And instead, what do we find? We find that the Bible is a very human book, full of obscurities and contradictions . . . God chose to reveal himself through the frailty of human words, just as he chose the humble poverty of the manger for his Son.
>
> The mystery of the divine love is a mystery of humiliation. God undertakes to lift his creatures to himself by first of all stooping down to them — he speaks their language, he shares their flesh. God gives himself to men in the Bible in the same way that he gives himself to men in his Son.[13]

If God does choose "to reveal himself through the frailty of human words," then it is not a disservice to faith but a responsible exercise of it, to examine those words, in all their frailty, to see how they witness to God incarnate in Jesus Christ.

But it is not enough for us simply to justify Biblical criticism. We must ask how it proceeds. For we are faced with the disturbing fact that there are many different levels within Scripture. Most

Protestants do not take seriously the miracle of the sun standing still (Joshua 10:12–14) and even express polite vagueness about the sin against the Holy Spirit (Luke 12:10) which (like the original infallible document of the fundamentalists) no man has seen at any time. They question the notion that it was really God's will for Saul to slay all the women and children of the Amalekites (1 Sam. 15:3), they doubt if happiness is truly to be found by dashing the heads of little children against the rocks (Ps. 137:9), and they notice marked discrepancies between the pessimistic outlook of the author of Ecclesiastes and the optimistic outlook of the author of Romans. They are suspicious of the ecstatic fervor of the early church, and they would like to have a doctrine of the Holy Spirit (who was responsible for the ecstasy) considerably more sophisticated than that of the book of Acts. How, then, does one possibly "adjust" this conglomeration of points of view into a satisfactorily consistent whole?

The most radical answer to the question has been offered by Rudolf Bultmann.[14] He asserts that we must "de-mythologize" the Scriptures, i.e. strip them of the mythological imagery of a prescientific world-view (with its three-story universe, its ascensions into heaven, its descents into hell), and then restate the enduring truth that remains when we have removed the accidental trappings of prescientific thought. In suggesting this, Bultmann is not trying to remove the "scandal" of the faith. On the contrary, he is sure that there is a "scandal," the scandal of the cross, and he wants to make sure that people do not come to the erroneous conclusion that in rejecting the pseudo-scandal of a prescientific world-view they have rejected the Christian gospel. The gospel is independent of the world-view in which it was originally formulated. From this Bultmann goes on to attempt a restatement of the Christian faith in categories drawn from the existentialist philosophy of Martin Heidegger. His attempt is a creative one, although it is open to question whether Heidegger is any more intelligible to "modern man" than St. Paul, and whether Bultmann has not simply clothed the gospel in another perishable garment that must be shed when the next philosophical fashion comes along. This is not said as a cavalier dismissal. It is meant only to suggest that no Christian can avoid Bultmann's challenge, even though not all Christians are prepared to accept Bultmann's answer.

We can find further help at this point from the Reformers, even if we make a slightly different use of their insight than they did. The Reformers made a great deal of the principle *Scriptura scripturae interpres* (Scripture is the interpreter of Scripture). By this they meant that there is a consistent witness shining through Scripture *as a whole.* When the character of that central thrust and concern has been discerned, it is then possible to interpret the rest of Scripture in the light of it. The obscure and "difficult" parts of Scripture can be more readily understood by the light cast on them from the clearer parts.[15] Now if (as we have seen with Luther) Scripture is primarily to witness to Christ, and if (as we saw in the previous chapter) the God of the Bible is the gracious God whom we know through "the grace of our Lord Jesus Christ," then we have a basis from which to approach Scripture and from which to evaluate its various parts. On these terms we know very well that we are not to slay modern Amalekites, that dashing children's heads against the rocks is no part of the divine will, that the author of Romans is to be preferred to the author of Ecclesiastes, and that the reality of heaven is not in the least jeopardized by a recognition that it is not located in the stratosphere. To be sure, not all of our critical problems will be solved this simply, but at least we will have a basis on which to keep trying to solve them.

3. It might appear thus far as though the interpretation of Scripture were simply a matter of careful scientific study. It is that, for the Christian, but it is something else as well. This something else, of which the Reformers were particularly aware, is an awareness that *the Holy Spirit continues to speak through Scripture.* Protestants read the Bible with the recognition that even though "the letter killeth, the Spirit giveth life." Anyone who reads the Bible discovers that more often than not the words are flat and lifeless and say nothing whatever to him. But on another occasion, as he reads *the same passage,* it "comes alive," speaks in most direct terms to his condition, and gives him a real sense of what God's purpose for his life really is. When this happens, the Protestant does not attribute the change simply to his improved "insight," or

to the fact that he has made himself more psychologically receptive, important as those things may be: he attributes the change to the activity of the Holy Spirit.

He attributes it to the fact that the living God is once again, as he has so often done in the past, using Scripture to make known his will. The words on the printed pages are nothing until God the Holy Spirit gives them life. Of all the Reformers, Calvin probably saw this most clearly:

> As God alone is a sufficient witness of himself in his word, so also the word will never gain credit in the hearts of men, till it be confirmed by the internal testimony of the Spirit. It is necessary, therefore, that the same Spirit, who spake by the mouths of the prophets, should penetrate into our hearts, to convince us that they faithfully delivered the oracles which were divinely intrusted to them . . . [Scripture] obtains the credit which it deserves with us by the testimony of the Spirit. For though it conciliate our reverence by its internal majesty, it never seriously affects us till it is confirmed by the Spirit in our hearts.[16]

But the clearest understanding of the relationship of Word and Spirit comes from Calvin's liturgy, rather than from Calvin's *Institutes*. It was the practice in the Reformed liturgies (a practice that is properly being revived) to offer a "Prayer for Illumination" just before the reading of the words of Holy Scripture. The burden of this prayer was a plea that the Holy Spirit, who had moved the hearts of those who wrote these words, would also move the hearts of those who heard them, to the end that through the words of Scripture the living God might speak directly to his children once again as he had done of old.

This plea could stand as a symbol of all that is best in the Protestant approach to Scripture — the expectant hope that once again God will bring dead words to life and through them speak his living Word to men.

4. This means one thing more. If Protestants are to read the Bible expectantly, they cannot read it as spectators. They must read it *as participants in the drama that is unfolded within its pages*. This means that citizens of Chicago hear the word of God spoken through Amos to the citizens of Bethel just as though it were addressed through Amos to the citizens of Chicago. It means that warnings against the corruption in the state, whether uttered in

Jeremiah or Revelation, must be heeded with particular care in Washington, London, Moscow, Paris, and other centers of power. It means also that the promise of Jesus that he will be with his followers until the end of the age is a promise spoken to the reader today in his grief and in his great joy.

The Bible itself will help to involve us in this way. Reinhold Niebuhr has pointed out how the more we read the Bible, and look at the world in the light of what we read, the more we become aware of what he calls its "self-authenticating character." That is to say, the Bible shows us (a) the shallowness and inadequacy of non-Biblical ways of looking at life, and (b) it provides a platform from which we can see some sense of meaning in life.[17] Amid a great deal of uncertainty, tragedy, and caprice, we discover through the Bible some things that are certain, that are beyond tragedy, and that are charged with meaning. We find that contemporary events confirm the prophetic view of history, and that the God of all comfort comforts us in the midst of our twentieth-century distresses just as Paul assured the Corinthians that he did in the midst of their first-century distresses.

The risk of reading the Bible

We do not, then, dispose of the Bible because we no longer believe in a geocentric universe, or because we discover Biblical passages that are manifestly "dated." The more we eliminate disturbing things of that sort the closer we come to the disturbing thing we cannot eliminate — the fact that the Bible confronts us with a God who, while he makes promises, also makes demands. The disturbing note that sounds through the Bible is the call to *repentance,* the demand that we turn about and change our ways. Repentance comes hard, and the more urgent the plea for repentance becomes, the more frantic become our attempts to find reasons for evading it.

This, it must be insisted, is the *real* reason we seek to dismiss the Bible: not because it is out-of-date, but because it is much too up-to-date, because it describes far too accurately who we are and where we have gone wrong. It is not fanciful at all to talk about being "participants" in the Biblical story, for we are participants in that story whether we will or no — participants who are the objects both of the promises it puts before us and of the demands it no less urgently puts before us. "Have I experienced anything more important, incisive, serious, contemporary than this," Karl Barth writes, "that I have been personally present and have shared in the crossing of Israel through the Red Sea *but also* in the adoration of the golden calf, in the baptism of Jesus *but also* in the denial of Peter and the treachery of Judas, that all this has happened to me here and now?" [18]

If I have experienced these things — and it is the testimony of all sorts of witnesses that all of us have — then we must hear with utter seriousness the query Barth goes on to address to us: "Whether, after the Word of God has sought to provide us with the movement and meaning, we have perhaps evaded it?" [19]

7. The Sovereignty of God—and Some Implications

We are being forced in an uncomfortable direction. The gracious God of Chapter 5, who is also the Biblical God of Chapter 6, is now the sovereign God of Chapter 7.

This word "sovereign" is not a cautious word. It is an extravagant word. It describes one who has unlimited power, who is superior to all others, who is independent of everyone and everything. This is the way men used to talk about the lords of the earth. It is the way men still talk about the Lord of earth and heaven. He is the God who is in control, who brings to pass what comes to pass, who ordains all things.

It is when we put it in these terms that we begin to get uncomfortable. For if this was ever easy to believe, which is debatable, it no longer is. First of all, the evidence does not seem to point that way. God does not appear to have a very firm hand on things. We know too much about evil in the world to assent glibly to the notion that God is in control. Second, if God *is* in control, if the evil in the world is the work of his almighty hand, he seems more like a frightful monster than a good God. Third, if God is sovereign, we seem to be little more than puppets who move not in freedom but at the whim of his omnipotent power.

These and other difficulties are often due to misunderstandings of God's sovereignty. But Protestants have been responsible for their share of the misunderstandings, and we must disavow some of the things our forebears said, even while we insist upon the truth of what they were trying to safeguard.[1]

"His mercy is forever sure" — some things the sovereignty of God has meant

1. The first thing can be stated briefly. The sovereignty of God means *the freedom of God.* God is not bound by our insistence that he act as we expect him to act. That he is sovereign means that he is not subject to us or to anyone else. He is free to act toward us on his terms rather than on ours. What he does will be consistent with his will, but there is no reason why it must be consistent with our wills. To acknowledge God's sovereignty is to acknowledge that he is free to be God and that he cannot be limited by "our idea of God."

2. This does not mean that he is capricious. To believe in God's sovereignty is to believe in *the sureness of his love.* The Calvinists sang, and still sing:

> . . . The Lord our God is good,
> His mercy is forever sure;
> His truth at all times firmly stood
> And shall from age to age endure.

How can we sing this in a world where there seems to be so little evidence that it is true? Because, a host of Protestants have answered, we learn of God's love not from looking at the world, but from looking at Jesus Christ. We do not gaze at the world and then try to understand Christ in terms of the world. We gaze at Jesus Christ and then try to understand the world in terms of him.

The music of one of the greatest Protestant composers provides us with an analogy. Bach's *Passacaglia and Fugue in C Minor* consists of a number of variations on a short theme. At first the theme is distinct and clear. As the variations unfold, and the music gets more complicated, the theme is harder and harder to distinguish. Soon the music seems to have no direction or purpose whatever. But *if one is already acquainted with the theme,* he can hear it through all the apparent chaos, holding the music together, giving it direction and force.

Protestant faith understands the sovereignty of God in a similar way. What we see and hear often seems to be sheer chaos. Life apparently has no direction or purpose. But the Christian who is *already acquainted with the theme,* having seen and heard it in the life and death and resurrection of Jesus Christ, knows that the direction and purpose are there, undergirding the apparent chaos, sustaining it, holding it together. The Christian believes that the theme is still being played, even when his own ears can scarcely detect it. God's mercy is forever sure.

This is no academic matter. It makes a difference. Things often went badly for the Reformers. Their cause was challenged, their ideas were ridiculed, their books were burnt, their bodies were tortured. But this did not threaten their faith in God's sovereignty or the sureness of his love. That assurance came from another source. The Scottish Presbyterians sang, with death sentences upon their heads:

> My soul with expectation doth
> Depend on God indeed;
> My strength and my salvation do
> From him alone proceed.
>
> He only my salvation is
> And my strong Rock is He;
> He only is my sure defense;
> I shall not moved be.[2]

3. But there is something more to say about the sovereignty of God. *Sovereign love expresses itself in servanthood.* This surprises us, for we think of a sovereign as having servants, not as being a servant. Yet the greatest exercise of sovereignty turns out to be the greatest exercise of servanthood.[3] He who is highest of all consents to become lowest of all. He who rules all time and space becomes incarnate in one whose life is bound to a particular time (the reign of Pontius Pilate) and a particular space (a corner of the Mediterranean world about the size of Connecticut). This is the way the sovereign Lord redefines his sovereignty for us. He shows us that his is not the sovereignty of naked power, but the sovereignty of grace and love. Whatever we may think of other

sovereignties, we can no longer understand the sovereignty of God as impersonal omnipotence; the sovereignty of God is active, outgoing love, taking the form of a servant.[4]

The Biblical doctrine of election

The sovereign God whom we meet in the Bible is the electing God. The Bible is quite straightforward about this. God "elects," God chooses, and he elects a special group of people, the Jews. They are not chosen, we recall, because they are the biggest nation or the best nation. They are chosen because it is God's good pleasure to choose them.

Many persons are offended by this claim of the Jews to be a "chosen people." Sometimes they use it as an excuse for anti-Semitism. Sometimes they cite it as an example of spiritual arrogance that has no place in a religion of humility.[5]

Nevertheless, the Bible stoutly affirms, God did choose the Jews and he did set them apart as his special people, entering into a *covenant* or bond with them. The terms of human covenant-bonds are familiar to us: if *x* fails to fulfill his side of the bargain, *y* is released from obligation to fulfill his. Not so in the covenant-bond between God and Israel. Israel's side of the agreement was to be faithful to God and no one else. But in the pungent language of the King James version, Israel went "a-whoring after false Gods." Israel was faithless. *But God was faithful.* This was the difference: God continued to love his people when they no longer loved him. He would not forsake them. To be sure, in the process of trying to win them back he executed wrath and judgment, but the purpose was always restitution rather than punishment. Judgment, in the words of Psalm 73, was "judgment . . . to save."

Jeremiah speaks of the possibility of a *new* covenant (Jer. 31:31–34). God and man will someday enter into a new relationship because God is a God who forgives. The Christian church affirms that Jesus Christ transformed this future possibility into a present actuality. "This cup," he said at the last supper, "is the *new covenant* in my blood, shed for many for the remission of sins" (Mark 14:24). The Christian community is "the new Israel," the community in which the new covenant between God and man has been actualized.

Christians who dislike the notion of "the chosen people" are not only making a judgment on the Jewish community, but on the Christian community as well. They are repudiating what they themselves have been called to be. For the Christian church is the inheritor of the promise made to Abraham: "I will establish my covenant between me and you and your descendants after you, throughout their generations for an everlasting covenant to be God to you and to your descendants after you" (Gen. 17:7). The New Testament word for "church" (*ek-klesia,* from which we get "ecclesiastical") means "called out." Christians are those who are "called out" by God into the new fellowship of the church in which the covenant promises have come true.

The minute we realize that *we* have been elected, we understand afresh that election is an act of sheer grace. No one, looking at himself, can assert that he deserves this election. No one, looking at the church, can assert that Christians deserve this election. No one deserves it, and yet it is given anyhow.

That is why it is an election of grace.

Some difficulties and some consequences

This is a heady doctrine. It has led men to reckless spending of themselves in utter humility for the glory of God alone. It has led other men to make recklessly arrogant claims about the unsatisfactory status of their fellow men in the sight of God. Most of the problems, indeed, that the doctrine of election raises grow out of the negative implication that if a few are chosen a good many are *not* chosen, and we shall examine some of these in an appendix to this chapter. But there are other difficulties to examine first.

1. Opponents of the doctrine of election often create the impression that until the time of the Reformation, God was a reasonably pleasant deity. Then, all of a sudden, the harsh Calvin produced the harsh God of harsh Presbyterianism. Calvin said a great deal about election and predestination, to be sure, but only because he found that the Bible said a great deal too. The doctrine, par-

ticularly in its negative implications, had been systematically formulated by St. Augustine, a thousand years before Calvin, and St. Thomas Aquinas in the thirteenth century had stated it in ways just as severe as those of Calvin.[6] The doctrine was no invention of the Reformers.

Part of the reason for the harsh way the Reformers often put it, is that the longer a doctrine has to be defended, the more "wooden" it tends to become. This rule seems to apply both to individuals and to the church as a whole. There is all the difference in the world between the brief treatment of predestination in Calvin's early *Instruction in Faith* (1537), and his lengthy, tortured defense of the same doctrine in the final edition of the *Institutes* twenty-two years later. As for the church, "A new insight," Charles Williams has said, "is quite sound when a master uses it, cheapens as it becomes popular, and is unendurable when it is merely fashionable. So Augustine's predestination was safe with him, comprehensible in Calvin, tiresome in the English Puritans, and quite horrible in the Scottish presbyteries." [7]

Defensive polemics are a poor way of describing the good news.

2. Many people interpret the doctrine of election to mean election to privilege, as though God had said to Israel, "You only have I known of all the nations of the earth, therefore I will see that it goes well with you" (Amos 3:2, revised). Actually, election in Biblical terms means election to responsibility. God chooses Israel to do special deeds for him. Israel is to be "a light unto the Gentiles," a "polished shaft" sent forth into the darkness of unbelief to illumine life for those who have not heard of God. This is now the task of the "new Israel," the Christian church, to whom a special responsibility has been bequeathed: "Go therefore and make disciples of all nations" (Matt. 28:19). The church has been "called out" so that others may be called in.

The consequence is that those who are involved in this mission are under more severe judgment than anybody else. What God actually said to Israel through Amos (and now says to the Christian church) goes, "You only have I known of all the nations of the earth, *therefore I will punish you for all your iniquities*" (Amos 3:2, original version). This is a surprising and disturbing conclusion. It means that to be among the "chosen" is not to be assured of an easier time, but to be guaranteed a harder time. Election is not to privilege but to responsibility.

3. Many people confuse election and fate. The ancient Greeks, and especially the Stoics, believed very strongly in fate (*moira*). They were convinced that the movements and activities of men were as rigidly ordained as the movements and activities of the stars. But the idea did not die out with the demise of the ancient Greeks. It stubbornly refused to die, and it still lingers on in the attitude of those who say, "Somewhere there's a bullet with your number on it," or "It's all in the cards, you can't do anything about it." Astrologers make a good living off these people in every age.

But when Paul is dealing with election (in Romans 9–11, for example), it is *against* this sort of belief that he is arguing. He sees that mankind has been in bondage to the "principalities and powers," and that demonic forces are continually trying to crush mankind. Paul's point is that in electing man, God has *liberated* him from the power of fate. The ultimate control over man's destiny is no longer in the hands of fate, but in the hands of the living God. The final word has been spoken, and it is a word that destroys fate, frees man from its clutches, and releases him to enjoy the glorious liberty of the children of God. Life is no longer a hopeless game with fate, a game fate is foreordained to win, but an exciting adventure to which God has called his children, so that they may be willing instruments in the fulfillment of his purposes.

4. This helps to explain the otherwise puzzling fact that people who believe in election are activists. They find it liberating rather than confining.

The Reformers preached about election not to bring terror to non-believers but to bring assurance to believers. Their message is still true — even though no one can deserve election, or secure it by his own efforts, we can believe in it because "the Lord our God is good, his mercy is forever sure." The message is a message about human insufficiency only so that it may underline the divine sufficiency.

If it were our task to earn salvation, the center of attention would still be ourselves. We would be loving our neighbor in order to show God how loving we were — which would not be loving our neighbor at all, but simply using him. And we would always be left wondering whether we had "loved" him enough.

The doctrine of election makes all that kind of worry and bother unnecessary. We need not brood over whether or not we are of the elect. Since salvation is God's gift rather than man's achievement, it is not presumptuous to believe in our election. The presumptuous thing would be to doubt it. The status of our souls can safely be left where it belongs — in God's hands. We can be free to live *as the elect,* to live as those for whom Christ died. If we have indeed been elected to special responsibility, then we must get on with the job, which is to help transform the world into the kingdom of Christ.

The belief lets loose reserves of courage as well as dynamism. If we believe that God has chosen us for special tasks, we can sit lightly upon the approval or disapproval of men. Success and failure are not in our hands but in God's. Our own failure may even be part of God's way of assuring his ultimate triumph. So be it. The cause is God's and cannot fail.[8]

A restatement of the doctrine

It is not enough to dissect and explain and justify past expressions of a doctrine. We must also indicate why it is still a "central Protestant affirmation." If this is to exemplify the spirit of Protestantism it must be done in confessional rather than merely analytical terms.[9]

The doctrine of election must therefore be approached Christologically. The God who elects is the God whom we know in Jesus Christ. It was because the Reformers failed to keep this Christological concern uppermost that they got into so many difficulties.

We do not start with a general notion of the "divine omnipotence," we start with a specific notion of the divine activity in Jesus Christ. What that divine activity in Jesus Christ tells us above all else is clear to see — it tells us that God is for us.

God is for us. God could, presumably, have been against us. He could have turned his back on us. He could have smitten us. He could have destroyed us. But he did not do these things. Rather, he came and lived among us, taking up our cause, choosing us to be his own. The life and death and resurrection of Jesus Christ mean that long before we know anything about it, *we are the objects of God's eternal love.*

This is a Christian description of who we are. It is not a "general truth." It is not the end product of an intricate bit of ecclesiastical logic. It is not at the periphery of our faith. It is at the center. It is not found in a few isolated spots in the New Testament. It is the reason the New Testament was written.

Anything else we say as Christians must be said in the light of this dazzling fact that God is for us. He is the gracious God who loves us with an everlasting love and persistently calls us into fellowship with himself.[10] We must, of course, go on to say many other things: men turn their backs on this persisting love of God, few people really give indication that they are loved by God, most Christians seem unresponsive to the divine call. But we must always note these other facts in the light of the basic fact that God is for us. We are the objects of his love.

In more traditional terminology, we are the ones for whom Christ died. The traditional terminology is important if we are to avoid sentimentalism in talking about God's love. For that love is not sentimental: it is holy, it is suffering, it is gracious. It is defined not as the indulgent overlooking of wrong, but as the costly embracing of wrong.

This means that the love of God can be very stern. God judges, God punishes, God is "wrathful." But the judgment is, as we have already seen, judgment to save, the punishment is for the purpose of redeeming ("He has torn us that he may heal us," writes Hosea), and the wrath is holy love expressing itself toward sin and wrongdoing. We must see the judgment, the punishment, and the wrath, but we must not see only the judgment, the punishment, and the wrath. We must see them in the light of the fact that God is for us, and that even judgment, punishment, and wrath are only the means he uses to draw us back to himself.

This too we must see in the light of Christ. If we want to see how God is disposed toward all men, we must see how God was disposed toward that one man. When we look at his cross, we find both judgment and love expressed there. We see God condemning sin, making it plain that we cannot stand before him on our own resources. And that is the judgment. But the judge does not simply condemn us. The judge takes our place as the one accused and is punished in our stead. The punishment we should suffer, he suffers on our behalf. And that is the love.[11]

If we want to know what it means to be cast away from the divine presence, to be "rejected" by God, we do not look around for some unworthy human being, we look to the one who said, "My God, my God, why hast thou forsaken me?" We discover that so total was his identification with us, that he even took the burden of utter rejection upon himself. By taking it upon himself he has lifted it from us.

Nor can we stop there. He did not do this just for a few eye-witnesses or for the handful of people who keep telling the story, generation after generation. He did it for the whole world. "In Christ, God was reconciling *the world* unto himself" (2 Cor. 5:19). Whether or not we believe it, whether or not we have even heard of it, reconciliation has taken place. God is for us, and he remains for us, even when we are not for him. We can dismiss the claim as nonsense. But that does not alter its reality. Christian preaching is not to effect reconciliation. It is to announce that reconciliation has been effected.

Is this only a sophisticated version of universalism? No. If our forebears were wrong to assert that some men *must* be damned, we would be equally wrong to assert that all men *must* be saved. Either statement is a presumptuous attempt on our part to dictate terms to God. We can more profitably remind ourselves of two incidents from Jesus' ministry.[12]

When we are too concerned about the ultimate destiny of *other* men, we should remember the rebuke Jesus addressed to Peter when Peter was too concerned about the ultimate destiny of John:

"What is that to you?" Jesus replied, "follow me!"

And when we are too smug about *our own* ultimate destiny, we should take seriously the question the disciples addressed to Jesus in the upper room when he said that one of them would betray him.

Their response was, "Lord, is it I?"

APPENDIX:

Double predestination and universalism: some pros and cons

Our main concern has been to treat the enduring affirmation growing out of the notions of sovereignty, election, and predestination. But a problem has always vexed those who took these emphases seriously: *If God chooses to save some, what happens to the rest?*

One solution to the problem was to deny that there was a problem, by asserting categorically that all men were saved. Historically, this has always been a minority opinion, although we shall presently examine a modern reformulation of it. It had no wide currency either in medieval Catholicism or Reformation Protestantism.

Another solution appealed to those who wanted to preserve the majesty of divine judgment without making God unmercifully cruel. This solution affirmed that God chooses to save whom he will, and that he simply "passes over" the rest. The latter, being ignored by God, are excluded from salvation, but since God does not directly damn them he cannot rightly be called cruel or unloving. This solution could not satisfy tidy minds, even though it assuaged a few sensitive consciences. There was a much more clear-cut solution, which allowed the logic of the matter to be pressed as far as necessary, which was pretty far.

This solution started with the assumption that all men deserved damnation. That God willed their damnation and rejected them was therefore only just and right, since they were getting precisely what they deserved. This witnessed to the *justice* of God. But God also willed to save some men, through no merit of their own. And this witnessed to his *mercy*. Thus were both the glorious mercy and the glorious justice of God shown forth in the doctrine of the "double decree." The doctrine of reprobation, of the actual *rejection* by God of many (usually most) men, hardened into a belief in "double predestination," a claim that before the foundation of the world God had predestined whom he would save and whom he would condemn.[13]

Save for very conservative thinkers, most Protestants today insist on a far-reaching modification of the traditional doctrine of double predestination. We will examine three such reappraisals.

1. Emil Brunner [14] rejects the doctrine on the grounds that double

predestination cannot be found within the Bible. He believes that it is a false inference drawn from the doctrine of election, for there is no *eternal* decree of rejection in the Bible. Brunner believes that the Bible speaks clearly enough of heaven and hell, but *not* that men have been rejected by God in advance. Otherwise, God becomes the author of sin and he ceases to be the author of love.

Brunner does not feel, however, that the alternative is a doctrine of universal salvation. If the latter alternative is accepted, the meaning of human responsibility is undercut just as decisively as in the case of the "double decree." For if men are to be saved regardless of what they do, there are no remaining grounds for ethical concern. "Logically satisfying, although terrible for the heart," concludes Brunner, "is the doctrine of the double decree. Logically satisfying, although devastating for the conscience, is the doctrine of the certain salvation of all men." [15]

2. H. H. Farmer,[16] however, finds it intolerable that God's concern to win all men to him should be forever thwarted. Nor can he believe that the "saved" could accept their state while there were some eternally "lost": "The existence of hell surely makes heaven impossible."

Farmer considers various objections to the universalist position. One of these, which disturbs Brunner, is the feeling that the *sure* victory of God over every recalcitrant soul plays havoc with the integrity of human freedom. If men are not really free to defy God as long as they choose, they are not really free. Farmer replies that the ways of love are such that presumably God's patient love can finally elicit a freely given "yes" from all men. Everyone acknowledges that God saves some men without infringing on their status as creatures. He can surely do the same with others as well.

Another objection to universalism, also urged by Brunner, is that it undercuts the urgency of the Christian call for decision: men can do as they please, since they will be saved anyhow. Professor Farmer replies that this fails to take account of the fact that men are saved at infinite *cost*. Salvation is not simple or automatic. There is a cross at the heart of it. The man who is confronted by the love of God and uses it as an excuse for lax living has failed to understand what *suffering* love really is.

A third objection to universalism is the fact that certain passages seem to teach eternal punishment (cf. Mark 9:43–48, Matt. 25:46, etc.). But there are other New Testament passages that suggest a universal restoration, notably Romans 9–11, the longest single passage dealing with the problem. And even if certain passages suggest the possibility that some persons may be lost, they do not demand a belief that in fact any persons are thus lost.

3. Other Protestants have tried to redefine the problem by asking whether we must assume that the issue is finally decided by physical death. It is clear that many people die unreconciled to God. But is this the end of the matter? If God is Lord of life and death, his active concern for men does not cease when they die. There may be other ways and places in which God can continue to seek and to save those that are lost. The problem is set in a different key if we assume that God has all eternity to continue seeking those who reject him in time. This would not necessarily lead to a universalistic conclusion if men still possessed the right to say "no." But it seems increasingly arbitrary to assert that the issue is eternally decided on this side of the grave.

8. The Priesthood of All Believers

No word sounds less characteristic of the spirit of Protestantism than "priesthood." The Reformers' phrase, "the priesthood of all believers," grates on modern Protestant ears as a most un-Protestant notion.

And yet, when properly understood, the notion of "the priesthood of all believers" expresses the genius of Protestantism as few other notions can.

Two distortions of the meaning of grace

The meaning of grace in the life of the church is open to distortion in two ways.

The first of these occurs when *grace is institutionalized.* The church, rather than receiving grace as a gift, claims it as a prerogative. The church asserts that it controls grace and can dispense it or withhold it at will. The dispensing or withholding is concentrated within the hands of a special group designated as priests. This is the distortion to which Roman Catholic Christianity is always susceptible.[1]

There is another distortion of the meaning of grace that is the particular temptation of Protestantism: rather than being institutionalized, *grace is individualized.* It ceases to be "the grace of our Lord Jesus Christ" and becomes the emotional content of a vague or a vivid religious experience. The experience may come on a golf course or on a mountain top — or in a church. But it is basically individualistic. There is no need for a community save as it may incidentally create a psychological atmosphere conducive to the right sort of experience. Rather than making grace dependent on what men do, this view makes grace independent of what Christ does.

As we shall see, the best safeguard against these institutionalized and individualized distortions of the meaning of grace is a proper understanding of the "priesthood of all believers."

What is a "priest"?

But a proper understanding of the "priesthood of all believers" is not easily come by. Protestants who assume that the word "priest" disappeared from Protestant vocabulary in the sixteenth century have an obligation to rethink the meaning of the word. The task is difficult, perhaps the most difficult task we face in this entire book, but it is essential.[2]

In most cultures it is recognized that something has gone wrong in the relationship between God and man, and that an intermediary is necessary to set things right again. Such an intermediary is a priest. He is *God's representative to man,* the one who has authority to communicate and interpret God's will to the people. But he is also *man's representative to God,* the one who intercedes on behalf of the people and offers sacrifices to the deity in the hope of placating him and procuring his forgiveness.

We get into serious difficulty, however, if we try to impose the latter conception on the Old Testament. There the main concern of the priest is God's Word, and his priestly and liturgical functions are to mediate that Word to men. Only in relation to the Word, and in illustration of it, does he properly offer sacrifices.[3] To be sure, the offering of sacrifice as a means of "influencing" the deity is described many times in the Old Testament, but it is also one of the things against which the Old Testament prophets inveigh most eloquently.

The highest understanding of the matter is not that the priest procures forgiveness for the people. Rather, his cultic acts demonstrate to the people that the power of *God* avails to forgive sin.

When we turn to the New Testament, two further conclusions emerge.

1. *Jesus is the great high-priest.* All the functions of the Old Testament priesthood devolve on him — and are transformed by him. He is now the priestly mediator between God and man. No other priesthood is essential save his. In the fulfillment of his high-priestly calling he has done all that needs to be done to restore right relations between God and man.

He, too, is *God's representative to man.* He mediates the Word, as the Old Testament priest was meant to do, but more than that, he *is* the Word, the Word made flesh. As such he offers himself to man in sacrificial love. He himself is the sacrifice that God provides.

He is also *man's representative to God,* the one who offers a sacrifice to God, as the Old Testament priests did. But the sacrifice is no longer a goat or a lamb, it is himself. *He* is "the lamb of God who takes away the sins of the world" (John 1:29). He is both sacrificer and sacrificed. He is the high-priest who comes as the suffering servant and offers himself, sacrifices himself, on behalf of those to whom he has come.

2. *All believers share in this priesthood.* The members of the Christian community are "a royal priesthood." They too offer sacrifices, in this case "spiritual sacrifices acceptable to God through Jesus Christ" (1 Pet. 2:5). They participate in Christ's ministry and priesthood by serving him and by joining their sacrifices with his. They continue his high-priestly work by offering *themselves* to God and to their fellow men. Priesthood in the church is participation in the life of the suffering servant. Everyone who is baptized is baptized into this ministry. It is a "priesthood of all believers."

> You are a chosen race, a royal priesthood, a holy nation, God's own people, that you may declare the wonderful deeds of him who called you out of darkness into his marvelous light. Once you were no people but now you are God's people; once you had not received mercy but now you have received mercy.
>
> (1 Pet. 2:9–10)

The high-priesthood of Christ and the royal priesthood of all believers are inseparable. They are not identical but they are part of the same activity. "We may conclude, then," T. W. Manson writes, "that the priesthood of all believers lies in the fact that each believer offers himself as a sacrifice according to the pattern laid down by Christ; and — what is equally essential — that all these individual offerings are taken up into one perpetual offering made by the one eternal high-priest of the New Covenant." [4]

A misunderstanding of the priesthood of all believers

There is a widespread misunderstanding of the Protestant doctrine of "the priesthood of all believers" that goes like this:

> Roman Catholics need a priest to mediate between themselves and God. They must confess their sins to a priest, be granted absolution by a priest, and receive the sacraments from a priest.
>
> But Protestants don't need anyone else to mediate between themselves and God. They can be their own mediators because they are all priests. Everybody can be his own priest.

The unabridged Webster's, which should know better, gives this misunderstanding respectability by stating that in the period since the Reformation "priest" has meant "any Christian believer, as each Christian is his own priest."

Our discussion of the New Testament understanding of priesthood indicates how wide of the mark this individualistic interpretation is. Not only does it misinterpret the New Testament, but it also misinterprets what the Reformers were trying to do when they reintroduced the New Testament notion of the "priesthood of all believers."

The phrase does not mean that "every man is his own priest." It means the opposite: "every man is priest *to every other man.*" It does not imply individuality. It necessitates community. Christians are to offer themselves to one another, to pray for one another, to sacrifice themselves on behalf of one another, so that through them all, the high-priesthood of Jesus Christ may be more effectually communicated to them all.

We must be clear about another thing. It is sometimes charged that the Reformers dragged the priesthood down to the level of the laity, so that there were no priests left, and that the real result was "the priesthood of no believers." Actually, they did the reverse:

they raised the laity up to the level of the priesthood, and in the most literal sense of the words, restored the long-neglected New Testament conception of "the priesthood of *all* believers." The church became again what it had been in the beginning, "a chosen race, a royal priesthood, a holy nation, God's own people" (1 Pet. 2:9).

We must therefore disavow the individualistic interpretation of the phrase, and recognize the priesthood of all believers for what it is — an emphatic declaration of the indispensability of Christian community.[5]

The church in which priesthood is exercised

But "community" is too vague a word with which to conclude a discussion of the priesthood of all believers. To talk about the priesthood of all believers means to talk about the church.

It is not easy for a Protestant "to talk about the church." He can talk about his own denomination. But if he is honest, he must admit that there is no such thing as a Protestant *doctrine* of the church. There are only Protestant *doctrines* of the church, and they are far from identical.[6] Even so, we can state certain things about which most Protestants would be agreed.

1. *The church is Christ's church.* This is the most important as well as the most Protestant thing to say. The church is not the creation of men nor is it dependent upon them for its survival. The church is the creation of God, who has made Jesus Christ the head of the church. The church is the "body" of Christ — the means through which he continues to do his work on earth. It can never be more than his servant. It should never be less.

Another way of stating this dependence on Christ is to recall the formula of ancient Christendom, *ubi Christus ibi ecclesia* ("where Christ is, there is the church"), and insist that this is a descriptive statement for modern Protestantism as well.[7] When Christ left his disciples he promised them the gift of the Comforter, the Holy Spirit, who would lead them into all truth, and it is the activity of that same Spirit that makes Christ the eternal contemporary of believers in the fellowship of the church. The church is the place where the Spirit dwells.

2. *The church exists where the Word of God is truly preached and the sacraments are rightly administered.* Almost all Protestants would accept this Reformation statement as a proper definition,[8] and it lends more precision to our understanding of the church as Christ's church.

But the statement is not as innocent as it sounds. The loaded words are the adverbs. Who decides whether or not the Word of God has been *truly* preached? Who determines whether or not the sacraments have been *rightly* administered? Different denominations answer these questions in discouragingly different and apparently mutually exclusive ways.

3. *The church is a community of sinners.* There is no way of avoiding this conclusion, and every branch of Christendom makes some acknowledgment of the fact.

> The church is not an organization of good people [writes Charles Clayton Morrison], it is a society of sinners. It is the only organization in human society that takes sinners into its membership just because they are sinners. It is the only organization that keeps on saying week after week, year after year, age after age: "We have left undone those things which we ought to have done and we have done those things which we ought not to have done . . ."
>
> Let us not claim moral virtue for church members or for the church. Let us rather glory in the fact that the church is a society of sinners, who claim no virtue but humbly rest their broken and burdened lives upon the grace which God has eternally revealed in Christ Jesus.[9]

The idea can be put in even more characteristically Protestant terms by stating that *the church is a sinful community.* Roman Catholics and Orthodox might balk at this way of putting it, but Protestants should not, for to deny the fact would be to make the assertion, impossible from a Protestant standpoint, that the church, somewhere or other in its life, is exempt from sin.

Protestants do not glory in the fact that the church is a sinful community. They do glory in the fact that God deigns to dwell even within a sinful community and employ it for the doing of his will. One of the greatest marks of the divine condescension is the fact that God works through the poor means men place at his disposal in the church.

4. *The church is one, holy, catholic, and apostolic.* So say all Christians, whether Protestant, Roman Catholic, or Orthodox. But their agreement is short-lived, for Protestants, Roman Catholics, and Orthodox mean different things by each of these four "marks" of the church.[10]

It sounds outrageous to claim that the church is *one,* yet few things were more strongly insisted upon by the Reformers. They clearly recognized that there could not be two churches of Christ, or twenty-two or two hundred and twenty-two. They clearly recognized that men could fracture and weaken the visible unity of Christ's church. But they also clearly recognized that *the church is one in spite of what men do to it.* Indeed, the impetus of the modern ecumenical movement is based upon this very fact: Christians are already one in Christ, and must strive to make that unity ever more manifest.[11]

It sounds equally outrageous to claim that the church is *holy,* particularly after we have been at such pains to assert that it is not only a community of sinners but also a sinful community. But in Christian vocabulary to be holy (i.e. to be "sanctified" or a saint) is not to be perfect but to know that one is not perfect. Saints are persons who recognize that they are sinners, and yet who also recognize that they are forgiven sinners. To call the church a holy community is not to call it a "good" community, but to point out that it is a community conscious of the fact that its goodness comes from God alone.

Our earlier discussion of the meaning of *catholic,* in Chapter 2, can be amplified by a comment on the meaning of *apostolic.* Protestants have too quickly dismissed this notion in the past, and one of the healthiest exercises in which modern Protestantism could engage would be an attempt to discover what apostolicity could mean in its own life.[12] The apostles of Christ were the "eyewitnesses to his majesty," and their task was to give a faithful account of what they had seen and heard. The significant thing about them was their *testimony.* Their authority was based not so much on who they were as on what they reported, and what they reported is recorded for us in the pages of the New Testament. The church is "apostolic" when it is a faithful transmitter of the apostolic testimony, and the presence of Holy Scripture in the church means that the church must test the content of its proclamation at all times against the content of the apostolic proclamation. Apostolicity ought therefore to be one of the most characteristically Protestant marks of the church.

5. *The church has a visible structure.* One of the disservices of the Reformers was their perpetuation of the distinction between a "visible" and an "invisible" church. This is a convenient escape valve for contemporary Protestants who, when confronted by some of the manifest weaknesses of the visible church, assert that what they *really* mean by "the church" is not the wretched visible church but the glorious invisible church.

This is too cheap a victory. God reveals himself on earth through flesh and blood realities, as the incarnation long ago made clear. He is not above using structures, and very visible structures at that, for the fulfilling of his purposes. The church is and has such a visible structure and no one should feel obliged to deny the fact.

There are three types of government or polity through which the visible structure of the church has been expressed. Those who advocate a *congregational* type of government claim that the Holy Spirit works through every member of the church and that the community as a whole must be responsive to his leading. Decisions are made at a "church meeting," and all members have equal voice. In a *presbyterian* system of government, elected representatives or "elders" (our translation of *presbuteros*) are responsible for the government of the church. Presbyterian government is "representative" democracy rather than the "pure" democracy of the church meeting. *Episcopal* churches are governed by "bishops" (our translation of *episkopos*), duly elected by representatives of the church, and consecrated by their fellow bishops.

Until the advent of Biblical criticism, advocates of each of these polities frequently tried to maintain that they were reproducing the actual polity of the early church. It is now clear, however, that there were elements of all three in New Testament Christianity. Most churches today, in fact, have a mixture of all three. Certain Episcopal dioceses have incorporated "presbyteries" into their structure, and many congregational churches have in practice adopted a system of presbyterian representation and possess leaders who fulfill many of the traditional functions of bishops. One of the things that makes the Church of South India such a hopeful portent of the future is that it has successfully combined elements of all three types of polity within its structure.

"Clergy" and "laity" — some right distinctions, some wrong distinctions, and some problems

When we have become as down-to-earth as all this, we have come to a place where we can no longer avoid an embarrassing problem.

We have seen that there is one essential priesthood in the church, the ministry of Jesus Christ, the great high-priest. We have also seen that every believer shares in this ministry of sacrifice, so that the priesthood is a priesthood of all believers. What we have not yet seen is that a distinction is made *within* the priesthood of all believers — conventionally described as the distinction between "clergy" (from *kleros,* meaning those set apart for the service of God) and "laity" (from *laos,* meaning ordinary people).

Here is where the embarrassment begins. Here is where Protestants are most confused. Here is where discussion about Christian unity is always jeopardized. For here is where the most serious differences within Protestantism emerge — over the way in which we are to distinguish between "clergy" and "laity."

We must first of all call into question the conventional way of making the distinction. In the New Testament, *laos* ("laymen") does not mean church members who are non-clergy. It means everybody. *Kleros* ("clergy") does not mean church members who are in a special category. It means everybody. Both words are used in the New Testament, but *they are used to describe the same people,* the whole people of God.[13]

If we examine the New Testament word for "ministry" (*diakonia*), we are led to a similar conclusion. Originally, *diakonia* (from which our word "deacon" derives) meant waiting on table (cf. Luke 17:8). It gradually came to mean one who serves others, one who ministers. In the early church everything that led to the upbuilding of the Christian community was *diakonia,* service, ministry. Every Christian participated in this *diakonia,* so every Christian was a servant, a "minister."

Thus we are led to conclusions similar to those we discovered in our examination of priesthood, and we may draw the two threads of the argument together by employing Hendrik Kraemer's remarkable phrase that "the church is ministry." [14] He does not say that the church *has* a ministry, but that *the church is ministry.* This ministry is rooted in Christ's ministry and it expresses itself in two different ways — the ministry of the ordained clergy and the ministry of the laity. *These are not two different ministries. They are two forms of the same ministry.* The New Testament makes this clear:

> Now there are varieties of gifts, but the same Spirit; and there are varieties of service but the same Lord; and there are varieties of working, but it is the same God who inspires them all in everyone. To each is given the manifestation of the Spirit for the common good.
>
> (1 Cor. 12:4–7)

So much for the New Testament. But with the passing of the centuries a distinction grew up between "clergy" and "laity" that transformed them from different forms of the same ministry into different ministries altogether, one superior, the other distinctly inferior. We shall trace some of the consequences of this in the next chapter. Indeed, so wide did the cleavage become that the notion that the church *is* ministry was replaced by the notion that the church *has* a ministry, and that its ministry is exercised only by the ordained clergy.

This is the misunderstanding that the Reformers were trying to repair. Their plea to the church was a plea to recover the New Testament stress on the priesthood of *all* believers as exercised within and under the unique priesthood of Jesus Christ.[15]

But along with this the Reformers were realistic enough to recognize that within the priesthood of all believers there are still "varieties of gifts" even when there is "the same Spirit." They therefore set apart certain of their members to carry on a specialized form of ministry usually described as a "ministry of Word and sacrament." Certain persons, qualified by conviction and training, were "set apart" by ordination to preach the Word of God and to administer the sacraments. This remains a necessary distinction simply from the point of view of order in the church. If every individual administered the sacraments whenever he pleased, there would be chaos in the church. So these tasks are delegated to certain persons appointed to perform them. *But the ministry of Word and sacrament is not a "higher" ministry than the ministry of the laity, it is simply another form of the church's total ministry.*

All Protestants would agree that ordained clergy fulfill at least the functional purpose within the life of the church described above: they are "set apart" to do certain things. The difficulty begins where the italics begin, and the words have been italicized to underline the issue. For many Protestants want to say much more than this. They may agree that there is a priesthood of all believers, but they insist that there is a special order of priesthood, instituted by Christ and "set apart" from the laity in a much more radical way than the above description would suggest. To this special order are committed certain powers that are essential to the ongoing life of the church, without which the church would cease to be the church in all its fullness. The possession of these powers is communicated by episcopal ordination, i.e. ordination at the hand of bishops. The bishops are the guardians of the life and teaching of the church, and it is their presence that assures apostolicity, since they stand in an apostolic succession going back to Christ himself.

Upholders of this position, while recognizing that non-episcopally ordained ministries may have been used by the Holy Spirit, insist that there is something irregular about the status of such ministries, and therefore make acceptance of episcopacy a condition of reunion. Those within non-episcopal traditions feel that the demand impugns the validity of their own ordinations and are normally reluctant to consider the claims of episcopacy seriously. This is the most grievous impasse in modern ecumenism.

If a way is to be found beyond this impasse, it is more likely to come from the experience of the "younger churches" than from the older ones. Most of the latter give the impression of being more concerned to vindicate their own pasts than to listen for a fresh leading from the Holy Spirit. The formation of the Church of South

India, for example, represents progress if not arrival. The church recognizes the priesthood of all believers: "All share in the heavenly High Priesthood of the risen and ascended Christ, from which alone the church derives its character as a royal priesthood." But it also makes a place for special ministries within this universal priesthood: "God is a God of order; it has been his good pleasure to use the visible church and its regularly constituted ministries as the normal means of the operation of His Spirit." When the Church was formally constituted in 1947, the members of the four merging denominations (Methodist, Congregational, Episcopal, and Presbyterian) all acknowledged that they found "regularly constituted ministries" within the other three, and that there would be no "re-ordination." But they also agreed that after the new church was constituted, all subsequent clergy would be episcopally ordained.

A somewhat different way of meeting the problem is proposed for the United Church of Ceylon. When this church is created there will be a laying on of hands and a commissioning of men who are already ordained, by a formula such as the following:

> Forasmuch as you were called and ordained to the ministry of the Church of God in the ——— Church, and are now called to the ministry of the Church of God as Presbyter within the Church of Lanka (Ceylon); receive from God the power and grace of the Holy Spirit to exercise the wider ministry of this office.[16]

Such measures as these do not solve all the problems. But they demonstrate that Christians are wrestling with the problems. If they are truly wrestling with the Word, it may be that like Jacob at the ford of Jabbok the blessing of God will be pronounced over their efforts.

The shape of a Protestant contribution

The full depth of meaning in the "priesthood of all believers" has not yet been plumbed by Protestants. It is one of those areas of Protestant thought and life where "the Reformation must continue."

The Protestant contribution to the total perspective of Christendom on this matter will surely be its insistence on the Biblical truth that there is only one essential ministry within the church, which is the ministry of its risen Lord, that the "priesthood of all believers" is a participation in that ministry, and that whatever distinctions are made between clergy and laity must be made *within* a recognition that although there are varieties of working it is the same God who inspires them all in everyone since to each is given the manifestation of the Spirit for the common good.[17]

We can suggest this pictorially by an architectural analogy.[18] Like most other abbeys, the abbey at Iona, an island off the coast of Scotland, has a chancel and a nave. In the Middle Ages the clergy sat in the chancel, near the altar, and the laity were confined to the nave. To make sure that no one strayed over the boundaries, there was a screen between the two. After the Reformation, the building fell into disrepair. It has recently been restored by Protestants, but with one significant change: *there is no screen.* Now all sit together and worship together without distinction, for *all* are "a chosen race, a royal priesthood, a holy nation, God's own people."

9. The Calling of the Christian Man

When St. Paul exhorted his Christian friends "to lead a life worthy of the calling to which you have been called" (Eph. 4:1), he was not referring primarily to fishing or tent-making or spice-trading. He was referring to the style of life that must characterize the Christian in *all* that he does as a Christian.

It is a linguistic catastrophe that the word "vocation," or calling, has come to be no more than a way of describing how a man earns a living, what he does when he is not on vacation. Originally it meant the calling of the Christian *to be a Christian,* to be a part of the people of God, and to serve God in every activity of life, a vocation from which there is obviously no vacation.

If a man today is asked, "What is your vocation?" he is almost certain to reply, as the case may be, that he is a lawyer, a lathe operator, or a chemist, and to feel that it would sound highly affected to say, in answer to the same question, "I am a witness for Jesus Christ." And yet, if a Christian is taking his primary vocation seriously, that is precisely what he is.

The problem, of course, even if he understands his primary vocation, is how he is to be a witness for Jesus Christ in the law office, the machine shop, or the laboratory. This is no small problem. It is perhaps the most perplexing problem the contemporary Christian faces.

The medieval church had one answer to the problem and the Reformers had another. A look at each of them will give us a better basis for tackling the problem in contemporary terms.

The medieval answer: a double standard

The Middle Ages worked out a comprehensive answer to the problem of vocation. It involved a distinction between "sacred" and "secular" callings, much like the distinction in old mansions between "above stairs," where the life for which the house had been built took place, and "below stairs," where the kitchen, scullery, and servants' quarters were located.[1]

On these terms, the medieval view of the "sacred" calling was like the upper part of the mansion. The kind of life for which the mansion of this world had been made, was "above stairs," removed from kitchens and domestic squabbles. To follow a "sacred" vocation was to become a monk and live a life of renunciation of the world. The true service of God was a life devoted totally to him, in worship, meditation, and work within the cloister. Here one could pray for the evil world outside, but one was not contaminated by the evils it represented. This, then, was the pure "religious" calling, devoid of sinful compromise, and more pleasing to God than any conceivable alternative.

But not everyone had the conviction or fortitude to do this, and so there was a second way of being a Christian. This was to remain in the secular world, involved in all of its compromises, and following some "worldly" occupation. Those who could not measure up to the demands of "sacred" vocations could at least live passably Christian lives "below stairs." Thus one might be a butcher, soldier, historian, or ox-cart driver, but these were second-rate "secular" callings, rather than first-rate "sacred" ones. They were the refuge of those who were weak in the flesh or weak in the spirit, and the butchers, soldiers, historians, and ox-cart drivers depended upon the *fully* committed Christians in the monasteries to pray them into heaven. So there were two types of vocation, one "sacred" and one "secular."

Before we leave this point of view, it is worth noticing that modern Protestantism, ironically enough, has adopted the medieval pattern. The phrase "full-time Christian service" means to modern Protestants something very similar to what the phrase "sacred calling" meant to a medieval Catholic. The alternatives put to Protestant young people are "full-time Christian service" (i.e. minister, missionary, church worker) or some lesser vocation (i.e. butcher, soldier, historian, or taxi-cab driver). The latter occupations, while necessary and useful, are ranked several pegs below the former, and are by implication only "part-time Christian service."

The reaction of the Reformers to the medieval view will be sufficient commentary on the modern variant of it.

The sixteenth-century answer: the doctrine of the calling

The Reformers also worked out a comprehensive answer to the problem of vocation. It involved an abolition of the distinction between "sacred" and "secular" callings. No longer was there an "above stairs" and a "below stairs." All the activities of life were held to take place on the same level, much like the plan of a modern ranch-type house in which kitchen and living room, washing machine and hi-fi set, are on the same level and are used by the same people. The Reformers felt, in other words, that there was a wholeness or unity to life, *and that God could be served equally well at any place within the whole.*

This meant for Luther that *all* callings were "sacred" callings, and that Christian vocation could be fulfilled whatever one's "station" in life:

> What you do in your house is worth as much as if you did it up in heaven for our Lord God. For what we do in our calling here on earth in accordance with His word and command He counts as if it were done in heaven for Him . . . Therefore we should accustom ourselves to think of our position and work as sacred and well-pleasing to God, not on account of the position and the work, but on account of the word and faith from which the obedience and the work flow. No Christian should despise his position and life if he is living in accordance with the word of God, but should say, "I believe in Jesus Christ, and do as the ten commandments teach, and pray that our dear Lord God may help me thus to do." That is a right and holy life, and cannot be made holier even if one fast himself to death.

However numerous and arduous they [vows of monkery and priesthood] may be, these works in God's sight are in no way whatever superior to a farmer laboring in the field, or a woman looking after her home. Rather all are measured by him by faith alone . . . Indeed it occurs quite frequently that the common work of serving man or maid is more acceptable than all the fastings and other works of monks or priests where faith is lacking.[2]

So the shoemaker can praise God through what he does at the cobbler's bench, just as the priest can praise God through what he does at the altar. Mending soles and saving souls are part of the same task, and through them both God can be praised.

Calvin pointed out that it was not necessary to enter a monastery to serve God, for the whole world was God's monastery. Therefore, one was to serve God within the world. This could be an ascetic life, in the sense that it involved discipline and self-denial, but it was what the historian Troeltsch has called "intra-mundane asceticism," i.e. a disciplined life lived to God's glory *in the world.* It was not necessary to "leave the world" in order to serve God. Indeed, it was quite wrong to leave the world. The place to serve God was precisely in the midst of the world he had created as a dwelling place for men.

Twentieth-century difficulties with sixteenth-century answers

So the Reformers. Their answer reclaimed the whole of God's world as an arena for his service. It was an exciting breakthrough. But the answer that served their needs adequately is not an answer that will serve our needs adequately, for at least three reasons:

1. Although it was originally radical teaching, the doctrine of the calling gradually became a way of justifying the *status quo.* Before long the Puritans were reasoning like this: Since I can be about my Heavenly Father's business by working in my earthly father's business, I can serve God very acceptably by making a tidy profit. If I make a tidy profit, is this not a sign that God is pleased with my diligence and is rewarding me? If my competitor happens to show a loss during the same period, is this not a sign

that God is displeased with him? Can I not best continue to serve God by making my business more successful than ever? And if I can serve God in *my* calling cannot a chimney sweep serve God in his? And why should the chimney sweep need an extra shilling a week in order to glorify God more effectively?

The doctrine, in other words, was a particularly gratifying doctrine for those on top of the economic heap, because it (a) assured them that they belonged there, and (b) absolved them of responsibility for those lower down. Protestants in the nineteenth century used to sing:

> The rich man in his castle,
> The poor man at his gate,
> God made them, high and lowly,
> And ordered their estate.[3]

What had originally been a fresh rediscovery of the equality of all men's service to God became a way of perpetuating men's inequality before one another.

2. Again, the Industrial Revolution has intervened between the sixteenth century and our own. In a technological society it is sheer romanticism to describe the shoemaker sitting all day at his bench and transforming it into an altar. Rather, we have to describe a workman sitting in front of a moving belt, repeating a certain flick of the wrist 32 times a minute, 1,920 times an hour, 15,360 times a day — never seeing the finished product, and never seeing how his wrist-flick is related to all the other tasks involved in creating the finished product. The words "Glorify God in your calling" have a hollow ring in the ears of the wrist-flickers.

Furthermore, the sense of boredom, of frustration, of simply going through the motions, of being a depersonalized cog in an efficient but inhuman machine, is no longer limited to assembly-line workers or shipping clerks. It has become an occupational hazard for executive vice-presidents as well.[4] From shipping clerks to executives, the advice to "Glorify God in your calling" is dismissed as nonsense.

3. Not only has there been an Industrial Revolution since the sixteenth century, but there has been an Atomic Revolution in the twentieth century. To be sure, only a relative handful of people

are directly manufacturing instruments that can annihilate the human race. But the import of what they are doing is raising vocational dilemmas for an increasingly large proportion of the population. Every man in the armed forces is committed to the use of atomic weapons against civilian populations, if this becomes a "military necessity." More and more physicists, research chemists, and laboratory technicians discover that their lives are in fact dedicated to the perfection of yet more deadly explosives. An increasing number of corporations are involved in the construction and distribution of atomic weapons. Every time an atomic bomb is "tested," the radioactive fallout further poisons the atmosphere, so that every effort to deter possible aggressors by a show of force is another step toward the genetic distorting of yet unborn generations.

It is frightful to the conscience to realize that *this* may be the end product to which the vocational resources of twentieth-century man have become directed. And it is a travesty of Protestant faith to ask men to accept the proposition that all this redounds to the glory of God.

Toward some twentieth-century answers

So the traditional answers will not do today. This does not mean that the Reformers were wrong for their day, but that "the Reformation must continue," if what they said for their day is to have any meaning for our day. The following pages are an attempt to discuss "the calling of the Christian man" against the backdrop of the twentieth century.[5]

1. This attempt must be made in recognition of "the priesthood of all believers." Theologians cannot work out solutions for laymen. The people who will make significant contributions here are the people who confront real vocational dilemmas *in their own lives,* and who are willing to join ranks with the theologians in working toward some new insights. Protestant lawyers and theologians together could make a fruitful study of legal ethics; Protestant labor leaders and theologians together could break new ground on the ethics of power. This sort of thing is beginning to happen in the

United States, and more sustained efforts have been made in Great Britain.[6]

It is in Europe, however, and particularly in post-war Germany, that the most significant attempts have been made to bring laymen and theologians together to deal with Christian vocation in realistic, twentieth-century terms. In 1945, many Christians in Germany realized how ineffective the church had been in reaching more than a handful of those who still occasionally "went to church." Out of this concern for relevance a number of "Evangelical Academies" have been created. These are centers where Christians and non-Christians, clergy and laymen, can gather in an informal atmosphere to discuss the relation of the Christian faith to the world of modern men. This is done in most down-to-earth and practical terms. At the Evangelical Academy at Bad Boll, for example, a series of typical conferences in a given month might go something like this:

Trade-union workers: the challenge of automation
Village mayors: the temptations of bureaucracy
Farmers: the problem of reassigning widely separated landstrips
High-school students: the place of the individual in a mechanistic age
Women factory workers: the rival claims of family and job
Department-store clerks: pressures of cut-throat competition and cheap goods

What does the gospel say about automation, bureaucracy, and landstrips, about depersonalization, industry, and competition? No abstract answers will help here. The answers must come out of the experience of those who confront the problems by wrestling with the Biblical faith *in relation to the particular problems.* To see this actually happening is to realize that the academies are indeed what the seal of Bad Boll depicts: a bridge between the church and the world.[7]

2. This joint effort does not mean scrapping the past. It means, among many other things, appropriating all that is still valuable in the Reformers' answers. The core of those answers is still sound: the Christian works out his salvation by responsible involvement *in* the world, not by retreat *from* the world. If the world was God's world in the sixteenth century, it is still his world in the twentieth

century, and his will is therefore still that his children serve him in the world that he has made. We have seen that romantic talk about the world of the self-sufficient shoemaker is irrelevant. The world in which a new sense of Christian vocation must be worked out is the world of IBM, lunar probes, economic boycotts, summit conferences, *apartheid,* and atomic-powered submarines cruising under the polar icecap. *This* is the world in which "Christian vocation" has to be understood. If this fact is recognized, many things can be learned from a fresh study of the Reformers, not because they provide tidy twentieth-century answers, but because they attack the problem in the faith that this is God's world. In our current passion for being realistic, we are often tempted merely to attack the problem.

3. Too often in the past, the problem of vocation was considered merely as the problem of an individual, to be solved in individualistic terms. This will not do. The fact of vocational problems must be consciously related to the fact of the church. For if one's basic calling is a calling to be *a Christian,* then he is not so much an individual as he is a member of "the household of God," part of the people who gather together to worship, pray, sustain one another, bring their cares and burdens to Christ's Table, and take away from that Table his presence and grace. They are furthermore a people who, having done this, go back into the world of business and professional life. If the household of God is a true household, they do not go back as "individuals," but as members of a fellowship that sustains them through the coming week. When one member of that fellowship faces a difficult decision at his desk or in his shop, he should know that he is upheld by the rest, and that their prayers are supporting him. Even more, he should know that they will support him with more than just their prayers, if the decision gets him into trouble. That he is a member of the church does not just mean that he has somewhere to go on week ends; it means that he is part of a community that goes everywhere with him on weekdays. And this has much to tell us about "the calling of the Christian man."

4. The Reformers' assumption that God can be served in any calling needs a fresh look. It was a needed corrective in the sixteenth century: it may be fatuous nonsense in the twentieth century.

Luther actually employed a criterion of discrimination in assessing the worth of different kinds of callings — the criterion of service to others. And although Luther felt that God could be served in any calling, he admitted perplexity when it came to applying this to thieves and prostitutes.

The problem today extends far beyond the categories Luther questioned. Should a man, as a Christian, be encouraged to manufacture useless objects, to sell luxury items while men are starving to death, to take a job in which lying and deception are the accepted rules of the game, or to market goods designed to wear out rapidly? Here is where Christian discrimination is called for. It is a necessary but dangerous kind of discrimination. It is necessary because some jobs are inherently more worth doing, and more in need of being done, than other jobs. It is dangerous because risks of self-righteousness, moralism, and pharisaism are inherent in any attempt to decide in which category a given job belongs. But these risks must be taken if Protestantism is to offer relevant guidance to the people faced with vocational decisions that will affect the remainder of their lives. Simply to tell them that they can glorify God in any calling is a sure inducement to take the most attractive job rather than the most important job.

It is not the task of this book to suggest a specific hierarchy of vocations. But it is the task of this book to suggest that it needs doing, however tentatively and cautiously, and to issue the warning that such an attempt must not reintroduce the old Protestant heresy that "full-time Christian service" means no more than working in the church. Failure to make the attempt will perpetuate the opposite heresy, that any job is morally equivalent to any other job.

5. The luxury of "choosing a significant vocation," however, is not open to most people. They now have jobs which, for quite valid reasons, they cannot change. Can Protestantism say anything to Christians already working in situations that are morally precarious or morally dubious? Here we come to a delicate area of discussion, particularly when it involves a so-called "ethic of compromise."

There are no jobs in which all the ethical choices are "pure." This applies to the missionary as well as to the miner. In a fallen world, every situation will involve compromise, even though some compromises have more agonizing and far-reaching implications than others. It is one of the most devastating consequences of human sin that it infects our "goodness" as well as our evil. This means that no one can have the luxury of an easy conscience. Even if one is not directly doing evil, he is involved and implicated in a system in which much evil is done.

In his recognition of this fact, the Christian has to draw a very fine line. Before God he can never stand "justified by his works." He sins and will continue to sin. And the resource with which he copes with this inescapable fact is the reality of divine grace. He may not sin bravely that grace may abound — but he *will* sin, and grace *will* abound! And the fine line must be drawn between *the inescapable reality of his sin, and his complacent tendency not to worry too much about it since it is inescapable*. Different Christians will draw the line at different points, and there are degrees of compromise beyond which the ethical tensions become too great. A point comes at which they have to erect a barrier and say, "Thus far and no farther." Some Christians may erect the barrier prematurely; others will need prodding to realize that any barrier is necessary. But even those who come, perhaps at great personal cost, to the point of seeking a "less compromising job" must bear in mind two things: (a) there will be a new set of ethical dilemmas in the new situation, and (b) someone else will have to cope with the ethical dilemmas remaining in the old situation.

Perhaps this problem seems unreal to many readers. They must be reminded that there are others for whom this is the sorry stuff of their daily existence. This may be the area where "the priesthood of all believers" is most needed in the Protestant community.

6. Finally, there are many people whose jobs are boring and necessary. The jobs must be done, but there is nothing exciting or creative in the doing of them. Protestant talk about glorifying God seems particularly thin in relation to them. Sir George MacLeod of the Iona Community often takes the least enthralling of the daily work jobs in the community, cleaning the latrines, "so that," as he says, "I will not be tempted to preach irrelevant sermons on the dignity of all labor."

Once the minimal "meaning" of such jobs has been recognized, Protestants must think carefully about ways in which off-the-job compensations can give people condemned to drudgery a greater sense of Christian vocation in the *whole* of their lives. A man on the assembly line may find that his Christian vocation is less realized through eight hours of wrist-flicking than through his union activities in the evenings. A garbage collector may be able to use the muscles thus acquired to demonstrate the fine art of batting to potential juvenile delinquents. The danger will be that the job itself will be written off as a dead loss, but this danger must be run unless many people are to be condemned to sheer meaningless drudgery.

"Love Him in the World of the Flesh"

We must still affirm, with the Reformers, that it is *in the world* that "the calling of the Christian man" is exercised. Few modern writers have seen this more clearly than W. H. Auden. His Christmas oratorio *For the Time Being* emphasizes the fact that because Christ came into the world, the world has been invested with new significance. "The garden is the only place there is," and it must be affirmed rather than denied. Because we are capable of

> Remembering the stable where for once in our lives
> Everything became a You and nothing was an It . . .

the world in which that stable was lodged has ultimate meaning. Therefore,

> In the meantime
> There are bills to be paid, machines to be kept in repair,
> Irregular verbs to learn, the Time Being to redeem
> From insignificance . . .

We can affirm these tasks because we can affirm the Incarnate One:

> He is the Life.
> Love Him in the World of the Flesh;
> And at your marriage all its occasions shall dance for joy.[8]

10. Loving God with the Mind

There is one piece of corporate misinformation about which many Protestants seem to be agreed: since (a) theology is a dull business, (b) it can safely be left to the specialists who (c) disagree so much anyway that their claims and counterclaims do not really matter.

As far as dullness goes, it can be countered that this is the least appropriate word to describe theology. Thinking which asserts that a man rose from the dead, that sins are forgiven, and that God became man may be fantastic, improbable, or untrue, but it is not dull.[1] That theology is not just for "the specialists" will be the particular concern of the following pages. As for theological disagreements, these may be a sign of vitality rather than irrelevance. When men disagree it is usually a sign that something important is at stake. Men disagreed about Adolf Hitler.

What theology is

So the claims of theology at least deserve a hearing. The word itself comes from the Greek words *theos* (god) and *logos* (word or knowledge). So theo-logy is the *logos* of *theos,* which simply means the study of our knowledge of God, just as anthropology is the *logos* of *anthropos,* or the study of our knowledge of man. But a more helpful definition would go: theology is our attempt *to love God with our minds.* We are, of course, to love him with our hearts and souls and strength as well, so theology is not our total response to God. That total response includes prayer and worship and active concern for the neighbor. But theology is *part* of our response, and it involves thinking — thinking as rigorously and honestly as possible about the meaning of God for our lives. We are not entitled to stop thinking once we "believe." Only after we believe do we really start thinking.

This means that we may define theology in a second way as *faith seeking understanding*. The phrase itself has a long history. It occurs in an eleventh-century tract by St. Anselm, was popular in the fourth century when in the negative form it was widely used by St. Augustine, who discovered it in a Latin translation of the Old Testament, where it is found in the writings of Isaiah several hundred years before Christ. In other words, throughout the Judaeo-Christian tradition there has been a recognition that it is not enough just to "have faith." Faith must seek understanding. The one who believes must be able to give account of his belief. The claims of faith must be subject to scrutiny. When this privilege is denied, as it often has been, faith becomes sterile and rightly deserves all the scorn that is often so wrongly heaped upon it.

The layman as theologian

The minute the matter is put this way, it is clear that theology cannot be left to "the specialists." For if theology means loving God with the mind, then *every* Christian is called upon to do this. If theology is faith seeking understanding, then no one is exempted from the demand that he seek to understand the faith that is in him. Someone once suggested that faith is so important to the Roman Catholic that he could not possibly take final responsibility for what he believed, whereas faith is so important to the Protestant that he could not possibly let someone else take final responsibility for what he believed.

This is no more than a half-truth in either case, but it does remind us that the Protestant must make *his own decision* about the Christian faith, and that he cannot do this apart from the life of the mind. He cannot, in other words, decide *not* to be a theologian without deciding not to be a Christian. His options are never, "Shall I be a theologian or not?" They are only, "Will I be a good theologian or a bad one?"

Even those who disavow theology are theologians. The man who says, "I don't bother with theology; I just try to live up to the Sermon on the Mount," is making a host of theological assertions. He is saying, among other things, (a) that man is capable of living up to the Sermon on the Mount, (b) that the speaker of the Sermon was a teacher rather than a redeemer, and (c) that such other items of the Christian faith as the suffering love of God are irrelevant. That these are *theological* assertions is beyond question (they treat, respectively, the doctrines of anthropology, Christology, and soteriology). That they are *adequate* theological assertions is another matter.

The layman must love God with his mind; the layman must seek to understand his faith. In doing these things he is certainly entitled to the help of the "specialists," and to all the resources that are available as a result of the experience of generation after generation of Christians wrestling with the problems of belief and unbelief. But he cannot simply "rely on the specialists" to solve his own problems of belief and unbelief, which means that he cannot buy his faith secondhand. The experts cannot do his wrestling for him. The most they can do is teach him some of the rules for proper wrestling.[2]

The importance of theology

If individual Protestants cannot avoid being theologians, corporate Protestantism cannot avoid being theological. The community of faith has a particular responsibility to think through the meaning of its faith, so that it may declare to the world where it stands and why. The times when the church's message has been weak or vacillating have usually been times when the church's theology had been flabby or gone askew.

This is one reason why so much church history is the story of attempts to define what the church believes. The church must try to speak coherently rather than incoherently, to make statements that do greater rather than less justice to its subject matter. Early Christians, for example, were confronted with the claim that in Jesus of Nazareth, the carpenter's son, God himself had appeared on the human scene. How were they to describe this in terms that

Greeks could understand, and in ways that would avoid the misunderstandings of the fact that were already rampant? This was the problem behind the creedal controversies of the early church. Similarly, when the Reformers rediscovered the faith Christendom had forgotten, they had to give an account of it. How were they to share the treasures God had given them? What happened was that the various Protestant groups wrote confessions of faith, setting down as coherently as they could what they believed.[3] Roman Catholicism, forced by these events to clarify its own understanding of the faith, set forth systematically both those things it believed and those things it repudiated, through the deliberations of a Council that met sporadically for eighteen years.

This kind of thing must always go on. The church, too, must love God with its mind and seek to understand the faith it proclaims. Theology is important.

The unimportance of theology

But theology is also unimportant. There have been few instruments more effective in insulating men from God than total theological "systems" that answer every question, plug every loophole, and promise the believer that if he accepts the system his problems are at an end. Theology is always tempted to forget that "we have this treasure in earthen vessels," and to confuse the earthen vessels with the heavenly treasure. Since God stands above and beyond all statements that can be made about him, the statements are always trivial in comparison with him, and in this sense theology is supremely unimportant. But the value of true theology is to make this fact evident — that God *is* more than we can contain in our statements, and that therefore the statements are no more than pointers toward him. That we have pointers pointing in a right rather than a wrong direction is important. That we confuse the pointers with the reality itself is blasphemy.[4]

There are two reasons why we must not claim too much for theology. The first of these is the fact of *human finitude*. We are finite creatures trying to understand the infinite — a comic disproportion at best. If we "see in a mirror," it is only "dimly" and not "face to face." If we "know," it is only "in part" (1 Cor. 13:12). "Shall our tremors," Charles Williams asked, "measure the Omnipotence?" The only possible answer is, "Of course not."

But there is a more important reason than this. The real distinction to be made is not between the infinite God and finite man, but between the holy God and sinful man. The real problem is *human sin.* The notion that only the pure in heart shall see God is a formidable barrier to full theological insight. Our vision is not only inadequate, it is distorted. All that we know, we know with hearts that are less than pure, with wills less concerned for God than for ourselves, with minds less eager to find what is there than to find what we hope is there.

Since this is so, the basic ingredient for the theological enterprise is humility — a recognition that whatever we learn will not be a discovery by our brilliant minds but a disclosure by God's gracious condescension. As St. Augustine sought continually to remind himself, "God resisteth the proud but giveth grace to the humble" (cf. Proverbs 3:34, James 4:6, 1 Peter 5:5). There are few things more arrogant than theological treatises on humility.

Half a dozen ground rules

Theological enterprise is not without its perils, and more is demanded than the plea that laymen become self-conscious about their theology. A few ground rules may help to make the enterprise less perilous for newcomers.

1. Clear theology comes from clear minds. It requires thought, and highly disciplined thought at that. This means that *Protestantism and education must go hand in hand.* They have, in fact, gone hand in hand from the start.[5] Initially the emphasis was on the need for a "learned ministry." Not only was this concern a reaction against the intellectual mediocrity of medieval clerics, it was also a positive recognition that learning is necessary if one is rightly to expound the Word of God. Consequently high educational standards were demanded of those entering the Protestant ministry. In Geneva, an "academy" was established to educate prospective

clergy. The Puritans carried a concern for the education of ministers from England to New England. By 1636 they had founded Harvard College "to advance learning and perpetuate it to posterity, dreading to leave an illiterate ministry to the churches when our present ministers shall lie in the dust." [6] The story has been the same wherever Protestants have settled: churches first, but colleges soon after.

There was concern for the education of the laity as well. The Geneva Academy had a regular course of instruction and soon became a full-fledged university; Harvard has by no means limited itself to preparing men for the Protestant ministry.

But it is not merely the fact that "laymen have a right to an education, too." The point can be made more persuasively by placing the Protestant conception of "the priesthood of all believers" alongside the Protestant conception of the "learned ministry." For we may not limit the tasks of the "learned ministry" solely to the incumbents of the pulpit. If there truly is a "priesthood of all believers," if all men share in the church's ministry and have a responsibility for the propagation of the faith, it follows that all men stand in need not only of inner conviction about the reality of God, but in need of *learning* as well, so that they may communicate the faith more comprehensively. Sound witness will hardly be effected without sound learning. *Every* Christian is to be a "learned minister."

2. The theology with which the "learned ministry" is to concern itself must be a *Biblical theology*.[7] We have seen that the very impetus for the Reformation came from the fact that men like Wycliffe, Luther, and Calvin read their Bibles. Periods of real renewal in the life of the church have always come at these times when the church was taking seriously the admonition to "search the Scriptures" (John 5:39). The life of the church, and particularly the theology of the church, must always reckon with the possibility that new things will be discovered as Scripture is searched. All creeds and doctrines must therefore be tentative to this extent, that they are always subject to correction in the light of Scripture. This may sound like a confining principle. Actually it has been a liberating one, for it has kept the church *free to listen,* and has helped the church to break through all manner of confining statements. The disclaimer in the Scots Confession (1560) is a case in point:

Protestand that gif onie man will note in this our confessioun onie artickle or sentence repugnand to Gods halie word, that it wald pleis him of his gentleness and for christian charities sake to admonish us of the same in writing; and we upon our honoures and fidelitie, be Gods grace do promise unto him satisfactioun fra the mouth of God, that is fra his halie scriptures, or else reformation of that quilk he sal prove to be amisse.

To be sure, Protestants have not always been this circumspect about their theological pronouncements, but constant reference to the Bible as the touchstone of faith has always been Protestantism's surest safeguard against theological imperialism and theological nonsense.

But it would not be honest to leave the matter there. For when different Protestants affirm the importance of Scripture, they do not always mean the same thing. We have seen, indeed, that Protestant fundamentalism's thoroughgoing dependence on Scripture can distort the very message it is trying to preserve, and lapse easily into Bibliolatry.

Some Protestants, for whom Bibliolatry is not a temptation, feel strongly that to make the Bible the *sole* source of Christian truth is to confine the vision of the church to unnecessarily narrow perspectives. They might be willing to assert that the Bible is the *supreme* source of truth. But they would go on to assert that God has nowhere left himself without a witness, and that Christians should gratefully acknowledge and appropriate whatever they can learn of God through such things as an examination of the human conscience, the wonders of nature and creation, and the insights of other world religions.

Others, however, would assert that God has done his decisive deed "in the redemption of the world by our Lord Jesus Christ," and that our primary witness to this fact is Scripture itself. Since this is so, we must always start with Scripture in seeking to understand who God is and what he has done. To insist that first of all we must seek him elsewhere than in the place where he has sought us, is the height of ingratitude. This does not mean that the Christian never looks anywhere else, but only that he looks first at the Word (i.e. Jesus Christ as revealed in Scripture) and that he looks at the world only *in the light of* the Word. The Word is the means by which the world is to be understood, not vice versa.[8]

3. These comments already anticipate a third characteristic of Protestant theology. With whatever else it may concern itself, *theology must concern itself primarily with Jesus Christ.* By now, this should be so self-evident as to require little elaboration. *Christ*-ian theology is an attempt to understand God in the light of who Christ is and what Christ does. A theology that develops a doctrine of God without reference to God's revelation in Christ is to that extent a less than Christian theology. Protestant faith is not first of all faith in man or even faith in God, but faith in Jesus Christ as the one who binds man and God together. "The one doctrine which I have supremely at heart," Luther writes, "is that of faith in Christ, from whom, through whom, and unto whom all my theological thinking flows back and forth day and night." [9]

4. What about *theology and science?* Can theology, particularly if it is Biblical and Christo-centric, maintain its integrity "in an age of science"? Many people believe that modern science has developed the only truly reliable methods for discovering truth, and that theology, being prescientific in origin, must either adopt these methods or retire from the scene.

Christians are often needlessly defensive and nervous about this. If one so wishes, one can argue that theology is actually "scientific" in the best sense of the word. One of the cardinal principles of scientific investigation is the principle that the method of investigation used must be appropriate to the subject matter being investigated. It is proper scientific procedure for a biologist to employ different methods in studying the human body than a geologist employs in studying rock formations, and for a physicist to employ different methods in studying cloud formations than a psychologist uses in studying the human mind. It would be quite unscientific to demand that the geologist study the Paleozoic era in accordance with the methods used by the psychologist to investigate neurotic disorders.

Now the subject matter of Christian theology is the living God in his relationship to men, and an investigation of this subject matter must use categories appropriate to it. In the nature of the case these will be categories dealing with the personal, and with personal relationship. Impersonal categories would be manifestly out of place. When, therefore, someone demands that the personal claims of Christian faith be vindicated by reference to algebraic equations or slide rules, the theologian can properly reply that this is no more appropriate than would be a demand on his part that the principles of microbiology be vindicated by reference to the book of Leviticus. Consequently, the language and method of theology must be closely related to commitment, trust, prayer, personal relationship, worship, and praise. To try to divorce theology from these would actually be the most "unscientific" thing one could do.[10]

5. *Some theological statements are more crucial than others.* One could, perhaps, state the heart of the Christian message in a phrase such as "In Christ, God was reconciling the world unto himself" (2 Cor. 5:19), or even in Luther's five words, "Christus Gottessohn ist unser Heiland." It would be hard for Christians to disagree over such affirmations as these. But the further one goes away from such a center, the wider the area where there may be understandable differences of opinion. Almost all Protestants, for example, would agree that one enters the church through baptism. A good many might differ as to whether the water should be administered by sprinkling, pouring, or total immersion. Only a few would maintain that the saving power of the sacrament is dependent upon the number of cubic centimeters of water employed.

Not all theological concerns, then, are of the same order of importance. Some will be at the heart and center of the faith and cannot be abandoned without abandoning the gospel. But others will be at the periphery and can be the objects of legitimate disagreement. In the popular mind, Calvin is usually pictured as the exponent of absolute fixity of belief on all points. It is particularly helpful, therefore, to hear his recognition of the need for theological discrimination between essentials and non-essentials:

> All the articles of true doctrine are not of the same description. Some are so necessary to be known, that they ought to be universally received as fixed and indubitable principles, as the peculiar maxims of religion; such as, that there is one God; that Christ is God and the Son of God; that our salvation depends on the mercy of God; and the

like. There are others, which are controverted among the churches, yet without destroying the unity of the faith. For why should there be a division on this point, if one church be of the opinion, that souls, at their departure from their bodies, are immediately removed to heaven; and another church venture to determine nothing respecting their local situation, but be nevertheless firmly convinced, that they live to the Lord; and if this diversity of sentiment on both sides be free from all fondness for contention and obstinacy of assertion? [11]

Calvin goes on to assert that "a diversity of opinion respecting these non-essential points ought not to be a cause of discord among Christians." [12]

6. In any discussion of theological responsibility, *the possible contribution of heresy* must be recognized. A heresy is not sheer untruth, but an overemphasis on one aspect of the truth. Christian faith, for example, asserts that Jesus Christ is both human and divine. To assert that Christ is divine is to assert part of the truth about him. But Christians sometimes make this assertion in such a way that in the name of what appears a genuine orthodoxy they are actually denying that the divine Christ was human also. It may then take a strident voice, proclaiming the opposite truth of the humanity of Jesus, to bring the church back to a realization that both things have to be said. For which recovery we must thank the heretic who has been perhaps the unwitting ally of the Holy Spirit.

But the heretic plays another role as well. For the church can proclaim both the divinity and the humanity of Jesus Christ in a way that is both impeccably orthodox and also hopelessly irrelevant. There is nothing quite so irrelevant as a self-conscious orthodoxy which becomes so wrapped up in niceties of formulation that it neglects the human beings all around it who are crying for a word from the Lord and receiving only the refined words of men. In such a situation, the heretic fulfills another needed function. There may be need for an individual with a Christian conscience to remind the church, for example, that men are being trampled under foot by political chicanery and that political involvement is a necessary part of churchmanship. In his very enthusiasm for this legitimate concern, the individual will probably become a little too sure that the Kingdom of God can be ushered in by human means, and that a change of federal administrations will do it. But in the process of stating such convictions, however one-sidedly, he will force the church to rethink its faith in terms of greater social relevance. "A live heresy," P. T. Forsyth once remarked, "is better than a dead orthodoxy."

There must therefore be a place within the church for "dangerous" ideas. This is the risk Protestantism must run in the name of devotion to the truth it is always stultifying. The compensating weight of heresy may be necessary from time to time to keep the listing ship of orthodoxy from foundering. If so, we can hazard the guess that God has a special kind of affection for heretics, and even that he raises them up to fulfill his purposes when his usual means have been hampered by human self-sufficiency.

APPENDIX: *The creative use of doubt* [13]

The problem of doubt is a major problem for twentieth-century Christians. This does not mean that faith came easily in the past, and that only within living memory has it suddenly become hard to believe. Nevertheless, there is urgent concern with the problem of doubt in contemporary Protestantism, and it would be inappropriate to conclude a chapter on loving God with the mind without some discussion of it.

It is often felt that doubt is an unworthy attitude in the life of the true believer. But it can more legitimately be contended that "faith without doubt is dead." Doubt need not be a way of avoiding commitment, although it sometimes is; doubt may be the price that mature faith must render to honesty.

From this perspective certain things may be suggested about the place of doubt in the life of faith:

1. The first word should be the sternest word. Pascal put it with shattering brevity: "Why is it so hard to believe? Because it is so hard to obey." This word must be spoken to those who indulge in dilettante doubts because it is more comfortable not to have to be committed. Doubt in these terms is evasion, and it must be unmasked for what it is. Many people who think they are going through intellectual turmoil are actually finding rationalizations for avoiding a commitment that would mean changing their ways. Augustine was more honest when he prayed, during his pagan days, "O God, give me chastity, but not yet."

2. The doubter must ask himself whether he is doubting the Chris-

tian faith or simply his own understanding of it. Many people have rejected the Christian faith on the mistaken notion that the Lord's Supper is cannibalism, or that if the whale did not swallow Jonah the Bible is unreliable, or that religious belief is simply a matter of environmental conditioning.

3. It may be that God is stirring up this discontent within the doubter's soul, and that the agonies of disbelief are necessary in order that the resultant belief may be firmer. A person's honest doubts may bring him closer to the truth than all the unruffled affirmations of faith he used to make. The doubter must ask himself why he is so concerned about the fact that he doesn't believe, if in fact there is nothing in which to believe. In the *Pensées,* Pascal puts on the lips of Jesus an initially — but only initially — curious assertion: "Console thyself," Jesus says to the agonized searcher, "thou wouldst not seek me if thou hadst not already found me."

4. In his doubt, the individual need not stand alone. He can receive help from the community of faith. He may take comfort from the experience of "the others," who do not live in such total faith as he is likely to assume they do. And he can learn from them that on the *other* side of doubt is a deeper security and faith than was present before the doubts intruded.

There is even a sense in which the doubter can be sustained by a realization that others within the church will, for the time being, "believe for him." This is not an evasion of the problem of doubt; it is an affirmation of the reality of the communion of saints. Many Christians can testify that during periods of unbelief they were upheld by the faith of their fellow Christians, praying all about them, and were thus sustained until they were ready once more to live within the life of faith. Thus Christians at different stages along the pilgrimage can help one another.

5. There is no such thing as "total doubt." Augustine tried to doubt everything, but he could not doubt the truth of his own skepticism, and it was rather shattering for him to discover that he had to doubt his doubts.

There will always remain *some* things the doubter can still affirm. He may doubt that Jesus Christ is Lord and Saviour, or that he rose from the dead: but he may believe in the historicity of a man who "went about doing good." He must then live on the strength of that affirmation. Sooner or later he will have to ask himself whether that affirmation alone is strong enough. As he recognizes the distance between Jesus' demands and his own fulfillment of those demands, the doubter may begin to see the significance of forgiveness, and the claim that Jesus forgave sin may begin to have a reality similar to the reality of his command that we love one another.

6. But the advice to "cultivate one's doubts," while it may sometimes be a first word, is never the last word. The last word is surely that if the doubter would seek God, he must be willing to look where God has sought him, for the Christian claim is that God has taken the initiative rather than leaving it to us. And the gaze of every man, whether believer, doubter, or seeker, must be directed toward the place where God's initiative was historically expressed in Jesus Christ.

When this claim is stubbornly resisted we understand why so many Protestant thinkers have described doubt as "rebellion" or sin. Sometimes the doubter turns his attention so much upon himself that he is unwilling to look elsewhere. He becomes, as Luther said, "curved in upon himself." From this perspective, there is a sense in which doubt is a radical denial of God in the name of a radical affirmation of the self over against God. The great error here is the assumption that the reality of God is dependent on how the doubter happens to feel about him at the moment. If God exists, he will not cease to exist just because the doubter is temporarily unconvinced of his existence. So at this point, the doubter must be urged to transfer his gaze outward for awhile instead of inward, to look more specifically in the direction of the One whom God has sent, to be willing to receive a gift rather than trying to create a faith, and to be content to take one step at a time.

11. The Worship of God

It is not enough to love God with our minds.

Talking about God is important, and talking about him as accurately as we can is more important still. But no one talks *about* God in authentic tones unless he has also talked *with* God.

Martin Buber, the Jewish thinker from whom Protestants have learned so much, goes as far as to say, "God cannot be expressed, he can only be addressed." [1] While the Protestant might want to amend this to read that God can be expressed only by those he has addressed, Buber's statement is still a healthy reminder that the final depths of the Christian life are not realized in the brilliancy of our thinking but in the maturity of our prayer.

If to know *about* God is not enough, to *know* God is not enough either. According to St. Paul, the important thing is "rather to be *known by God*" (Gal. 4:9). It is when we are known by God, and God makes us aware of the fact, that a new situation is created. For when people are known by God, they do not first of all write books or work out a philosophy of history or start analyzing their religious experience. They sing; or they pray; or they sing and pray at the same time — things like: "Thank you . . . Bless the Lord, O my soul . . . I am unworthy . . . Father, forgive . . . You are all and I am nothing . . . Empower me . . . Thy Kingdom come." Even the creeds are expressions of praise and devotion before they are theological statements; the creeds were originally meant to be sung. These acts — singing, praying, listening, adoring, confessing — we call *worship,* for they are an acknowledgment of the "worth-ship" of God.

That we are "known by God" means that he knows us before we know him. This in turn means that we cannot describe worship simply as "our response." It is that. But since God is the God of grace, our response is a response that he himself initiates in us. When we worship, we must realize that it is *God* who elicits and calls forth in us the response we could not possibly make unless his grace were at work in us.

No attempt to describe worship can be successful. What we think we see happening, and what really happens, are two different things. To read about worship does not mean that we know what worship is, any more than to read about God means that we are in personal relationship with him. There is only one way to find out what worship is, and that is . . . to worship.

The chaotic character of Protestant worship

An honest description of Protestant worship must begin with a judgment upon it. Few things seem more chaotic.

This is partly because different denominations use different liturgies. The word "liturgy" originally meant "the people's work," i.e. what the people *do* when they worship God. Any sequence of acts of worship is a liturgy. There are good liturgies and there are bad liturgies, but all of them are liturgies. It is inaccurate to contrast "liturgical" and "non-liturgical" worship. The proper distinction is between "free" liturgies (in which there is great latitude in the pattern of worship from week to week) and formal or "set" liturgies (in which a regularly ordered pattern is followed, with such variations as are prescribed by the different seasons of the Christian year). This distinction accounts for much of the seeming chaos of "Protestant worship." There is considerable difference between a Baptist testimonial service and a high church Episcopal eucharist.

But the chaotic character of Protestant worship is not explained by being explained away, and those who conduct worship must bear chief responsibility for the chaos that remains. There are at least three reasons for this:

1. Many ministers conduct worship without any apparent sense of mystery and awe and wonder in the face of what they are doing. If the worship of Almighty God is, as the opening sentence of one liturgy puts it, "the most solemn act of us his creatures here below,"

the sense of its solemnity and dignity and godly splendor ought to be apparent in the demeanor of the person conducting the service.

2. Many ministers have never worked out for themselves a satisfactory understanding of what corporate worship should entail, and the utter chaos of the services they "plan" betrays their lack of disciplined thinking. Something is wrong when a New England minister feels free to dispense with the reading of Scripture and to substitute "improving" selections from Robert Louis Stevenson.

3. Many ministers who have been trained in the meaning of corporate worship make no attempt to share with their congregations the fruits of their study. Too many Protestant laymen still look upon all acts of worship before the sermon as "the preliminaries," and have no idea why an assurance of pardon follows rather than precedes a prayer of confession.

How is this state of affairs to be remedied? It will not do to suggest that a uniform liturgy be imposed on all Protestants regardless of their temperament or heritage. But certain criteria can be suggested to all Protestants, in terms of which they can develop liturgies that have greater inner integrity. For the right ordering of Protestant worship, for example, it would be hard to improve on St. Paul's recognition that Christians are to stand fast in the liberty with which Christ has set them free (Gal. 5:1), and his recognition that all things are to be done decently and in order (1 Cor. 14:40). Some ordering of public worship is necessary and right, but no single way of ordering public worship is the only necessary and right way.

Within these boundaries, there are three kinds of resources available to Protestants of all traditions:

> Those responsible for the ordering of the public worship of God should emphasize fidelity to the aspects of public worship that are emphasized in Scripture; maintain receptiveness to the historic experience of Christendom, appropriating for their own such elements from the past as have been found consistent with the right showing forth of the gospel; and in the light of these resources of Scripture and ecumenical experience, endeavor to serve the needs and situation of their own worshipping community.[2]

The double intent of Protestant worship

Is it possible to discern a common intent behind the varieties of Protestant worship ranging from Lutheran to Methodist, Anglican to Congregational, Disciples to Presbyterian? We can discern at least a double intent in them all: *to give God glory* and *to lead to amendment of life*. The order of priority is important.

Worship is an acknowledgment, as we have seen, of the "worth" of God. "Great is the Lord and greatly to be praised" (Ps. 48:1). The word "praise" has the same root as the Middle English word *preisen,* meaning to value highly. In worship, men acknowledge that they value God so highly that no one else can be compared to him. The greatest hymns are hymns of praise. The hymnbook of the Jewish people, the Psalter, is saturated with the note of praise:

> O give thanks to the Lord, call on his name,
> make known his deeds among the peoples!
> Sing to him, sing praises to him,
> tell of all his wonderful works!
> (Ps. 105:1–2)
>
> I will extoll thee, my God and King,
> and bless thy name for ever and ever.
> Every day I will bless thee,
> and praise thy name for ever and ever.
> (Ps. 145:1–2)

This is really the heart of the matter. There is a "given-ness" about God that nothing men do can change. We cannot cause him to appear or disappear at our bidding. We cannot bend his will to ours. We cannot dictate terms to him. But we can glorify him. We can praise him. We can "ascribe to the Lord the glory of his name" (Ps. 29:2). We can gather together to praise God, aware that nothing else we do on earth so clearly defines the meaning of our "human-ness." We can, with no thought of self, give all thought to him. Whether this moves us, or inspires us, or changes us, is for the moment beside the point. For the point is that we fulfill our true destiny as children of God when we give God glory.

But worship must lead to amendment of life as well. Nothing is a greater travesty of worship than Sundays that bear no relationship to weekdays. Something is wrong when on one day Protestants pray to the father of all men—and deny for the next six days that he is in fact the father of more than a few men, i.e. "our sort." The day at worship must challenge the days at work or it is worthless.

The Psalter knows this too:

> Search me, O God, and know my heart!
> Try me and know my thoughts!
> And see if there be any wicked way in me,
> and lead me in the way everlasting.
> (Ps. 139:23–24)

To give God glory . . . to lead to amendment of life. Neither has integrity without the other. But neither is properly defined without the other. We discover that when these two foci of Protestant worship are properly related, they blend together so as to be almost indistinguishable. To give God glory is to seek to do his will — which means amendment of life. And it remains as true as ever that "to work is to pray" (*laborare est orare*). We know that something is wrong when work becomes a substitute for prayer, or prayer becomes an alternative to work. The avoidance of these imbalances is a constant challenge to the integrity of Protestant worship.

Distinctive emphases in Protestant worship

One way to learn about Protestant worship is to study the liturgical materials of various denominations, such as *The Book of Common Prayer* (Episcopalian), *The Book of Common Worship* (United Presbyterian), or *The Book of Common Order* (United Church of Canada). But the only adequate way is to worship with those who use such materials. The secondhand comments that follow are better than nothing — but not very much better. No secondhand description can do justice to firsthand experience.

There are at least five things we can describe as characteristic of Protestant worship, the last of which is important enough to be treated in a separate chapter.

1. *The offering of prayer.* Prayer is a primal response to God. It need not take the form of specific words uttered in a specific posture, though it often does. Any acknowledgment of the presence of God is a form of prayer. It is not surprising that much of the attempt to give God glory should consist of praying to him.

There are many kinds of public prayer. In some traditions, the prayers are offered by the minister on behalf of the congregation. He may prepare these himself, or he may draw on the liturgical heritage of Christendom. If he belongs to a certain school of thought, he may pray *ex tempore,* hoping that the Holy Spirit will supply him with the proper words. This hope is not always fulfilled.

But almost always the congregation will pray too. The ways in which it prays will depend upon the tradition in which it finds itself. Some Protestants kneel for prayer. Many congregations sit. The Puritans used to stand.

More important than the posture of the pray-ers is the content of the prayers. They may be mimeographed for the occasion or printed in the order of service. They will often be the pure gold that has been refined by the fire of centuries of liturgical experience. Familiarity need not dull their impact — worshippers testify that the experiences of life add new meaning to old phrases.

The opening prayers in public worship are usually prayers of *adoration,* acknowledging the incomparable greatness and goodness of God. Adoration is the "purest" form of prayer, and therefore the most difficult. Truly to adore God is to be made acutely aware of one's own shortcomings, and so a prayer of *confession* usually follows. This should be prayed by all since all have sins to confess. It can include confession not only of sin-in-general but of sins-in-particular. Often the minister follows it with an "assurance of pardon," declaring God's forgiveness to those who truly confess their sins. This in turn leads to prayers of *thanksgiving* for the gift of forgiveness, the gift of grace, the gift of Jesus Christ, and the very specific gifts that God has given to his children. Thanksgiving is perhaps the most characteristic expression of the spirit of Protestantism — since all is of grace, the only response can be gratitude. Prayers of *supplication* or *intercession* should come toward the end of the service. After worshippers have been confronted by the promises and the demands of the gospel, they realize that they bear responsibility, under God, for their fellow men. It is appropriate to lay those concerns before God before going back into situations where they will be called upon to translate their prayers into deeds.

Someone has noted that the above sequence of prayer (adoration-confession-thanksgiving-supplication) is an acrostic of the word *a-c-t-s,* as useful a reminder as any that prayer involves both giving God glory and being renewed for amendment of life.

2. *Congregational singing.* Before the Reformation, congregational participation in worship had practically disappeared. The mass was performed *by* the priest *for* the people. The congregations were spectators. The music was extraordinarily beautiful but extraordinarily complicated, and could be sung only by trained choirs. The Reformation repaired this situation by *giving back to the people* their right to participate in the praise of God through song.[3] The task of the preacher was to expound the Word; the task of the congregation was to "sing the service." When the "priesthood of all believers" was reaffirmed, the liturgical responsibility of all believers was re-established.[4]

Luther was an accomplished musician and wrote both words and music for many chorale tunes. The new hymnody was simple, and untutored laymen could praise God through song in ways not only pleasing to the Lord but not too displeasing to their fellow men. *Von Himmel hoch* (1536) is an example of the simplicity and dignity of Reformation song. The first phrase uses only four notes, while the last is simply a descending octave with one tiny twist. Anyone who can carry a tune can sing it after hearing it once or twice. Common street tunes were often adapted for worship — a notable way of destroying the barrier between sacred and secular. A café drinking song, originally in ¾ time, was reharmonized by Johann Sebastian Bach, set to words dealing with the death of Christ, and became the passion chorale, "O Sacred Head Now Wounded."

The Genevan Reformers likewise emphasized congregational singing, and provided metrical versions for the psalms. Those who object that the Strasbourg and Genevan liturgies seem to lack the note of joy, should be reminded that congregational singing supplied this note. The best example of Reformed psalmody is *Old*

Hundredth, a metrical version of Psalm 100, set to music by Louis Bourgeois. The words quickly dispel caricatures of early Reformed worship as dour:

> All people that on earth do dwell,
> Sing to the Lord with *cheerful* voice,
> Him serve with *mirth,* his praise forthtell,
> Come ye before him and *rejoice.*

Strong words and strong music likewise characterized the hymnody of the Scottish Reformation. The tune *Dundee* (sometimes called *French*) is typical of the Scottish Psalter. In Great Britain, many of the more than 4,000 hymns written by Charles Wesley have stood the test of time and remain staples of modern Protestant worship the world over. During the revival of pietism in Europe, hymns that laid stress on the personal faith of the worshipper became popular, and have remained so in many Protestant circles.

The point of this historical excursion is to provide a reminder that Protestants have a musical heritage they too often overlook. It is difficult to establish criteria for distinguishing between "good" and "bad" hymns in that heritage. But a warning should be posted when hymnody becomes intensely subjective. This will mean that attention has shifted from God to man. "Gospel hymns" are a genuine expression of religious feeling, but the question remains whether a hymn should be primarily an expression of "religious feeling" or an expression of the majesty and the love of God in a musical idiom worthy of its subject matter. Music that is characterized by chromatic thrills and syncopated responses suffers from comparison with the music of Luther or Bourgeois.

There was a time when the "paid quartet" was a hallmark of Protestant worship. This was a reversion from the Protestant intent, worse even than the situation the Reformers had tried to repair, for the music sung by "paid quartets" is almost always inferior to Gregorian plainsong. It is cause for rejoicing that professional singers are being replaced by choirs drawn from the congregation. For the choir is not a group of "performers" to relieve the congregation of its responsibility to praise God through song; the choir is that part of the congregation entrusted with helping the rest of the congregation "sing the service."

3. *Scripture and sermon.* The integrity of Protestant worship requires that we say "Scripture and sermon *and sacrament,*" as the next chapter will emphasize. But whether or not the sacraments are observed each Sunday, Scripture is read each Sunday. No branch of Christendom whose forebears cried *sola Scriptura* can ignore its dependence upon the Bible. The Robert Louis Stevenson cults are few in number.

The Bible permeates the whole of Protestant worship. Opening sentences and benediction, hymns and prayers, responses and litanies, all are couched in Biblical language and draw on Biblical imagery to mediate Biblical themes. But the influence of the Bible is not merely indirect. At least one portion of Scripture is read aloud, frequently two (Old and New Testament lessons), and sometimes three (Old Testament, Epistle, and Gospel). Some denominations leave the choice of lessons to the minister. Others follow a "lectionary" or prescribed order of lessons, read in regular sequence. The advantage of the lectionary is that the congregation is exposed to the fullness of the Biblical message, and is not at the mercy of the minister's whim.

The Bible is read. It is also expounded. The minister preaches a sermon in which he deals with Biblical material, or with contemporary issues, or (in optimum situations) with the relation of the one to the other. Many people would call the sermon the most distinctively "Protestant" thing about Protestant worship. What then is a sermon, and how does it differ from an ordinary speech?

Empirical evidence does not always yield a convincing answer. After touring the United States, Alec Vidler reported back in Britain that the message of a good many American preachers seemed to be, "Let me suggest that you try to be good." [5]

But a wider sampling than the American pulpit makes clear that the sermon *is* a distinctive form of address. Its distinctiveness lies in the fact that it is not a man reporting his thoughts about God, but a man reporting God's deeds among men. A sermon is an unfolding of a portion of Scripture — a book, a chapter, a verse, even a word. It is a means through which a Word of the Lord in Scripture becomes, by the grace of God, a Word from the Lord to the congregation. Protestant preaching has most characteristically been "expository preaching," i.e. an "exposition," a laying open, of a portion of Scripture so that those who hear it will know that it is being addressed to them.

Protestants should remember two things about expository preaching. *First,* there is no guarantee that a sermon based on Scripture will "speak" to them. Such are the weaknesses of flesh and mind that expository sermons can be deadly dull. But such is the humility of God that he relies upon weak flesh and weak minds to expound and hear his Word, and bears the indignities worked upon that Word with exceptionally patient grace. For when Scripture is laid open, the Word of God has at least a fighting chance to be heard amid the words of men. *Second,* comfortable American Protestants need to remember that churches under tribulation return to expository preaching. The Bible is recognized as the only adequate vehicle of faith, and it speaks with power. A Lutheran pastor behind the Iron Curtain describes what has happened there:

> God's Word has assumed a strange straightforwardness, whether it be in church school, the sermon, in group Bible study, or in personal conversation. The thick walls of nineteen hundred years have come down. Nothing stands between us and the biblical Word. The Bible speaks to our situation as never before. It seems as if the biblical characters have again become alive among us, drawing us to their side as actors in the divine drama, almost against our will. Many of us can testify of an instance when suddenly we find ourselves mirrored in Scriptures, and with us, the estranged, the indifferent, and the enemies.[6]

Modern preaching seems flat and insipid when it loses this Biblical dimension. If there is a revival of Protestant faith, it will be due to a revival of Biblical preaching.

4. *The offering of gifts.* An outsider observing Protestant worship might report, "At a certain point in the service, money was collected."

He would be wrong. That is only what it looks like. What actually happens is that money is *given.* "The offering," not "the collection," is the way this part of worship is described.

Not all people agree that it is a proper part of worship. They feel that the clinking of coins, or more hopefully, the rustling of bills, is an intrusion of the "secular" into the realm of the "sacred." Earthly things like budgets and bank balances have no place, they feel, in a spiritual experience like worship.

But they are wrong, too. It is not being funny or ironic to say that churches are concerned about money. It is simply affirming that in the Protestant way of looking at things no line can be drawn between sacred and secular, earthly and spiritual. Life in God's world is all of a piece, and money is part of it.

The offering of gifts is an act of worship rather than an interruption of worship for at least three reasons:

a. The offering is a very conscious way of bringing the "affairs of the world" into the life of the church, a dramatic means of emphasizing that there can be no gap between what goes on "in church," and what goes on elsewhere.

b. Even more important is the fact that the offering symbolizes the giving of the *self* to God. What men offer is not just money; the offering of money is a way of dramatizing the offering of their lives. The dollar bill or the quarter or the ten dollar check stands for the giver. It shows that at least a part of his talents and time is being offered to God. Because God gave himself, men give themselves in return.

c. The offering is the means by which the work of the church goes on. It is a simple fact of life that churches need funds. To give is to affirm a belief in what the church does, and to support the church in the doing of it. Churches are also expected to help one another. This is how Protestants give *tangible* expression to the communion of saints and the bearing of burdens. There is often pseudo-pious talk about how a designated offering becomes a substitute for a dedicated life. But true piety realizes that when another person is in real difficulty it may not be enough just to "pray for him." Purse strings are as important as heart strings.

"Private worship" as an extension of "corporate worship"

The Protestant not only worships in company with others. He worships by himself. At least, he *should* worship by himself, as well as in company with others. Since Christian faith is a communal faith, priority must be given to corporate worship. But since Christian faith is personal faith, a relationship with God must be established in individual terms as well. This is the life of private prayer.[7]

Protestantism has both a strength and a weakness here. The *strength* lies in the fact that a Protestant can pray anywhere at any time. He does not need a church building, nor does he need a "religious atmosphere." He is not dependent on a group of persons or a set of words. All of these can help, but none of them is essential. Since God is always near, he can be reached in a crowded subway as well as in a crowded church.

The *weakness* lies in the fact that since a Protestant can pray anywhere at any time, he is likely not to bother praying at all, unless he is in difficulty. God is always accessible, so God need not be sought, except in emergencies. As far as one can tell, not many people do pray in a subway.

One evidence of this weakness is the fact that Protestantism has been less productive of saintly lives than has Roman Catholicism. Protestants are sometimes a little condescending about the "props" Roman Catholicism makes available for cultivating the life of the spirit. They fail to realize that there is great practical wisdom in setting apart certain places for prayer, in providing "set" prayers that can be memorized, and in commending spiritual exercises such as the Rosary or the Stations of the Cross. These are genuine means of grace for many Roman Catholic souls. When all the properly Protestant comments have been made about the possible abuse of such devotional exercises, the final comment must be that praying in such ways is surely preferable to the Protestant alternative of not praying at all.

This does not mean that the way to overcome Protestant spiritual barrenness is to consecrate Lady Chapels or introduce prayers to the saints. It does mean that Protestantism must ask whether in fact it gives sufficient help to those who are concerned with the life of devotion from Monday through Saturday. To do this more amply, and to do it in Protestant terms, means *transforming the Protestant weakness into strength,* by dealing creatively with the fact that one can pray anywhere at any time.

One way to do this is to emphasize the fact that if one turns to God at certain regular times, he is more likely to turn to God at other times as well. *A disciplined life of prayer* is the hard-won prerequisite for that spontaneity in prayer that many Protestants wrongly imagine to be their natural inheritance.

A second and particularly Protestant resource for individual prayer is *the availability of the Bible.* Nowhere are the words of Scripture more likely to become the Word of God than in the life of prayer. The "prayer for illumination" does not belong only to the public reading of the Word. Bible study and prayer, prayer and Bible study, are inseparable in Protestant "personal religion."

A third resource for the Protestant is a recognition that *in his life of private prayer he is not alone.* Not only is God there with him, the communion of saints is there with him too. He prays as part of a praying community of believers. He prays for them. They pray for him. What he does alone is only an extension and continuation of what they all do together.

A final Protestant resource is the practice of *family worship,* which represents a kind of bridge between "private" and "public" worship. There was a time when the most typical portrayal of Protestant living would have been the Puritan father reading from the family Bible or offering grace at the head of the table before a meal. If modern Protestants feel that there is something overly patriarchal in such pictures, the answer is not the destruction of the picture itself but a sharing within the family of responsibility for the reading and the praying. To be sure, "grace before meat" can become threadbare and perfunctory — as can all the gifts of the Spirit. But it can also be a thrice-daily offering of thanks to God for the very gift of life itself and for the means of sustaining life.

Both food and prayer are mysteries to us. But when they are close together their glory shines.

12. The Worship of God (continued): The Sacraments

To devote a separate chapter to the sacraments is to flout an important theological principle in the name of an important typographical principle. The theological principle is this: Word and sacrament belong together. The typographical principle is this: chapters should not be too long.

It must also be clear that to consider the sacraments at the conclusion of a section on "central Protestant affirmations" is meant to be climactic, not anti-climactic. The sacraments are not afterthoughts that must be validated by something else. They validate everything else.

The unity of Word and sacrament

The conviction that Word and sacrament belong together is a basic Protestant conviction.[1] Article 5 of the Lutheran Augsburg Confession states that they are the means by which the Holy Spirit is imparted. Lutherans have maintained this principle vigorously. But other traditions have the principle as well, even though they are not always able to incorporate it in practice.

An examination of Calvin's Genevan liturgy, for example, shows that the sacrament of the Lord's Supper was intended to be the culminating point of the service, and that it was to be celebrated each Lord's Day. Although Calvin's elders, for reasons best known to themselves, would not permit such frequent celebration, Calvin insisted to the end of his life that the full service of the Word should include not only Scripture and sermon but the sacrament as well.[2]

The same intent is apparent in the Episcopal *Book of Common*

Prayer. The central expression of Episcopal worship is the service of Holy Communion, the Eucharist, and this service quite properly has provision for a sermon. Word and sacrament belong together. But there is a shorter service, Morning Prayer, originally intended as an "early service" before the main one, that has neither sermon nor sacrament. In one of those curious ironies of history, the place of the two services became reversed. "Morning prayer" became the main service (usually with a sermon added on afterwards) and Holy Communion became an "early service" for the faithful few (usually with the sermon omitted).[3]

There are signs in these two traditions of a concern to relate Word and sacrament as they were originally intended to be related. Churches in the Calvinist tradition are taking more seriously the recognition that the integrity of their worship demands frequent rather than infrequent celebration of the sacraments, and in Episcopal churches there is increasing emphasis on the Holy Communion as a family service which includes at least a brief sermon. In Protestantism as a whole there is a growing conviction that when Word and sacrament are separated, something basic in Christian worship has been debased. T. F. Torrance goes so far as to say; "Just as the head without the body is useless, so the Word without the Sacraments is an abstraction, and the Sacraments without the Word are a torso." [4]

What is a sacrament?

1. In treating as controversial a question as this, it is well to take as ecumenical a starting point as possible, and St. Augustine, who certainly fits such a description, defines the sacraments as *the Word made visible*.

The Word, we have already seen, is Jesus Christ, the Word made flesh. We "hear" in Scripture and sermon that he gave up his life for us, but we "see" in the breaking of the bread that his body was broken on our behalf. He it is who is "made visible" in the sacraments, and they exist to witness to him and to his saving power. P. T. Forsyth was pointing in this direction when he stated that there was really only one sacrament, "the sacrament of the Word," which was conveyed through the media of Scripture, sermon, Lord's Supper, baptism. All of these are important in the life of the church because they witness to the Word.

An imaginative translation by Donald Baillie has also caught the point. He suggests that in view of the way we now use the word "remembrance," the words "Do this in remembrance of me" could more properly be rendered, "Do this for my recalling." The sacrament of the Lord's Supper is not merely a "remembrance" of things past. It is a "recalling," *a making present,* of the living Christ. A past event (the presence of the Lord with his earliest disciples) becomes a present event (the presence of the Lord with his contemporary disciples). The Word is made visible.

2. The Reformers frequently described the sacraments as *seals.* In their day, when a king issued a decree, his words were written down and read aloud to the people. But the decree was not official unless "the king's seal" had been affixed to it. The seal made the proclamation *authentic.* If the seal was affixed, the hearers knew the proclamation was not spurious, and that the king himself was speaking to them through it.

In the same way, the sacraments are seals. They authenticate the proclamation of the gospel in Scripture and sermon. They are part of the full showing forth of that gospel. They make clear that the King himself is speaking to us, for they are his seal upon what has been said. The promises from the pulpit are sealed to us by the action at the table.

3. The sacraments have also been described as *outward and visible signs of inward and spiritual grace.* "The grace of our Lord Jesus Christ" is not just talked about in Protestant worship. It is given an outward manifestation. This is in keeping with Jesus' own ministry. He did not just talk about the Kingdom of God, he gave outward and visible signs of its presence. When he cured a leper by touching the leper and thus taking the leper's misfortune upon himself, he was giving an outward sign of what the Kingdom of God is like — that in the Kingdom of God the Lamb of God takes the sins of the world upon himself.

Christ has given similar signs to the church. The church does not just talk. It acts. It acts in the way its Lord acted. Since "the Lord Jesus took bread . . ." so does the church. It acts in the way he told it to act. Since he said, "This do for my recalling," the church does this to recall him. The sacraments are the outward signs of "the grace of our Lord Jesus Christ."

4. Protestants are agreed in observing *two sacraments,* the sacrament of baptism and the sacrament of the Lord's Supper.[5] This measure of Protestant agreement is unfortunately purchased at the price of disagreement with Roman Catholicism and Eastern Orthodoxy, both of which affirm a belief in seven sacraments.

The differences here stem from contradictory interpretations of the New Testament material. The Protestant insistence on two sacraments is based on a firm belief that only baptism and the Lord's Supper are given explicit warrant in the teaching of Jesus.[6] None of the other sacraments practiced by Roman Catholicism and Orthodoxy (penance, confirmation, matrimony, ordination, and extreme unction) appear to Protestants to have such warrant. They solemnize high moments in human life in a way that may often be the envy of Protestants, but they are not on that account to be elevated to the status of sacraments.[7]

To summarize: in baptism and the Lord's Supper, the two sacraments instituted by Jesus Christ for his church, Protestants discover the Word made visible, sealing and authenticating the promises of God, and serving as outward and visible signs of inward and spiritual grace.

Are the sacraments "necessary" for salvation?

There have been sharp differences in Christendom over this question. Roman Catholicism answers the question in the affirmative. In an emergency anyone — Roman Catholic or Protestant, believer or non-believer, priest or layman — can validly baptize, since without receiving the sacrament no one can be saved. Yet even Roman Catholicism introduces a qualification by making room for baptism of desire: a person who would desire baptism if he knew that it were essential for salvation, is accounted as though he had actually been baptized.

Very few Protestants indeed would hold that one who is cut off from the sacraments is denied the possibility of salvation. And yet few Protestants would assert that they are therefore optional appendages in the life of Christians, to be received or neglected at will. This seeming discrepancy is explained by an important distinction: *sacraments are necessary for church proclamation but not for individual salvation.* The full declaration of the gospel by the church necessarily includes the sacraments. The church not only speaks, it acts; the church not only proclaims, it "shows forth." A better way to put it might be to say that one way the church speaks is by acting; one way the church proclaims is by showing forth. Once again, Word and sacrament belong together. The church is derelict in its mission when it neglects either.

But as far as the individual is concerned, salvation is a gift conferred by God and not by sacraments. The sacraments show forth or ratify or "seal" the promise of salvation, but they do not guarantee it. Only God can do that. This does not, however, permit a cavalier attitude toward them. The individual who neglects the sacraments on the ground that they are not, strictly speaking, essential to his salvation, is neglecting the means God has ordained for the proclamation and reception of the Word, and in showing disdain for those means he is showing disdain for the God who provides them.

The reason behind the Protestant rejection of the claim that salvation is tied to the sacraments is an important one. To assert that grace is given only to those to whom the church dispenses the sacraments is to assert that what God can do is limited to what men have done. It is to make the church the manipulator of the promises of God rather than the humble recipient of those promises. It is to deny "the surprises of grace." [8]

The sacrament of baptism

That baptism should be charged with such meaning is surely one of the surprises of grace. It is usually an unexciting, even disappointing, ceremony. Some words are said, a few drops of water are sprinkled on someone's forehead, and the service is over.

If the service is in a Baptist or Disciples' church, the individual will be mature enough to know what is going on, and will make his own affirmation of faith. In some churches he may even be totally immersed. But in most churches the one baptized will be a tiny baby who is oblivious to what is going on.

With whatever outward differences, however, Protestants would agree that baptism represents the incorporation of the individual into the church, and that a valid baptism is performed if there is at least an application of water and a repetition of the baptismal formula, "———, I baptize thee in the name of the Father and of the Son and of the Holy Spirit." [9]

How is "the Word made visible" in this simple ceremony? How does this show forth the gospel?

1. Nothing the church does represents the gospel as a pure gift of grace more vividly than the baptism of an uncomprehending child. *The sacrament shows that the initiative belongs wholly to God.* Before the child is aware of God, let alone of God as a gracious God, God claims him for his own. Before the child seeks God, or seeks to please God, God has sought the child and pronounced him pleasing in his sight. In technical terms, baptism could be called the sacrament of prevenient grace, the grace that "prevenes," or comes before. In the baptismal service of the French Reformed Church, the pastor says:

> Little child, for you Jesus Christ came into the world, he did battle in the world, he suffered; for you he went through the agony of Gethsemane and the darkness of Calvary; for you he cried, "It is fulfilled"; for you he triumphed over death . . . For you, and you, little child, do not yet know anything about this. But thus is the statement of the apostle confirmed, "We love God because he first loved us." [10]

The child is claimed by God and initiated into the fellowship of those who have been claimed by God. Later on, the child will have to affirm or reject this activity of grace. If he rejects it, this will not alter the fact that the deed has been done, and that God claims him and will always claim him. If he affirms it, and the reality of his faith later wavers, he will discover that the reality of his baptism never wavers. (Luther, in his moments of greatest doubt, used to console himself by writing on a table in huge letters of chalk, "I have been baptized.") Whatever the child's response, it will be a response to God's prior activity.

2. The sacrament of baptism shows forth the gospel in another way. It demonstrates that the Christian life is a *participation in the death and resurrection of Jesus Christ,* and therefore a dying to self and a rising to newness of life in him. *This* Word is most clearly visible when baptism is administered as total immersion. The meaning it conveys can surely be extended to the act of sprinkling, but the dramatic force is considerably lessened.

The early church acted out the meaning of the gospel in baptism. Since Christ by his death and resurrection had broken the bonds of sin and death, the initiate, as he was incorporated into the body of Christ, participated in Christ's victory. He was submerged beneath the water — an act that truly symbolized his death, since it cut him off from the source of life. Thus he shared in the death of Christ, and entered into the tomb with him. But then the initiate was raised up from the water, symbolizing his resurrection from the dead, his rising to walk in newness of life with Christ. He was now a new creature, a "new being" in Christ Jesus.

This is the imagery behind a number of Paul's otherwise difficult statements about baptism.

> Do you not know that all of us who have been baptized into Christ Jesus were baptized into his death? We were buried therefore with him by baptism into death, so that as Christ was raised from the dead by the glory of the Father, we too might walk in newness of life.
>
> (Rom. 6:3–4; see Col. 2:12)

This is why hymns about the resurrection are more appropriate at a baptismal service than hymns about little children.

The picture of the initiate submerged beneath the waters suggests another dimension of the gospel. For the waters imply the "washing away" of sin, so that the initiate rises cleansed of all the stains of the past, forgiven and made clean.

3. If the baptism of an infant stresses the prevenient grace of God, "believer's baptism" stresses *the necessity of human response to what God has done.* When an adult is baptized he is publicly affirming his desire to accept what God has graciously offered him.

A service of confirmation for those baptized in infancy helps to illumine the same point. We have stated that a baptized child grows up with the realization that something *has been done* for him. He cannot undo it. But he can affirm it himself, accept the gift that has been given him beyond any deserving of it, and promise to live as one for whom this deed has been done.

4. Baptism is *an act of the church and an act for the church.* It is an act *of* the church, for although the minister does the actual baptizing, he acts not in his own right but on behalf of the church. Furthermore, when someone is incorporated into the church by baptism, the members of the church must take active responsibility for his growth in the faith. In some denominations, "godparents," speaking on behalf of the whole community, promise to do this, but in others the full congregation pledges to help in the nurture of the baptized.

Baptism is also an act *for* the church. The meaning of the sacrament is primarily a meaning for the congregation — particularly in the case of an infant baptism. The sacrament becomes an "enacted sermon," the Word made visible. It reminds those present that the relation between God and this child is precisely the same as the relation between God and them. They too have been called and chosen long before they were aware of it. They are called upon to reaffirm the faith in which they were baptized, just as the child will some day be called upon to do the same thing.

The sacrament of the Lord's Supper [11]

Baptism is the act of incorporation into the membership of the body of Christ. As such it occurs but once. The Lord's Supper is the act whereby that membership is sustained and nurtured. As such it occurs many times.

What "happens" at the Lord's Supper?

Men break bread together. They share wine together. They claim that as they do so the risen Christ is in their midst.

This has been true ever since two men, walking along a dusty road, invited a stranger home for supper and then recognized who the stranger was. How did they know him? "He was known to them in the breaking of the bread" (Luke 24:35). When he "took the bread and blessed, and broke it, and gave it to them . . . their eyes were opened and they recognized him." As other men have broken bread together and shared the cup, they have found that Christ is present.

THE PATTERN OF THE SERVICE

How does all this come to pass? Whether the service is a simple one around a kitchen table in a "house church," or a high mass at the altar of a Gothic cathedral, it follows the pattern of what Jesus did in the upper room on the night of his betrayal. There are four steps in this action, as it is reported in 1 Corinthians 11:23–26, our earliest account:

1. Jesus first of all *"took bread,"* just as later on he took the cup. Similarly the minister "takes" the elements of bread and wine, preparing them for the holy use to which they are appointed. Sometimes the elements are "taken" from the rear of the church and brought forward by those assisting in the service.

2. Next, Jesus *"gave thanks."* The mood of thanksgiving is the true mood of the service. Several Protestant traditions, in fact, refer to the service as "the eucharist" (from the Greek *eucharisteo,* meaning "to give thanks"). The Lord's Supper is not a wake, recalling a sad death; it is a joyous feast, celebrating the good news that death has been swallowed up in victory. From earliest times, it has been celebrated on Sunday morning, the day of Christ's resurrection.

Within the prayer of thanksgiving, most Protestants include a prayer of consecration, during which the elements are offered up to God for his blessing, so that rather than being mere bread and wine they may now stand for the body and blood of Christ, and represent his real presence.[12]

3. After Jesus had given thanks for the bread, *"he broke it,"* just as later he poured out wine and gave it to his disciples. Similarly, the minister breaks a piece of bread in view of the people, and pours out some wine, as enacted reminders of what happened to the one whom the elements now represent. Christ's body was broken just as the bread is broken, and his blood (i.e. his life)

was poured out, just as the wine is poured out. His love for men was this costly a love. It cost him his life.

4. Finally, Jesus *"gave"* the bread and wine to his followers and they ate and drank. The bread is his body, broken for them, the cup is the new covenant in his blood, the new bond between God and man based on God's forgiving love. This is a love made visible in portent by the poured wine, and made visible in actuality by the life poured out upon a cross. To receive these elements is to receive the one who gave them.

GOD'S ACTION — AND OURS

It seems a strange thing over which to make such a fuss, this act of eating bread and drinking wine. Surely God could have acted in more spectacular fashion. Whether he could have or not, *this is how he chose to act.* This is not God "saying" what he is like, this is God "doing" what he is like. Here the Christian gospel is transformed from word to deed, from promise to actuality, from hope to fulfillment. God's forgiveness, to take one example, ceases to be an idea and becomes a reality. Once again we find that the reality is pure grace, unmerited, but given anyhow. Communicants pray, "We do not presume to come to this thy Table, O merciful Lord, trusting in our own righteousness, but in thy manifold and great mercies. We are not worthy so much as to gather up the crumbs under thy Table . . ." But on those terms they are welcome at Christ's Table, not because they have a right to be there, but because they can trust in God's "manifold and great mercies." They are not refused because they are sinners. They are welcomed because they are forgiven sinners.

This is how God chose to act — through simple elements of bread and wine. But this is also how we are to act. And what we do tells us more about the meaning of the sacrament.

1. *We are united with Christ.* As we take the bread and wine into our physical bodies we indicate our desire that Christ, whom the physical elements now represent, may enter into us and dwell with us, so that we may be united with him and he with us. Rather than simply talking about it, we act out our desire that Christ "dwell in our hearts by faith."

This takes place "between a memory and a hope," but in the act that unites us with Christ we find all moments of time focused. We remember the *past*. We re-enact what Christ did, recalling his words, remembering his actions, rethinking their meaning for us. But we invest the *present* with new meaning, for what was true then becomes true now. We do not just remember that Christians were once united with Christ; now, in the present, we too are united with him. We anticipate the *future* for we "proclaim the Lord's death until he comes." Our oneness with Christ, which is now real in part, will one day be fully realized in ways beyond our imagining. God continues the work he has begun in us and will bring it to fulfillment.

We continue to live "between the times" of his coming and his coming again and during these periods we can be united with Christ.

2. But not only with Christ. In the action of the sacrament *we are also united with our fellow believers*. Calvin describes this in a figure of speech used since the earliest days of the Christian era:

> For there the Lord communicates his body to us in such a manner that he becomes completely one with us, and we become one with him. Hence, as he has only one body, of which he makes us partakers, it follows, of necessity, that, by such participation, we also are all made one body; and this union is represented by the bread which is exhibited in the sacrament. For as it is composed of many grains, mixed together in such a manner that one cannot be separated or distinguished from another — in the same manner we ought, likewise, to be connected and united together, by such an agreement of minds, as to admit of no dissension or division between us.[13]

This is more than an arresting figure of speech. It has arresting consequences. For if this is so, Calvin goes on, "it is impossible for us to wound, despise, reject, injure or in any way offend one of our brethren, but we, at the same time, wound, despise, reject, injure and offend Christ in him."

We are not only united with our fellow believers here and now. We are united with all Christians across the corridors of space and time. For a moment on earth, we are praising God with something like the praise continually offered him in heaven. "With angels and archangels and all the company of heaven," so goes one phrase in the service, "we laud and magnify thy glorious name." This extensive reality of the communion of saints is further expressed in a widely used prayer: "We beseech thee mercifully to accept this our sacrifice of praise and thanksgiving, as, *in fellowship with all the faithful in heaven and on earth,* we pray Thee to fulfill in us, and in all men, the purpose of Thy redeeming love."

Printed words cannot communicate what it means to say that incorporation into the body of Christ means union with our fellow Christians across space and time.[14] This cannot be reduced to cold type or warm prose. But it is a reality known to many, particularly those who have walked through the valley of the shadow of death and realize that it is there that God prepares a table for them.

3. In what God does, and in what we do, *we are showing forth what life is meant to be*. We bring forward the elements of bread and wine, for example, and place them upon the Lord's Table. In this action we are also bringing forward all of the unpromising immediate situations that these earthly materials represent, and offering them up to God. It may be the day-to-day routine, or the dingy office, or repeated calls at police headquarters, or frustrating encounters with the local political boss.

We lay these on the table. And out of such unpromising materials, God gives something back. He gives back the bread and wine, the day-to-day routine, the dingy office, and all the rest. But they are no longer *just* the bread and wine and the dingy office. These commonplace things are now vehicles through which the risen Christ comes into our midst. Christ is present in the day-to-day routine and in the people who interrupt it. The dingy office is the place where he dwells. The police headquarters is vibrant with his presence. The local political boss is one for whom he died.

This is the way life is meant to be seen. Our eyes are so clouded with sin that we seldom see it this way. The sacrament is the means whereby the scales are lifted from our eyes.

This was vividly illustrated to the author during the first communion service he celebrated as a chaplain during World War II. The scene was a destroyer escort. Since the service was being conducted by the after gun turret, there was only room for three men to come forward at a time to receive the elements. The first three who came were the commanding officer of the ship, a fireman's apprentice, and a Negro steward's mate. In the social life of the ship, as on all Navy ships, there was a rigid hierarchy that went, from top to bottom: (1) white officers, (2) white enlisted men, (3) Negro enlisted men. At the Lord's Table that hierarchy disappeared. The three men knelt side by side in an absolute equality of need. For a moment there was neither bond nor free, white nor black, officer nor enlisted man. For a moment those men were precisely what God intended them to be, men who were united in Christ and united in one another.

One must not become too romantic about such an experience. When they had finished worshipping, the men went back to a world where the old barriers remained. And yet, to whatever extent they took seriously their oneness in Christ, they could never again rest comfortably with the utter incongruity of the segregation that was elsewhere imposed upon them.

The scandal of division

The Lord's Table is the place where Christians should be most united. They are not. The Lord's Table is the place where they are most divided.

It is a shocking fact that many Christians cannot sit at the Lord's Table with their fellow Christians. There may be occasional moments at the Lord's Table when there is neither white nor black, officer nor enlisted man. But the moments are even fewer when there is neither Lutheran nor Baptist, Episcopalian nor Congregationalist. Here denominational pride and ecclesiastical arrogance are most pronounced — just where they should be overcome by a recognition that it is the Lord's Table to which men come and not their own table. Men do not sit at the Lord's Table by right, nor do they gain admission to his banquet by producing proper denominational credentials. They sit there only by the gracious condescension of the One who has invited them.

Disunion here is a scandal in the life of Christendom. While it lasts, the sacrament is a vehicle of judgment as well as a means of grace. Perhaps only those who have sat at the Lord's Table can understand that there is no contradiction in saying both things.

PART THREE

Ongoing Protestant Concerns

13. Protestantism and Roman Catholicism

Protestantism has been shaped by the New Testament. But it has also been shaped by its reaction to medieval Christendom.

Roman Catholicism has been shaped by the New Testament. But it has also been shaped by its reaction to the Protestant Reformers.

If we cannot understand the Protestant return to the Bible apart from the medieval neglect of the Bible, no more can we understand the Roman Catholic Council of Trent apart from the Protestant challenge that made the statements of that council necessary.

For better or for worse, then, Protestantism and Roman Catholicism are bound up with one another's destinies. This is not simply an historical judgment. It is also a contemporary description. But unfortunately the contemporary description must be broadened to include the fact that neither group is particularly happy about the presence of the other. On almost every level of relationship there is irritation and ill will, if not active dislike.

We must therefore see what issues are at stake in this relationship and what can be done about them by both groups. In such an undertaking, the guiding principle here as elsewhere must be not only to speak the truth, but to speak the truth in love.[1]

The present impasse

The conventional Roman Catholic stereotype of Protestantism goes something like this:

Protestants are responsible for disrupting the unity of the church founded by Jesus Christ. In refusing to give their allegiance to the vicar of Christ, sixteenth-century Protestants created new sects founded by man rather than God. Protestants continue to do the same thing, whether the founder in question is Luther or Calvin or Henry VIII or Joseph Smith or Aimee Semple McPherson. As a result, it is difficult to know what Protestants believe, because they have always disagreed among themselves, and start new churches if the disagreements get too violent. About all they really believe in common is that the extension of Roman Catholicism must be stopped by whatever means are necessary.

Protestants talk a great deal about tolerance, but they are intolerant of Roman Catholics who run for public office, and of Roman Catholic parents who want to give their children a Christian education by sending them to parochial schools.

If this seems to the Protestant a less than adequate description of his faith, let him imagine the Roman Catholic reaction to the conventional Protestant stereotype:

Roman Catholicism is a rigid, authoritarian system, much like communism. Everything is decided by the Pope. All other Roman Catholics have to believe whatever they are told. They believe that the sacraments are magic and that all non-Catholics are going to hell. They perpetuate this kind of brainwashing through parochial schools, whose purpose is to keep Roman Catholics ignorant of the truth so that they will believe whatever the priest tells them.

Roman Catholics want to dominate the world. When they get enough power they will force everybody to believe as they believe. Since they don't have a democratic church, Roman Catholics don't believe in democracy, and Roman Catholics who say they do will be tolerated only so long as they are a minority.

As long as such attitudes predominate, things can only get worse: each side stops shouting just long enough to gather fresh ammunition. The disturbing thing is that there is just enough truth behind some of the charges on both sides to lend plausibility to the arguments *in toto*.

In the United States, the situation is further complicated by a sociological factor. American Roman Catholics were originally a small minority group, and (to a greater degree than Protestants like to acknowledge) a persecuted minority group. Even today, memories of active opposition, discrimination, and segregation persist among American Roman Catholics. Thus, even though Roman

Catholics are now the largest single religious group in the United States, they retain the defensiveness, and the reflexes, of a persecuted minority. This fact increases the tensions and misunderstandings on both sides.[2]

Ingredients for dealing with the impasse

But the picture is not all bleak. There are a number of things that both Roman Catholics and Protestants can do without violating the integrity of their faith, that will at least put the disagreements properly into focus.

1. Both Protestants and Roman Catholics *must be responsible representatives of their own faith.* This is not as innocuous as it sounds. The theological illiteracy of most Protestant laymen, for example, is appalling. Very few could give an adequate accounting of the faith they hold. So long have they been captives of the symbol of "the right of private judgment" that they have assumed that "beliefs" are of secondary importance so long as the church "gets on with the job." But why the church should get on with the job, or what the job is, seems to escape them. As long as Protestants allow this situation to prevail, they will have only themselves to blame if their Catholic neighbors come to the conclusion that Protestants have no convictions worth bothering about.

If Protestant laymen do not think doctrine worth bothering about, Roman Catholic laymen think it very much worth bothering about, so much so that they are content to let the Roman Catholic theologians bother about it full time — and thus excuse themselves from further responsibility. Although the average Roman Catholic has "learned the answers" more assiduously than his Protestant counterpart, he has seldom given much thought to the reasons for the answers. Since the church has worked it all out for him, he need not bother to work it out for himself.

Protestant: Why do you believe the dogma of the assumption?
Roman Catholic: Because it's true.
Protestant: How do you know it's true?
Roman Catholic: Because the church says so.

There are good Roman Catholic reasons for the Roman Catholic answers, but they will not be self-evident to the Protestant. The Roman Catholic who wants to be a responsible representative of his faith will need (a) to try to make clear *why* he believes something "because the church says so," and (b) to be able to explain some of the reasons why the church has defined the dogma in question. If he can also (c) indicate the contribution that the dogma makes to his own devotional life, he will have performed a work of supererogation.

2. Both Protestants and Roman Catholics *must be responsibly informed about each other's faith.* Misinformation about the other's faith simply compounds the mischief already done by ignorance about one's own faith. The Protestant who does not know what the "priesthood of all believers" is about knows all about the immorality of Renaissance popes; the Roman Catholic who never heard of the Liturgical Movement has heard how Martin Luther founded a new church so that he could marry a nun.

There has been enough lance-tilting at imaginary windmills. A Protestant who wants to assess Roman Catholicism must find out from Roman Catholic sources what Roman Catholicism really is, and his right to speak and be heard will be in direct proportion to the amount of homework he has been willing to do.[3] He need not do this homework furtively, as though his Protestant loyalty were rendered suspect because he had read some "Catholic books." On the contrary, it is his obligation as a Protestant to be well informed. He will probably discover that Roman Catholicism is not what he thought it was, that Roman Catholics are not the fools he imagined them to be, and that his own convictions must be re-thought as a result of this exposure to another faith. Most important, he will now be able to grapple with Roman Catholicism as it really exists, and not with a figment of his own imagination.

The effort must be made from the Roman Catholic side as well. It will be more difficult from that side, because in certain Roman Catholic quarters it is considered an act of disloyalty to read Protestant literature. But in other Roman Catholic quarters there is a determined effort under way to understand Protestantism rather than annihilate it. Roman Catholics who do not yet feel venturesome enough to read the kind of Protestant literature cited in the notes of this book, ought at least to expose themselves to the responsible Roman Catholic treatments of Protestantism that are appearing in ever increasing numbers, so that they do not perpetuate the stereotypes of another generation.[4]

3. Both Protestants and Roman Catholics must bring to the present impasse a double awareness that can be put like this: we *disagree* in the faith, but we disagree *in the faith.*[5]

We disagree. No service will be rendered to anyone by ignoring this fact. The differences between Roman Catholicism and Protestantism are not based on misunderstandings that can be resolved by a little effort. A little effort can get rid of caricatures, but it will also pinpoint how deep the basic cleavages really are, once the false cleavages have been disposed of. Nor must either group count on the fact that the other will "change" in any basic way as a result of being exposed to rational opposition. Protestants are naïve if they think that discussion with Protestants is going to lead Roman Catholics to modify their dogmas in order to make them more palatable to Protestants. The real differences between us will remain. We disagree.

But we disagree *in the faith.* This fact is just as important. For there is a very special context to Roman Catholic–Protestant dialogue that is not present in dialogue with Hindus or Buddhists or even Jews. For, whatever their differences, Roman Catholics and Protestants share a faith in Jesus Christ. As Dom Aelred Graham put it, quoting Pius XII: "What makes non-Catholics near to us of the Catholic Church is not simply that common brotherhood in a human nature which we all share alike, but something much more significant, a 'faith in God and in Jesus Christ.' "[6]

Roman Catholics and Protestants believe in the same God, the God who has revealed himself supremely in Jesus Christ our Lord. We have all been baptized in the triune name. We share substantially the same Scriptures. We pray many of the same prayers. Protestants read Pascal and von Hügel and feel real kinship; Roman Catholics read Kierkegaard and Tillich and find themselves addressed. Protestants believe that Roman Catholics are a part of the church of Jesus Christ; Roman Catholics describe Protestants as "separated brethren" — with the emphasis increasingly on the noun rather than the adjective. We disagree *in the faith.*

Militant proclamation of disagreement alone can imply that discussion is not worth the effort; saccharine proclamation of agreement alone can imply that discussion will resolve all differences. However, the only road Protestants and Roman Catholics can helpfully walk today is the road of recognition that *we disagree* in the faith but that we also disagree *in the faith.*

Two issues that divide us

To say these things does not remove "Protestant-Catholic tensions," but it makes it possible to confront them with more charity and clarity. The most visible areas of tension may be designated as the beer-ballots-birth-control-and-bingo areas, and many communities have suffered grievous wounds because of them.[7] But we shall not linger with them here, for painful as they are, they are only symptomatic of deeper distresses, two of which we shall try to isolate.

1. *Protestant fears about "Catholic power."* For many American Protestants this is the crux of the matter. They look at countries in which Roman Catholicism has a large majority, and they see many distressing things: Protestant minorities discriminated against and denied the right to proclaim their faith, Protestant Bibles confiscated, Protestant seminaries closed, individual Protestants persecuted and even tortured or killed. Protestants conclude that the same thing will happen in America if or when Roman Catholicism gains a clear majority. This fear lies behind much Protestant opposition to "Catholics in public office." It is the fear that Roman Catholic legislators will enact legislation favorable to Roman Catholic groups and unfavorable to non-Roman Catholic groups, and that one day, too late, Protestants will discover that they can no longer preach, witness, or evangelize, without being deprived of property or sent to jail.[8]

This is a widespread attitude. It is fostered by (a) occasional unhelpful comments by a minority of the American hierarchy, (b) frequent unhelpful comments by a majority of the Spanish hierarchy, (c) a Protestant image of Roman Catholicism as rigid and unchanging, and (d) a healthy respect for the right of dissent. The attitude contains some truth and a good deal of inaccuracy. To separate what is true from what is inaccurate will require the combined efforts of both Protestant and Roman Catholic men of good will.

The Protestant act of good will consists of a willingness to believe Roman Catholic spokesmen who say that the suppression of minorities is not representative of the whole of Roman Catholicism though it is regrettably typical of a part of Roman Catholicism, who say that they would deplore this kind of activity in the United States, and who further say that they deplore it wherever it now exists.

This does not sound like a particularly difficult exercise of charity, and yet the prevailing Protestant attitude is to accept whatever Spanish Roman Catholics say as normative, and to discount whatever American Roman Catholics say to the contrary as "expedient" — something they either do not mean or something the hierarchy will deny them the right to say when it is safe to silence them. There are enough instances in Roman Catholic history of such voices being silenced, to give a measure of substance to the Protestant concern.[9] But to predicate the case solely on this fact is to assume that history stands still and that modern Roman Catholicism is systematically engaging in a shocking kind of double-dealing.

When the Protestant hears American Roman Catholics speaking out for religious liberty, he must, then, either assume that they are speaking in integrity, or that they are charlatans. If he does the latter, he not only impugns the motives of the Roman Catholic church, but by his wholesale attack upon it he forces *all* Roman Catholics (whatever their views on religious liberty) to close ranks in defense of their beleaguered church, and this means a victory for its most reactionary spokesmen.

The fact of the matter is that Roman Catholicism does *not* have a united point of view on religious liberty or on the relation of church and state. Very different attitudes prevail, for example, in Spain, Ireland, France, and the United States. It is neither logical nor helpful to conclude that the Spanish pattern is destined to become the American pattern. Nor is it logical or helpful to conclude that because there were inquisitions in the sixteenth century, there will be inquisitions in the twentieth or twenty-first century. Contemporary Roman Catholicism is presently undergoing a vigorous internal debate on the allied subjects of tolerance and religious liberty. Many of its foremost thinkers are engaged in this debate. Great good can come of it, and the Protestant act of good will must be to accept the fact that the debate is being conducted in integrity.[10]

Here is where the Roman Catholic must likewise engage in an act of good will. His particular responsibility will be to see that the voices that offer a creative alternative to the "Spanish line" get a wider hearing both within his own church and outside. If he possesses such a voice, he must speak loudly enough so that his Protestant neighbors can hear. If he wields a pen he must not only wield it for scholarly journals buried in seminary libraries, but for popular journals exposed on public news-stands. If he only knows that such voices exist, he must help to make their message more audible to both Protestants and Roman Catholics.

2. *The problem of authority*. As we have just seen, there can be significant realignments within Roman Catholicism on the issue of "Catholic power" and religious liberty. This is not true of the problem of authority, which is governed by irreformable dogma, and for which, therefore, no change is possible. We must anticipate the discussion of authority in the following chapter, to the extent that it impinges upon issues of Roman Catholic–Protestant relations.

In contrast to the Protestant understanding of authority, which is hazy indeed, the Roman Catholic position has the virtue of being unambiguous and clear-cut. It asserts that when the Pope (understood as the vicar of Christ and the successor to Peter) speaks under specified conditions on matters of faith and morals, he speaks infallibly. That is to say, dogmas proclaimed by him are irreformable and beyond possibility of error.[11]

This is a part of Roman Catholic faith that will never change. And it is no disservice to the Roman Catholic–Protestant dialogue, to say forthrightly that it is a position the Protestant can never accept. The reasons for the Protestant refusal have been made plain, particularly in Chapter 4 above. By the dogma of papal infallibility, Roman Catholicism has adopted a position incompatible with the notion that the church is *semper reformanda,* always to be reformed. It has asserted not only that the church *need not* be reformed, but that it *cannot* be reformed, for in its highest reaches it is by definition "irreformable." The Protestant can only interpret this to mean that Roman Catholicism has become master of the gospel rather than servant. Instead of believing that judgment must begin at the house of God, it has proclaimed that the house of God is the one place where there is no need for judgment. In terms of a distinction previously elaborated, there can be peripheral reforms *in* the church, but there can be no basic reform *of* the church. Here, then, is the heart of the difference: the dogma most distinctive of Roman Catholicism, the infallibility of the Pope, is the dogma that separates it most decisively from Protestantism and the whole of non-Roman Christendom. The place where the Roman Catholic feels that the voice of the Holy Spirit is most clearly discerned is the place where the Protestant feels that the voice of the Holy Spirit is most surely stifled.

These seem like harsh things to say about the beliefs of one's fellow Christians, particularly when one sees the wonderful riches of grace and humility that the Roman Catholic church imparts to individual lives. But there is nothing to be gained by refusing to say them, and there is everything to be gained by saying them to try and locate the core of the problem — at the point of greatest disagreement.

Creative possibilities remaining — some specific suggestions

Does this make the impasse so great that nothing can be done about it? Not at all. It means more than ever that there must be creative dialogue between Roman Catholics and Protestants. There are at least three areas where this can occur, and both groups should take advantage of them.[12]

1. There is a meeting ground for Protestants and Roman Catholics in the fact that they share substantially the same Scriptures. The Roman Catholic canon is larger than the Protestant, but it includes all the books in the Protestant canon. Recent Protestant theology has rediscovered the Bible, and there has been a renewed

emphasis on Biblical studies in Roman Catholic theology, much of which makes use of the Biblical research of Protestant scholars. There have been new Roman Catholic translations of the Bible, the most notable by the late Ronald Knox, and there are even proposals under discussion that Roman Catholics and Protestants collaborate on a new translation. Holy Scripture is, as Père Daniélou has said, a "meeting place of Christians." He points out (and the Protestant can only agree) that when men are trying to listen to Scripture, there is no way of telling what may happen. "To speak otherwise," he concludes, "would be to doubt the creative power of the Holy Ghost." [13]

2. Another level of Roman Catholic–Protestant exchange is theological. For the immediate future this will chiefly concern the theologians, but in time the results of such exchange will make themselves felt in the life of both communions. Roman Catholics, for example, have begun a new examination of the Reformation. Previous treatments derogated the concerns of the Reformers in general, and heaped abuse on Luther in particular. More recent Roman Catholic treatments, while naturally not approving of what the Reformers did, make a genuine effort to understand them. There is often high praise for certain of their insights, and a recognition that they did restore elements of the gospel that had been neglected by medieval Christendom.[14]

There is also growing Roman Catholic interest in the Protestant ecumenical movement. While Roman Catholicism does not officially participate in the World Council of Churches, it pays careful attention to the activities of the World Council, and has even sent official observers to a number of its conferences. There are an increasing number of Roman Catholic books dealing with the ecumenical movement both in terms of description and appraisal.[15] There is likewise increasing Roman Catholic attention being given to contemporary Protestant theology. The fullest appraisals yet made of the theology of the Protestant theologian Karl Barth have been written by Roman Catholics.[16]

3. Roman Catholic and Protestant laymen have an important role to play. For one thing, they can let the spirit of charity infuse their relationships and discussions more actively than it has in the past. More important than this, they can pray for one an-

other. The week of January 18–25 is known in the Roman Catholic liturgical year as the Christian Unity Octave, during which Roman Catholics pray for the return of the separated brethren. Of even greater significance is the "Week of Prayer for Christian Unity," held at the same time, and initiated in 1936 as the result of efforts by a remarkable French priest, Abbé Couturier.[17] The World Council of Churches has prepared Protestant materials for this occasion, and each year increasing numbers of Protestants pray for unity, "in accordance with Christ's wishes and through the means that he chooses." The Week of Prayer for Christian Unity can also include conferences, retreats, and vigils of prayer. No one can build any fences around what might result from a joint facing by Protestants and Roman Catholics *in prayer* of the scandal of the disunity of Christendom.

Oscar Cullmann, a French Protestant Biblical scholar, has recently proposed that on the Sunday of the Week of Prayer for Christian Unity, Protestant and Roman Catholic parishes take up offerings for the poor of *each other's* parishes. Such action would underline the *solidarity* of Roman Catholics and Protestants in their concern for one another as persons, even when they cannot affirm their *unity* as churches. The experiment has been tried in a number of places in Europe and is perhaps the most feasible "next step" toward greater understanding.[18]

The need of Roman Catholicism and Protestantism for one another

Roman Catholicism and Protestantism are going to co-exist for a long time. Whether it is to be peaceful or antagonistic coexistence will depend on Roman Catholics and Protestants. A hopeful portent of peace would be a recognition by each group that it needs the other.

A Protestant can acknowledge that Protestantism is helped by the leaven and challenge of Roman Catholicism. Protestant enthusiasm sometimes leads to a one-sided expression of the gospel, and Roman Catholicism is a healthy corrective in such situations, as H. Richard Niebuhr has shown:

Roman Catholic theology, with its great stability, has at times maintained Christian truths close to the heart of Protestantism with greater effectiveness than Protestantism itself. There have been many periods in history when the Roman Church has known, better than many of us who are outside it, how important the truth of "justification by faith" is. When Protestantism, or parts of it, tended in the direction of humanism, it was Roman Catholicism which maintained the principle of the sovereignty of God. Sometimes it was this Roman Church, more than the Protestants, that resisted human authority when this conflicted with the authority of the Word of God.[19]

It is harder for the Roman Catholic to acknowledge that Roman Catholicism "needs" Protestantism. Why should a church in possession of infallible truth "need" the existence of churches in error? There is evidence, however, that Roman Catholicism is truer to itself where it exists in tension with other branches of Christendom. It is more creative in Great Britain than in Spain; it is more vital in Germany than in Argentina. In countries where it dominates the culture, Roman Catholicism can easily become decadent. Under challenge it can rise to magnificent heights.

Deep cleavages remain between Protestantism and Roman Catholicism. The terms of reunion offered by each are incompatible with the deepest convictions of the other. But the alternative to organic union need not be animosity, and the task of the present generation is to make dialogue the alternative. No one can tell where such dialogue will lead. No one need try to predict where it will lead. Everyone must believe that the Holy Spirit can do more with it than the participants have any way of knowing. We do not know just what use God will make of attempts to offer up to him a discussion of our similarities and differences, but we do know that nothing that is offered up to God in humility and charity and prayer is ever offered up in vain.

14. Authority: The Achilles' Heel of Protestantism

Achilles' mother was told that if she dipped him in the river Styx he would be protected from harm in battle. She did as she was told, but she had to hold him by the heel in order to immerse him. As a result, he remained vulnerable at this point and was finally shot in the heel by an arrow. An "Achilles' heel" is therefore a point of vulnerability or weakness.

Reasons for Protestant difficulty

Protestantism has an Achilles' heel. It is located in the Protestant understanding of authority. There are a number of reasons for this.

One of these is that a clear-cut contemporary answer to the question "What is your ultimate authority?" is lacking. People with a built-in Protestant reflex still instinctively reply, "The Bible," but they are hard-pressed to say what that answer means. Others reply, "My conscience," without reflecting on the dilemmas conscience can create and not resolve. Still others say, "The church," before they examine the more convincing defense of that answer that can be given by Roman Catholicism.

Another reason why authority is an Achilles' heel for Protestantism is that the original clear-cut Protestant answer to the question is inadequate today. "The sole authority of Scripture" cannot be defended any longer without careful reformulation. No satisfactory reformulation has yet been achieved.[1]

A third reason for Protestant difficulty in this area is that clear-cut answers of any sort must be subjected to a built-in Protestant suspicion of clear-cut answers. This may not have been a difficulty for Protestants in the seventeenth and eighteenth centuries, but it is a difficulty for Protestants today. To suggest that the "problem" of authority had at last been "solved" would be to suggest that the ongoing Reformation had reached a final resting point. This is a contradiction in terms, and a denial of the conviction that the spirit of Protestantism represents constant renewal at the hand of God.

A final source of strain for Protestantism is that the only real "answer" to the question simply presses the question further. The Protestant who is asked, "What (or who) is your ultimate authority?" may be able to give the only proper answer a Christian can give, which is, "Jesus Christ." But this does not solve the problem. It only states it. The deeper problem remains: *how* does the authority of Jesus Christ become an authority for us today?

The traditional answers to the problem

Christians have coped with this deeper problem in three ways, each of which we must examine.

THE AUTHORITY OF THE CHURCH

The most precise answer to the problem is an assertion that the authority of the church guarantees that the claims of Jesus Christ are valid. We need not rely upon our own uncertain judgments, nor need we rely upon interpretations of Scripture so varied as to leave us more confused than ever, for we can rely upon the voice of the church. The church speaks clearly, undividedly, authoritatively. Only as we stand on this firm rock are we saved from the quicksand of mere probability. We can believe what the church says because what the church says is true.

How do we know that what the church says is true? The Roman Catholic answer to this question is the clearest answer that has ever been formulated.

Since the truth sought is truth about Jesus Christ, Roman Catholicism has a high regard for *Scripture* as a source of knowledge about him. Indeed, official Roman Catholic statements concerning the inspiration and inerrancy of Scripture would satisfy the most rigorous Protestant fundamentalist.[2] But Roman Catholicism also has a high regard for *tradition.* This can be understood as the "apostolic tradition," i.e. those things affirmed by the apostles and recorded in Scripture, but it can also be understood as the process by which the apostolic teaching has been handed down through the centuries. "Tradition," Father Tavard has written, "is the art of passing on the gospel." [3]

Since the Christian faith is an historical faith, and since Christians are rooted in history, there is no way around this. The gospel must be "handed down" from generation to generation. Protestants who refuse to concede the fact for fear that it may have Roman Catholic consequences are living in a dream world.

The "Roman Catholic consequences" begin to emerge with the assertion that the church, through its bishops, is the guardian of tradition. The task of the church is to see that the gospel is handed down without being corrupted. Since not all the nuances of the faith are explicitly developed in the Bible, it is the contribution of tradition to take what is only implicit in Scripture, and make it explicit in the church. Thus tradition is creative and dynamic, and the church sees to it that tradition neither contradicts itself nor becomes inconsistent with the Biblical witness. This means that Scripture and tradition are two sources of truth and must not be separated. If they are, so the view maintains, disaster follows.

The Reformers asserted that tradition had distorted the Biblical witness. They rallied around the cry *sola Scriptura,* a view that Roman Catholicism consciously repudiated in Session IV of the Council of Trent (April 8, 1546) by affirming the joint authority of Scripture and tradition:

> The council follows the example of the orthodox Fathers and with the same sense of devotion and reverence with which it accepts and venerates all the books both of the Old and the New Testament, since one God is the author of both, *it also accepts and venerates traditions concerned with faith and morals* as having been received orally from Christ or inspired by the Holy Spirit and continuously preserved in the Catholic Church.[4]

Although there is a kind of formal equality between Scripture and tradition, it is the church that determines the meaning of

Scripture in the light of tradition. Later in the same Session, the delegates asserted, "Furthermore, to keep undisciplined minds under proper control, the council decrees that no one should dare . . . to distort Sacred Scripture to fit meanings of his own that are contrary to the meaning that holy Mother Church has held and now holds."[5]

Scripture has authority, but the sense in which it has authority is determined by the church — a church that gives equal weight to the traditions that have developed subsequent to the writing of Scripture. A Protestant cannot escape the conclusion that *tradition has become normative for Scripture.*

Even if such a conclusion were a premature judgment at this point in the story, it is confirmed by subsequent events, culminating in the Vatican Council of 1869–70, which promulgated the dogma of the infallibility of the Pope.[6] There could be no clearer way of guaranteeing the authority of the church than to assert that all authority inheres in its head, and then to assert that when that head speaks *ex cathedra* on matters of faith or morals, he speaks infallibly and irreformably, beyond any possibility of error. This is a guarantee that the church will not introduce error in its unfolding of the truth.[7]

We now have an answer to our question, "How do we know that what the church says is true?" We know that what the church says is true because God protects the church from error. He assures that dogmatic utterances made by its infallible head are as true as from the lips of Christ himself.

This position has many strengths. (a) It is clear-cut and unambiguous (particularly in comparison with Protestant hedging on the same issue) and it commands the allegiance of millions of Christians. (b) It has an impressive degree of historical plausibility, particularly when examined apart from Protestant presuppositions. (c) It has the theological advantage that it stresses the continuing activity of the Holy Spirit at all stages in the life of the church. (d) It has great logical appeal. It is logical that Christ should found a church to carry on his work, logical that he should provide for the continuation of that work through a direct succession, logical that one person should have this power rather than a group of persons who might disagree, and logical that God should endow the head of the church with infallibility, in order to protect his church from error.

A Protestant reaction to this position must include at least the following observations:

(a) Criteria such as precision and wide acceptance are not necessarily criteria of truth. There are other precise and widely accepted points of view that happen to be false. This does not demonstrate that Roman Catholicism is false, but it suggests that Protestants are sometimes impressed by it for the wrong reasons. Ecclesiastical unanimity is so hard to achieve in the Protestant household that households possessing it are liable to appear attractive for that reason alone.

(b) Protestant scholars, and all sorts of other scholars, have raised questions about the historical justification for the position. There is not space for an examination of their queries, but data on which the queries are based are easily available.[8] Biblical scholars, for example, are far from agreement on the meaning of the crucial passage in Matthew 16, which is the basis of the papal claims: "You are Peter, and on this rock I will build my church" (Matt. 16:16). Some assert that the "rock," rather than referring to Peter himself, refers to Peter's previous confession of faith in Jesus as the Christ, and this was apparently the most widely accepted exegesis in the early church.[9]

Even if it be granted, however, that the rock is Peter himself, the passage gives no warrant for assuming that the unique position of Peter was to be bequeathed to his "successors," and this is the point on which the Roman Catholic claims must rest.[10]

The Protestant can discover no historical grounds for accepting the validity of a Petrine succession, and plenty of theological grounds for questioning it. We may reverse our earlier assertion and say that the historical plausibility of the position is less impressive when examined apart from Catholic presuppositions.

(c) and (d) we may consider together. The problem — and it is the basic problem — is whether or not the dynamic and logical structure of the Roman Catholic position maintains or corrupts the gospel. The Roman Catholic eagerly opts for the first alternative. The Protestant must regretfully opt for the second. The Roman Catholic claims that tradition merely unfolds what is implicit in the apostolic proclamation. The Protestant cannot help feeling that the traditions of the church have *changed* the gospel, gradually but irrevocably, so that these new traditions are now irreformably imbedded in "Roman Catholic truth." There is no way in which the process can be arrested or redirected.

The development of Mariology is an obvious example. There is an annoying Protestant hysteria that often surrounds discussion of this issue, but quite apart from the hysteria there is valid Protestant concern that recent Roman Catholic teaching about the mother of our Lord not only goes far beyond what is even implicit in Scripture, but jeopardizes and must eventually discard the New Testament declaration that Jesus Christ is the sole redeemer of mankind. Roman Catholic tradition has gradually elevated Mary to a higher and higher position — most recently in the dogma of the Assumption of the Blessed Virgin in 1950 — and this whole dogmatic trend has the seal of papal infallibility upon it.[11] It seems quite clear, as a number of Roman Catholic theologians have already said, that the next step in the process will be the proclamation of Mary as *co-redemptrix* of mankind.

The Protestant rejects this trend, not primarily because he wants to believe *less about Mary* than the Roman Catholic believes, but because (in fidelity to the full catholic faith set forth in Scripture) he wants to believe *more about Jesus Christ* and the uniqueness of his once-for-all redemptive work, than he feels the Roman Catholic can now believe.[12]

This is merely illustrative of what happens when tradition becomes normative for Scripture. A church that takes this step need no longer listen to Scripture. It need only listen to itself.

THE AUTHORITY OF SCRIPTURE

The traditional Protestant answer to the problem of authority is an assertion that the authority of Scripture guarantees the claims of Jesus Christ as valid. This answer, as it was stated by the Reformers and their successors, was fully as precise as the Roman Catholic alternative it disavowed.

We have seen that their form of the answer is no longer a live option for Protestants. In Chapter 6 we examined some reasons for its breakdown, and made some preliminary forays in the direction of a restatement of it, and that chapter should be reread in connection with the present discussion. Such forays, however, can only be preliminary until we have related the view of Biblical authority outlined there more closely to the authority of the church and to the authority of personal experience. A full restatement of the authority of Scripture must therefore be deferred until we have examined the third traditional answer to the problem.

THE AUTHORITY OF PERSONAL EXPERIENCE

A third answer to the problem is an assertion that the authority of personal experience guarantees that the claims of Jesus Christ are valid, although the nature of this answer makes an immediate qualification necessary. It is more accurate to say that the authority of personal experience determines which claims about Jesus Christ are valid and which invalid, and that many religious claims can exercise authoritative force over us whether they are related to him or not.

This position has been the particular province of the mystics in all religious traditions, and of the sectarians and pietists in the Christian tradition. We can most helpfully examine it for our present purposes, however, in the form it took as a reaction against the traditional answer of an infallible church and an infallible book. The fervor with which it has been upheld must be understood not only in terms of its intrinsic appeal, but also in terms of the spiritual aridity of the alternatives against which it was reacting.[13]

Rejecting the notion that authority can be guaranteed by external means such as an institution or a book, advocates of this position insist that the believer must *look within* for the authentication of his faith. Only what is a part of his own experience can have authority for him. When the position is theologically grounded, appeal is made to the Holy Spirit, although the Holy Spirit is frequently understood apart from his relation to the Father and the Son. The consequence of this separation is that historical affirmations assume a secondary role. What is sought is not a rootage in the past, but contact with the eternal. And the latter is authenticated only by the personal experience of the eternal in the life of the believer. Dogmas claim scant interest here, being at best the second- or third-hand accounts of the experience of someone else, and at worst a series of abstractions related to the experience of no one else at all. The avenue of dogma leads to a religion of the head, rather than to a religion of the heart and soul, and externalizes what needs to be internalized.

This is a needed emphasis in Christian thought. It must always be urged that "faith" is an abstraction and an irrelevance until it becomes "my faith," and that a God who is only "out there" is a sorry substitute for a God who should also be "in here." Truth, in Christian terms, as has been said before in these pages, is not just information, but encounter with the living God.

Nevertheless, there are difficulties of such magnitude in the position as to preclude giving full Protestant approval to it. Reluctance to make personal experience the criterion of religious authority can be expressed in three overlapping ways:

1. The chief difficulty is that vividness becomes more important than content. What is *experienced* carries more weight than *what* is experienced. If two conflicting sets of experiences are vying for acceptance, the more vivid of the two wins the day.

Not only does this raise a problem about the implied equality of vividness and truth. It also raises a serious dilemma for the person from whose experience the vividness has disappeared, leaving nothing in its place. Does this mean that the former experience was an illusion? Does it mean that since nothing is now being experienced there is nothing in which to believe? The reed of personal experience is a very slender reed on which to found a faith. If it is occasionally a source of spiritual security, it can with the passing of the mood be transformed into its very opposite and become a source of real despair.

2. An allied difficulty is created by the unreliability of the *content* of personal experience. Are these experiences authentic intimations of the deity? Are they merely the product of wishful thinking? Or are they, perhaps, authentic intimations so badly distorted by our manipulation of them that they can no longer be trusted? One who speaks of "the religion of the heart" needs to be reminded that the heart is corrupt. This is not a recently discovered insight. It was asserted with considerable vigor by both Jeremiah (Jer. 5:20–29) and Jesus (Mark 7:21–23). Those who stress

the authority of personal experience often underestimate the degree to which the interpretation of all experience, and particularly religious experience, is corrupted by human sin.

3. The relationship of private experience to the corporate convictions of the religious community is a complex one. Those who assert the priority of "experience" over "external authority" claim that when there is a conflict between the two the burden of proof lies upon the community. Those who stand within the church reply that when an individual comes to conclusions contrary to the corporate wisdom of the community, the burden of proof is first of all upon the individual.

This may be an inevitable rebuttal, but it is also a dangerous rebuttal. The community, to be sure, always possesses the initial advantage of longer experience than the individual, but it may become the repository of untruth as well as truth. In the latter case, the voice of the individual may be the appointed means for bringing new light and life to the community. "There is always an initial presumption in favor of the tradition," writes Archbishop Temple, sounding exactly like an archbishop should, "for it represents the deposit of innumerable individual apprehensions." But he immediately goes on: "None the less it must be remembered that it is by fresh individual apprehensions that the tradition has been developed, and to reject the new intimation may be, not the suppression of human aberration, but a quenching of the divine spirit." [14]

Martin Luther is a convenient example of the complexity of this relationship. Roman Catholics usually indict Luther on the score that he was pitting his own ideas against the age-old wisdom of the church. If that were a completely accurate assessment, Luther might have deserved the indictment. But actually he was not voicing the private religious hunches of one lone individual. He was proclaiming that what he had found in Scripture was true, and that since it was true for him it must be true for all the church as well. This suggests a context for the authority of religious experience that we must presently examine in more detail.

The common difficulty with the traditional answers

All of these answers, whatever their strengths, share a common weakness: *instead of witnessing to Jesus Christ, they witness to themselves.* They should be means through which his authority is communicated; instead they are ends from which their own authority is radiated.

Whatever we call these authorities — church, Bible or experience, Roman Catholicism, Protestantism or sectarianism, ecclesiasticism, Biblicism, or mysticism — their story is the same. Not content to be earthen vessels holding a treasure, they claim to be the treasure itself. They all displace the object of their witness.

We can see this tendency at work in each of the answers we have examined.

The church can witness to the mighty deeds of God in Jesus Christ. But it has become an authority witnessing to itself. No longer does the gospel authenticate its claims within the church. Instead, the claims about the church authenticate the gospel. The gospel becomes what the church says it is, which means that men claim for the church an infallibility that can only belong to God. The object of faith becomes the church rather than the Lord who humbles himself to speak through the church.

The Bible can witness to the mighty deeds of God in Jesus Christ. But it, too, has become an authority witnessing to itself. No longer does the gospel authenticate its claims through the Bible. Instead, the claims about the Bible authenticate the gospel. The important thing is to hold correct views about the Bible, which means that men claim for the Bible an infallibility that can only belong to God. The object of faith becomes the Bible rather than the Lord who humbles himself to speak through the Bible.

Personal experience can witness to the mighty deeds of God in Jesus Christ. It, likewise, has become an authority witnessing to itself. No longer does the gospel authenticate its claim by transforming personal experience. Instead, the claims of personal experience transform the gospel. The gospel becomes whatever the experiencer says it is, which means that men claim for their own experience an infallibility that can only belong to God. The object of faith becomes the experience itself rather than the Lord who humbles himself to speak through personal experience.

These may seem overbold ways of making the point. But the point needs to be emphasized rather than underplayed. For *there are no resources within these alternatives to safeguard them from these conclusions.* That is the whole problem. Each of the traditional authorities, by becoming a witness to itself, forfeits the claim to be a faithful witness.

Toward a restatement of a Protestant doctrine of authority

To challenge these authorities is to run the risk that no authority can ever take their place. This is the Protestant risk. It involves a recognition that the final authority of Jesus Christ will overflow and even smash the vessels through which he comes to us. But this is also the glory of the Protestant risk. It is always the particular Protestant contribution to remind men that we have this treasure in earthen vessels, lest we claim the transcendent power for ourselves.

We stated at the outset that the problem was to find a way of asserting the final authority of Jesus Christ over human life. We have seen that in attempting to do this, Christians absolutize the vehicles through which they feel that his authority is channeled, and erect an infallible church, an infallible book, or an infallible experience. Is there a way to overcome this temptation? [15]

If such a way is to emerge, we can find it only by treading a precarious path — the path of using the earthen vessels, but using them in such a way that no one of them can claim to be the treasure. We must acknowledge the *relative* authority of each of the traditional answers, at the same time disavowing their claim to ultimate authority for themselves.

This will mean taking at least two steps:

1. We must recognize that *there is a convergence of testimony among the witnesses.*[16] If they cannot be permitted to point to

themselves, we must discover in which direction they are pointing. And we discover that they are pointing in the same direction.

To what are they pointing?

In answering this question, we make a judgment, but it is a judgment which the convergence of the various witnesses increasingly substantiates. We discover that they are all witnessing to "the gracious God," and more specifically to "the grace of our Lord Jesus Christ," through whom God has acted authoritatively, and to whom our response must be submission in gratitude and joy, acknowledging that his authority extends over all human life.

How do we know that he is our authority? We know it because the testimony of the various witnesses converges on him.

We are confronted by, and involved in, a *community* that proclaims his grace, and tries, in its own stumbling fashion, to respond to it. The church through all its members, creeds, and deeds, witnesses to the gracious God who nevertheless remains greater than anything the church can be, or do, or say about him.

The community is confronted by a *book* containing the accounts of how this grace was actively released in human life — accounts that not only contain information but are themselves the channels through which the power they describe becomes available again. The Bible through all its pages witnesses to the God and Father of our Lord Jesus Christ, who nevertheless remains greater than anything the Bible can say about him.

These two things, community and book, become authoritative as the grace to which they witness confronts men in their own *experience,* and demands the response of joyful obedience. In personal experience we receive the grace of our Lord Jesus Christ, who nevertheless remains greater than anything our experience can encompass or exhaust.

Thus it is the converging testimony of all three witnesses — community and book and experience — that establishes Jesus Christ as the true authority. The witnesses derive their relative authority as they witness faithfully not to themselves but to him.

2. We must recognize that *there is a priority among the witnesses.* This is the second step, and it is a distinctively Protestant one. It is necessitated by the fact that we manipulate each of the relative authorities to serve our own ends.

It is notoriously easy to manipulate our personal experience and make it mean what we want it to mean. The history of the church bears record of the ease with which men twist the gospel and fashion a new message from it. The use men have made of the Bible shows that with a little ingenuity they can make its message serve their ends.

Even so, it is through the relative authority of the Bible that the corrective power of the gospel has the best chance to manifest itself. It is more difficult to manipulate the content of Scripture than to manipulate the content of our own experience, and it is more difficult to manipulate the printed page than to manipulate the traditions men introduce into the church, because the Bible has a *given-ness* that does not change from generation to generation. Its given-ness does not depend upon our momentary mood or upon the currents of opinion prevalent within the church.

To be sure, we can interpret the Bible to suit our ends, as the history of Biblical interpretation makes all too clear. That history is full of instructive examples of men reading Scripture for what they want to find, rather than listening to Scripture for what they are afraid to hear. We will always face this temptation, and it will always be the peculiar Protestant temptation.

But we can never quite get away with it. The reason we cannot get away with it is that *the text is always there*. It retains its power to speak louder than the distortions we impose upon it. It speaks in accents we cannot succeed in stifling, no matter how hard we try or how momentarily successful we may appear to be. For just when men have succeeded in muffling its voice beyond all recognition, it breaks forth again with fresh and compelling power. No matter how hard we try to transform its message, the message will try harder to transform us. It was this impact of the Bible that made St. Augustine a Christian, that showed St. Francis an alternative to medieval pomp and circumstance, that gave direction to the life of Wycliffe, that empowered Martin Luther to be God's agent in the reformation of the church, that (in conjunction with some help from Brother Martin) "warmed" John Wesley's heart, that bound up the tattered fragments in the life of Blaise Pascal. The story has been told before and it will be told again. It is the clue to renewed vitality within the church.

If we are to give this relative priority to Scripture, we are under particular obligation to make sure that it does not lead to a new Biblicism. With Luther we must "urge the authority of Christ against the authority of the Bible." [17] With Luther also we must recall that the Bible is the cradle in which Christ lies. We must know something about the construction of the cradle, we must see how it fits together, we must be convinced of the integrity of those who built it. But we must not become so absorbed in its construction that we fail to notice the one who lies within it.

For the cradle is not empty. It holds Christ.

APPENDIX: *A convergence of the relative authorities*

Discussions of authority are liable to sound abstract even when they are dealing with the most down-to-earth realities imaginable. To forestall the possibility that the preceding pages have created this impression, I offer an example of the way in which the convergent testimony of these relative authorities served to manifest afresh to me the ultimate authority of Jesus Christ.

A number of years ago a colleague of mine died very suddenly, and I found myself confronted in a particularly shattering way by the harshness of death. The authoritative power of the gospel came home to me at the funeral service as each of the relative authorities became a witness to something beyond itself.

Here was the witness of the *church,* the fellowship of believers, gathering together to testify to its conviction that the power of God was stronger than the power of death, affirming in concert with the faithful down through the ages its belief in "the holy catholic church, the communion of saints, the forgiveness of sins, the resurrection of the body and the life everlasting."

Here was the witness of *Scripture,* speaking its Word to the church, as the church gathered together to listen and be sustained by a power not in its control: "Who shall separate us from the love of Christ? Shall tribulation, or distress, or persecution, or famine, or nakedness, or peril, or sword? . . . No, in all these things we are more than conquerors through him who loved us. For I am sure that neither death, nor life, nor angels, nor principalities, nor things present, nor things to come, nor powers, nor height, nor depth, nor anything else in all creation, will be able to separate us from the love of God in Christ Jesus our Lord . . . If we live, we live to the Lord, and if we die, we die to the Lord; so then, whether we live or whether we die, we are the Lord's" (Rom. 8:35, 37–39; 14:8–9).

Here finally was the witness of *personal experience,* mine and that of those about me, for whom all this in a new and overpowering way was being demonstrated and vindicated, so that these affirmations were now *our* affirmations, convictions not created by us but merely received by us.

Then and in succeeding days I had a reaction I can only describe by such words as, "It's all true, it's really true!" The things I had previously preached about, lectured about, written about, and talked about, had a new kind of reality. I didn't have to prove them. I could simply accept them and be grateful for them.

As the intensity of such a mood diminishes, the temptation is to try to recapture or re-create it. This temptation must be resisted, for it suggests that the truth of the gospel is dependent upon how vividly we "feel" its truth at a given moment. Not so. The recognition that it is all "really true" is based on nothing so slender as a private feeling, or a book, or an institution. It is based on the convergent testimony of all of these, as they witness not to themselves but to something greater than themselves — the reality of Jesus Christ as Lord of life and death.

Before that kind of thing one finally stops analyzing. One simply says, "Thank you," and gets on with the business of living.

15. Protestantism and Culture

The word "Puritanism" has an unpleasant sound on twentieth-century lips. It does not describe a faith that led men to cross the seas in search of religious liberty, or to stand fast against tyranny at home. It describes an attitude that frowns on the world, mortifies the flesh, and denies that life can be encompassed by joy.

Blue-nosed Protestantism

Many persons extend the stereotype from Puritanism in particular to Protestantism in general. There is considerable data in Protestant history to support the extension. Many states still have "blue laws" on their statute books that were enacted by Protestants in order to make sure that nobody desecrated the Sabbath. There are still many Protestants for whom the major sins are card-playing and going to movies. The visitor to the lovely Lady Chapel at Ely Cathedral in England will observe over a hundred headless statues, all decapitated by Protestants who wanted to make sure that nobody worshipped an image. In Scotland, the cathedral at St. Andrews was stripped of its images and other items of Catholic worship in 1559. There was little wilful destruction, but the cathedral gradually crumbled of neglect, its demise being hastened by townsfolk who, with no animosity in their hearts, carted off the stones to pave the streets, build a harbor, and erect private dwellings. Today the cathedral is a ghostly remnant, a reminder not so much of Protestant fanaticism as of Protestant indifference to things beautiful.

Reasons for Protestant suspicion

Why should this have been so? Why should Protestants have been so suspicious not only of the beauty of cathedrals, but of the beauty of other achievements of men in the realms of art, literature, drama, and sculpture?

The suspicion is by no means a Protestant invention. The second commandment, prohibiting "graven images" (Ex. 20:4–6), was graven deep in the experience of Judaism and was inherited by the early Christians, who were likewise suspicious of "images" on the ground that they might be worshipped and thus become idols. Another factor in the experience of the early church was the expectation that Christ would shortly return and that the pleasures of the present world, soon to pass away, should be disregarded in order to concentrate on the new world about to be ushered in. Even after the vividness of this hope had waned, there was a continued rejection of the present world throughout a large segment of Christendom, first on the part of the hermits and later on the part of the monastic communities, both of whom repudiated the world of the flesh for the sake of the world of the spirit. Dualism, the radical separation of these two worlds, was in the church to stay.

By the time of the Reformation another factor had entered to strengthen Protestant suspicion that the things of this world were likely to be unsuitable vehicles of God's grace. This was the scandalous abuse of images and relics in late medieval Christendom. There were enough pieces of the "true cross," as one writer put it, to build a fleet of ships. Half a dozen kneecaps of St. Peter were scattered across Europe. Even more serious was the fact that relics, statues, and pictures were invested with properties that in fact led people to worship them. The Reformers stoutly opposed the images and relics, for they felt that images were taking the place of God. Their motives were proper even if their zeal was excessive. A grave disease can only be cured by drastic measures.

The "sect" groups were the most active protagonists of a negative view of the world and things cultural. In the sixteenth century they felt that the Calvinists and Lutherans were accommodating themselves much too fully to the sinful world. In the twentieth century they look upon dancing as a sin, and folk dancing as a way of bringing sin into the church. Since movies are sinful and therefore to be shunned, the advent of television has created a new theological perplexity for the sectarian: he cannot always be sure whether he is viewing a "live" program in a state of grace, or endangering his soul by viewing a program that was filmed in advance.

A new danger: capitulation

It is not only the rejection of absurdities of this sort, but a wrong kind of concern for the world, that has led to a new difficulty in the relationship of Protestantism and culture. For in our day, the danger is not so much that Protestantism will shun culture too disdainfully as that it will embrace it too eagerly. There are encouraging signs of a growing Protestant appreciation of modern literature, drama, and art.[1] But there are also signs of a less sophisticated and uncritical acceptance by Protestants of the cultural patterns of their environment. We saw in Chapter 4 that Protestantism is always in danger of reflecting its environment uncritically, rather than challenging it in the name of the gospel, and nowhere is this clearer than in contemporary America. For American Protestantism today could almost be described as an amalgam of (a) the insights of Thomas Jefferson, (b) belief in "truth, beauty, and goodness," (c) the "American way of life," (d) positive thinking, and, sometimes, (e) a slight dash of internationalism and the Golden Rule.

This is a caricature but not very much of a caricature. If earlier Protestantism had no genuine interest in transforming the world, much contemporary Protestantism has been so transformed by the world that it has become virtually indistinguishable from it. The identification of religion with "Americanism," the indifferentism with which religion may be, interchangeably in the public mind, Roman Catholicism, Protestantism, or Judaism, the assurances by public officials that religion bolsters American security, the conviction that "belonging to a church" is one of the duties of a rising young executive — all this easy capitulation to the success standards of contemporary culture is at least as bad, if not worse, than the cultural indifferentism of former times.[2]

Transition: the affirmation and negation of images

What resources are available by means of which we can cope with the older Protestant attitude of cultural indifferentism and the newer Protestant attitude of cultural capitulation? A fruitful approach to the matter has been explored with great richness by the distinguished British writer, Charles Williams.[3] Williams described two ways of understanding the created world as a vehicle of God's revelation. The first of these he called the way of *the affirmation of images.* There are "images," experiences, events of human life, that can testify to us of God. Every created thing, according to this view, partially reveals God and can help us discover him. The greatest exponent of this way of affirmation, Williams believed, was Dante; Christendom first had to understand "the awful difference" between God and the world before it could be permitted, through Dante, to see "the awful likeness." [4] The image of Beatrice was the vehicle through whom the reality of God was revealed to Dante. As he gazed at his beloved, Dante saw for a moment a human being as God sees and intends that human being to be. The sight of her "filled him with the fire of charity; he became — and for a moment he knew it — an entire goodwill." [5] As he affirmed the image of Beatrice, Dante could say to God of her, "This also is Thou."

But there has been another way as well. This is the way of *the rejection of images,* of all images, that is, save God himself. If advocates of the first way must say, "This also is Thou," advocates of the second way must say, "Neither is this Thou." No created thing is more than an image, and every created thing can be perverted from an image into an idol, whom to serve is to be damned. So the images must be rejected. This has been the way of the mystic, the ascetic, the rejector of the world. Dionysius the Aereopagite dared not compare God to anyone or anything; he could only say what God is *not.*

Williams's point is that neither way can be followed to the exclusion of the other. *Both ways must be followed by everyone.* For if the way of affirmation leads to idolatry, the way of negation leads to a repudiation of the world God created and declared good. So the two ways must co-exist.

> Neither of these two Ways indeed is, or can be, exclusive. The most vigorous ascetic, being forbidden formally to hasten his death, is bound to attend to the actualities of food, drink, and sleep which are also images, however brief his attention may be. The most indulgent Christian is yet bound to hold his most cherished images — of food, drink, sleep, or anything else — negligible beside the final Image of God.[6]

The Christian must say of every image, "This also is Thou . . . neither is this Thou." Even St. John of the Cross, a follower of the way of rejection, was encouraged to remember that he liked asparagus.

Protestant resources for an approach to culture

We have observed that the Reformers had a relatively negative attitude toward culture and that here, more than at most other points, they are open to the charge of having thrown the baby out with the bath. At the same time, the picture must not be painted in blacker hues than the facts will allow. No one reading the *Table Talk* could justly accuse Luther of a negative attitude toward the world, and it is not hard to collect passages from Calvin's *Institutes,* and even more from his sermons and commentaries, in which he expresses gratitude to God for the good things of the created order. If the Reformation cost the statues in Ely Cathedral their heads, it also gave the world a Rembrandt and a Bach.

This suggests that there may be more resources within Protestantism for a positive approach to culture than have yet been explored, and we must now explore some of them.[7]

1. The first is *a Biblical resource: "Assyria, the rod of God's anger."* Since Protestantism makes a particular point of listening for the Word of God in Scripture, we may begin with a consideration of this important passage in Isaiah 10. The usual pattern for

the prophets is to assert that Israel must make God's will known to the pagans. But Isaiah 10 contains the unexpected declaration that *God's will is made known to Israel through the pagans.* Since Israel has forgotten God, God will use pagan Assyria to reveal to Israel just what his will is, and how heavy the consequences of flouting it can be. And so God stirs up Assyria and declares that Assyria will be his instrument, "the rod of my anger, the staff of my fury . . . Against a godless nation [i.e. Israel] I send him" (Is. 10:5, 6). To be sure, it never enters Assyria's mind that it is being used by God, and the Assyrian king would have been either contemptuous or amused at such a description of himself, for "he does not so intend, and his mind does not so think" (Is. 10:7). Nevertheless, the pagan is God's vehicle of revelation to Israel.

As then, so now. The modern "pagan" can be God's vehicle of revelation to the Christian. God's resources are not limited to the pious or the orthodox, for the pious and the orthodox may be clogging, rather than cleansing, the channels of revelation. The modern "Assyrians," the avowed non-Christians, may be the means God has chosen to reveal himself to the new Israel. To be sure, the non-Christian novelist, poet, sculptor, or dramatist may be either contemptuous or amused at such a description of himself, for he too "does not so intend, and his mind does not so think" (Is. 10:7, again). But this will no more lessen the effective use God can make of him that did a similar ignorance lessen the use God made of the king of Assyria.

This means that Christians must be considerably more receptive to non-Christian expressions of drama, painting, sculpture, verse, and even politics, than they have been in the past. The vehicles of revelation are not exclusively the theologians, preachers, and liturgists; they may include the William Faulkners, Jacob Epsteins, and H. L. Menckens. Calvin is often accused of having had a blue-nosed attitude toward culture, but he saw the point clearly:

> Whenever, therefore, we meet with heathen writers, let us learn from that light of truth which is admirably displayed in their works, that the human mind, fallen as it is, and corrupted from its integrity, is yet invested and adorned by God with excellent talents. If we believe that the Spirit of God is the only fountain of truth, we shall neither reject nor despise the truth itself wherever it shall appear, unless we wish to

insult the Spirit of God . . . If it has pleased the Lord that we should be assisted in physics, logic, mathematics, and other arts and sciences, by the labour and ministry of the impious, let us make use of them.[8]

2. There is also *a Reformation resource: an extension of the doctrine of the calling*. The Reformers, we recall, broke down the wall which medieval Christendom had erected between the "sacred" and the "secular," and insisted that God should be served *in* the world, rather than by retreat *from* the world. Their doctrine of the calling meant a positive view of the world, and suggests that when they or later Protestants took a negative view of the world, they did so in defiance of this central insight.

The principle behind this Reformation attitude toward vocation is an obvious resource for a contemporary Protestant approach to culture. If the world is what the doctrine of vocation assumes it to be — not only the arena in which God works but also the arena in which he calls upon men to work with him — then the Christian must have a high regard for this arena, and take seriously whatever is produced within it. There is nothing that is not potentially an instrument in God's hands, no human endeavor that may not, however indirectly, be witnessing to him. Men produce works of art. The men themselves may not be Christians, and their creations may not have God as their ostensible subject. But these works of art can tell us something about God's world, and, perhaps more important, something about the men who live within his world. Even if they only show us how broken our world has become, or how evil men can be, they will be telling us important things about the religious dimension of our existence. Paul Tillich has said that Picasso's *Guernica* is the most "religious" piece of art in the twentieth century.

The same thing would be true of a Protestant attitude toward other art forms. If the Protestant Reformation made it possible once again to take a positive attitude toward the world of men, by denying that it was "secular" and therefore inferior, then the contemporary Protestant can, in the name of this insight, reclaim the whole world of culture. Rather than condemning it arrogantly, he can appreciate it humbly, grateful that God works in so many ways for the achievement of his purposes.

3. There is thirdly *a sacramental resource: the use of earthly*

things. A proper Protestant concern for the sacraments offers a further resource for a positive approach to culture. It can be argued that a high doctrine of culture will go hand in hand with a high doctrine of the sacraments, and that where the sacraments are belittled, the Christian appreciation of culture will likewise suffer. The Roman Catholic stress on the sacraments may well be one of the reasons why Roman Catholicism has usually had richer cultural concerns than Protestantism. To acknowledge this does not commit us to a Roman Catholic view of the sacraments or even to the notion of a "sacramental universe," but it can prod us to examine ways in which a Protestant understanding of the sacraments can contribute to a Protestant appreciation of culture.

The sacraments represent God's use of earthly, tangible things to convey the reality of his grace. There are few things more down-to-earth than bread. We must have it to stay alive. We must eat it, chew it, swallow it, digest it. To stress this may seem vulgar to the fastidious, but it does not seem vulgar to God. He uses bread, and the actions of eating, chewing, and swallowing that go along with it, as means of manifesting his real presence in our midst. The highest point in our corporate experience as Christians is the moment when we are doing the most ordinary things imaginable — eating and drinking. If we want to know that Christ is in our midst, we do not sing hymns — we eat. If we want to know that his death is effectual for us, we do not pray — we drink.

God has deigned to use the commonplace vehicles of bread and wine and water, and the commonplace actions of eating and drinking, as his way of communicating with us. Matter is not alien to his works and ways, it is essential to them. Christianity, as William Temple has said, is the most "avowedly materialist" of all the world religions. To God, matter matters. To his children it cannot not matter.

It should not be hard to draw the appropriate conclusion: eating, drinking, growing grain, harnessing water power, distributing bread so that all can have enough — those are not only legitimate concerns of Christians but essential concerns. No one may call profane what God has made holy.

4. Finally there is *a negative resource: the judgment on "Assyria."* We have tried to suggest resources for a Protestant view

of culture that will counteract the rather jaundiced Protestant glances of the past. But along with all this must go a caution, for Protestantism must always stand in a certain tension with culture. Approval can never be more than qualified approval, for it must include a recognition that cultural forms, like religious forms, can become debased, and that there is always a danger of idol-worship, of an uncritical acceptance of whatever man has made.

Another look at Isaiah 10 can illustrate the point. Assyria is indeed God's instrument without knowing it, but Assyria becomes the victim of "haughty pride" (Is. 10:12). The king of Assyria boasts of his achievements: "By the strength of my hand I have done it, and by my wisdom, for I have understanding" (Is. 10:13). This attitude brings about his downfall, for "the Lord of hosts will send wasting sickness among his stout warriors, and under his glory a burning will be kindled, like the burning of fire" (Is. 10:16), and the last state of Assyria is worse than the first. The flail God had used against Israel is broken more disastrously than those who were chastized by it.

This is a necessary reminder that culture is not simply an end in itself, and that when it sets itself defiantly against the God who gave it birth, it has already sowed the seeds of its own destruction. This is also a reminder to Christians that they have not fulfilled their obligation to culture merely by receiving from it. They are also called upon to engage in a ministry to culture and to those who are the artisans of culture, to the end that they may see their true destiny, and employ their talents and skills in the conscious service of God the Father Almighty, who not only made heaven and earth, but in Jesus Christ redeemed all that he had made.

APPENDIX:
A case study of culture in the service of the gospel

Does Protestantism make discriminating use of the gifts of culture in the life of the church? One wonders. There is a head of Christ that has become a hallmark of the Protestant Sunday School. It portrays a man with graceful Nordic features that are at the furthest sentimental remove from the man of sorrows who was acquainted with grief. It is inconceivable that this man could have hung three hours on a cross, or uttered the woes against the Pharisees, or had the stamina to hike from Caesarea-Philippi to Jerusalem.

This kind of sentimentalism is not, of course, the exclusive property of Protestantism. Roman Catholic art in its turn has produced bathos beyond description, and with the wider subject-matter that Roman Catholic hagiography presents, there is a correspondingly wider area for the expression of artistic mediocrity. Nothing in Protestantism, perhaps, is quite so bad as really bad Roman Catholic art, but nothing in Protestantism is any better than really good Roman Catholic art.

One has a particular feeling of uneasiness in the face of Protestant church architecture. Two heresies are evident here, one old and one new. The old one goes: *If it isn't Gothic, it isn't a church.* Flying buttresses there must be even if they do not support anything. (Concealed steel beams now render the buttresses unnecessary.) Actually, Gothic is singularly ill-adapted for Protestant worship. The Gothic "split chancel," for instance, was appropriate for medieval monks who chanted their offices antiphonally; it is perhaps the most inappropriate arrangement possible for a Protestant choir. Likewise, the arrangement of a long nave with an altar at the far east end is scarcely conducive to the expression of a liturgy conceived in terms of the people of God gathered around the Table of the Lord. It is sometimes forgotten that Gothic itself was once "contemporary" and strange. Its advantage over Norman architecture was not so much its greater inherent beauty as the very functional consideration that it permitted more light to enter the sanctuary than had been possible before. If light is a criterion for church building today, there are newer and better ways of achieving it than Gothic. (One church journal recently printed on adjoining pages a picture of an ornate Baptist Gothic church and a picture of a modern glass skyscraper in New York built by a soap manufacturing company. The caption beneath the two pictures ran: "Cleanliness is better than Godliness.")

That the pro-Gothic school of Protestants is dying but not yet dead became evident during the building of the Protestant Inter-Church Center in New York City. The original plans called for a Gothic skyscraper. There was enough artistic resiliency in American Protestantism so that the resultant hue and cry led to the elimination of the irrelevant and structurally dishonest Gothic ornamentation. But the hue and cry was not great enough to achieve a building design of any freshness or originality whatever. The most that can be said is that although the present structure is undistinguished, it is at least not a relic of the past.

The alternative to building churches in thirteenth-century style (with the inevitable implication that the church is still living in the thirteenth century) is to build them in contemporary style. But this alternative introduces a second heresy. The new heresy goes: *So long as it's modern, it's all right.* In the face of this attitude, it needs to be said with all possible emphasis that the problem of building a suitable church is hardly solved by introducing the blessed words "modern" or "contemporary," and assuming that the resultant product will therefore render suitable praise to God, let alone provide a suitable place for worship.

The decision to "go contemporary," however, would seem to be a sound one for a faith that believes that since "Jesus Christ is the same yesterday and today and forever," his gospel must be proclaimed in an idiom that the day and age can see and acknowledge. *But this is the initial decision rather than the final one.* That decision made, the basic task for a given congregation, minister, and architect is to find an answer to the question, "What is a church *for?*" If the question is wrongly answered, the building will be a failure, no matter how contemporary it may be. Some modern churches have been no more than architectural showpieces, while others (by an improper use of glass) actually promote nature-worship and glorify a pagan deity. A modern church that is only a medieval floor plan in contemporary dress, no more provides a proper place for Protestant worship than does a medieval cathedral. A split chancel remains a split chancel whether it has a vaulted stone ceiling or aluminum I-beams.

If a church building is meant (a) to provide a place for the community to worship in the light of its own liturgical heritage, and (b) to show forth in tangible terms the faith of that community, then the building must be honestly designed to meet those two needs. Surely the task of church architecture is a functional one. A church is not designed to be a work of art. It is designed to offer the best use of space and light and form for the worship of God. Modern materials make this possible with a structural freedom unknown to previous ages.

If Protestantism really believes that it has an obligation to speak to culture, and to learn from culture, it must run the risk of using new media in the service of God, so that all created things may praise him. And the way Protestantism designs its churches will be one of the surest tests of its daring and its trust.[9]

16. Holy Worldliness: The "Highest" and the "High St."

Sir George MacLeod tells of a boy throwing a stone through a church window and smashing one of the letters in the caption so that the words GLORY TO GOD IN THE HIGHEST now read GLORY TO GOD IN THE HIGH ST.

He rightly laments that the window was repaired. At most, the new letter should have been mounted on a swivel, so that no one could read either ascription without being reminded of the other.

A similar concern lies behind Alec Vidler's plea for "holy worldliness." [1] He asserts that Protestants cannot settle for uncritical "world-affirmation" or for pious "world-renunciation," but must relate their faith both critically and creatively to the world in which they live. The idea is not new, but Protestants are so adept at avoiding it that it must continually be reasserted.

The case for involvement: a recapitulation

There is not a chapter in this book that is complete if it does not point toward "holy worldliness." Conversely, no chapter is more liable to misunderstanding, if read in isolation, than the present one. We can illustrate this connection in a variety of ways.

Since grace is God's free gift, offered to all irrespective of their merit, any structure of society claiming that some people are "better" than others because of social background, color of skin, or place of birth, is wrong. *Grace is the great leveler.*

Since God hallowed the world by his presence in it, "the calling of the Christian man" must be pursued *in* the world rather than *apart* from it, and business, economics, and politics are a direct concern of the gospel. *The place where God worked is the place where we work.*

Since Jesus Christ is Lord, no one else can be Lord. Whenever a society elevates another Lordship above his, that society must be opposed. *The Lordship of Christ is the agent of change.*

Since God can use "the Assyrians" to reveal himself to men, Christians cannot assume that the church gives automatic access to the Word of God. They will hear the Word in vain if they do not listen also in the marketplace and theater. *The God of all comfort is the God of all culture.*

Since the table of the Lord is the place where all are one in Christ, no one who has supped there can arise content to let his fellow men go hungry. *Bread from Christ's table must nourish the world.*

These comments are drawn at random from a few of the concerns of Chapters 5, 9, 4, 15, and 12, respectively. They underline the same point: *Glory to God in the highest is glory to God in the High Street.*

Romans 13 and Revelation 13

There are all sorts of High Streets. There are all sorts of alleys and slums behind the High Streets. Do we have the same attitude toward all of them? This is a question about the church and the world. To answer it we must say two things that sound perfectly obvious until we discover that we must say them together.

First of all, the church is *in the world*. Nobody who knows the church will disagree with this. The church is one of the visible, sinful, flesh-and-blood realities of space and time, making its share of mistakes, helping its share of people, operating in terms of budgets, squabbles, rivalry, love, and comfort to the afflicted.

But the church is also *against the world,* and this makes it different from the other communities it so often resembles. The church is the "interfering community," in Hendrik Kraemer's phrase, the community that refuses to let the world have the last word, the community that challenges the world in the name of another world, the community that sometimes says "no" to what the world asks of it, the community that brings affliction to the comfortable.

It is always an interesting commentary on a given church to discover what parts of Scripture it quotes to justify its attitude toward the world. When a church wants to be *in* the world and be relieved of the necessity of prophetic witness against it, Romans 13 is a favorite passage: "Let every person be subject to the governing authorities. For there is no authority except from God, and those that exist have been instituted by God. Therefore he who resists the authorities resists what God has appointed . . ." (Rom. 13:1–2). This appeals to comfortable, well-fed, let's-not-do-anything-disturbing Christians.

But when a church wants to be *against* the world and be relieved of the necessity of ministering to it, Revelation 13 is a favorite passage, for it depicts the state as a horrible beast that men worship, a beast that utters blasphemies against God and must therefore be totally repudiated. This appeals to holier-than-thou, let's-not-get-spotted-by-the-sinful-world Christians.

Neither attitude will do by itself. Both are irresponsible, one for succumbing too completely to the world, the other for shirking responsibility for the world. The only way to avoid these twin errors is the difficult way of recognizing that both attitudes must characterize the church. It is in the world and against the world simultaneously. Because God has placed it *in* the world, it has a responsibility for the world; and yet part of that responsibility will consist of speaking *against* the world when the world defies God — which is most of the time. What is involved here is indicated by the extraordinary advice given in 1 Peter, a letter written to the church in time of persecution. On a single line, the author writes, "Fear God. Honor the emperor" (1 Pet. 2:17).

If we can let "emperor" stand for the state as a whole, we can say that the whole difficulty and possibility of "holy worldliness" is compressed within the five words, "Fear God. Honor the emperor." [2] The priority of the commands is crucial: *first,* fear God, then, and *only then,* honor the emperor. In the light of allegiance to God, try to find proper ways of giving allegiance to the state. This must never be blind allegiance, but it can include proper respect for the state as a creative instrumentality in the hands of

God. Until it demands a type of allegiance that rules out the basic allegiance to God, the state is to be "honored." When that allegiance to God can no longer be given first place, there is a final word from Scripture, behind which there is no further retreat for the Christian, and by which he must make his uncompromising stand. This is the word, "We must obey God rather than men" (Acts 5:29).

No Christian can finally tell another Christian exactly when the time has come to say this, and the one who says it will probably have to say also, "Here I stand. I can do no other. God help me." But real wisdom in this matter, as in so many other matters, has been distilled by Reinhold Niebuhr. "The Christian," he reminds us, "must not disturb the established order irresponsibly, but the Christian must not accept the established order complacently." That may not be a blueprint for immediate action, but it establishes the boundaries within which the action must be determined, as both individuals and churches try to work out for themselves the meaning of "holy worldliness."

Protestantism and democracy: a case in point

A concern for "holy worldliness" cannot stay clear of politics, and it belies the frequent assertion by people who ought to know better, that "religion and politics don't mix."

We cannot study Protestantism very long without discovering that it has a political past, and that it was, among other things, a tributary in the development of political democracy. We cannot study it very long either without realizing that there were other tributaries as well (such as Hebraic prophetism, Stoic equalitarianism, and the philosophy of the Enlightenment), so we must not claim too much for Protestantism's contribution. But the interrelationship of Protestantism and democratic procedures is still a significant example of Protestant "holy worldliness." [3]

It would be folly to claim the Reformers themselves as champions of democracy. They had, on the whole, rather traditional views of government, and their fear of anarchy (quite proper for their own times) led them to give support even to despotic regimes.[4] Moreover, the Lutheran doctrine of two distinct realms of church and magistrate led to political quietism in areas under Lutheran control, while the Calvinism of Calvin's lifetime made only a minimal concession to the "lesser magistrates" to revolt against unjust government.[5] But this concession was the thin edge of a long and ever-widening wedge with which later Calvinists, like Knox, relentlessly pushed their way into the fortification of the divine right of kings and queens and asserted the rights of the common man. It was, in fact, the combination of Calvinism and Anabaptist radicalism that combined in left-wing Puritanism to help create the democratic heritage that Britain enjoys today, and the "non-conformist conscience" remains one of the noblest creations of Anglo-Saxon history. William Temple asserts that the "church meetings" of the dissenting groups were a fruitful training ground for democratic procedures,[6] and Wilhelm Pauck, commenting on the American scene, has pointed out that congregational church polity in New England Puritanism became the pattern for New England "town meetings," and thus a chief source of democratic practice in America.[7]

What was there in the Protestant ethos that led to these expressions of democracy? Two examples will indicate how the emphases of Reformation theology sowed seeds that later blossomed forth in democratic procedures.

1. Curiously enough, *the doctrine of election* furnished one of the most important contributions to political democracy. The doctrine of election, we recall, asserts that men have been chosen by God simply because he is gracious, and not because they are worthy. This conviction destroys any fundamental difference between commoner and king. Both stand in precisely the same status before God: sinners who are undeserving of God's love, but whom he loves anyhow. This is a new kind of equality, the equality of need, and it extends across all mankind. Therefore no privileged group inherits or deserves the franchise more than any other group. No longer can there be upper class versus lower class, upper-middle class versus lower-upper-middle class, organization man versus trade unionist, power élite versus blue collar. The doctrine

of election plays havoc with all such hierarchies. The fundamental notion of democracy, that one man equals one vote, is implicit in the doctrine of election. Election makes elections possible.

2. There are similar political implications in *the doctrine of man* that has characterized Protestant theology. Man is "created in the image of God," and this means that every man has unique worth. If any man is hungry, this is both a religious and a political concern, and out of a religious concern for one created in God's image, political means must be devised for ensuring that everyone gets enough bread — which is a suitable enough definition of the art of politics.

Protestant theology also affirms that man is a "sinner." Politically, this means that no man can be trusted with unlimited power, since he will abuse it. There must be ways of controlling the amount of power he has, such as "checks and balances" between the various departments of government, and frequent elections to ensure that no one has power for too long against the will of the majority. The American Constitution, Lord Bryce has observed, was the work of men who believed in original sin. Reinhold Niebuhr's famous epigram shows the relevance of both sides of the doctrine of man to political democracy: "Man's capacity for justice makes democracy possible; but man's inclination to injustice makes democracy necessary." [8]

From such foundations as these, the democratic edifice has been reared. The lesson is plain to all who read: no Protestant who takes his own heritage seriously can sit on the political sidelines.[9]

Politics — and evangelism

It can be objected — and it frequently is — that all the talk about political concern is premature: "If Protestants are really concerned about 'holy worldliness' they won't spend so much time on the political front. The root of the trouble is the heart of man, not the structures of society. There will never be a good political order until there are good people. So the first concern is not politics but evangelism. Convert individuals to the gospel, and the social order will take care of itself."

To which a number of things must be said. It must be acknowledged that persons, rather than social structures or political institutions, are what count. It must be acknowledged that evil persons are unlikely to produce good governments. (Reinhold Niebuhr has said that his book *Moral Man and Immoral Society* could more realistically have been called *Immoral Man and Terribly Immoral Society*.) It must be acknowledged that no Christian is entitled to ride lightly over the needs of a single individual for the sake of political ends.

But it must also be asserted that the whole framework of the objection is wrong. In modern life there is no such antithesis as "personal" concern versus "political" concern. They are wrapped up together. We cannot evangelize in a twentieth-century world without reference to the facts of life in a twentieth-century world, and those facts include the recognition that politics determines who gets bread and who starves, who gets justice and who does not, who votes, and who goes to jail.

If we define evangelism as "sharing the good news" (the word comes from *evangel* from which we get the word "gospel," meaning "good news"), it is clear that there are many ways in which the good news is shared. Calling individuals to decision is one of them, but it is not the only one, and it is unfortunate that individual decision has become the popular stereotype for the entire evangelistic venture. Indeed, modern Protestantism's particular heresy in this regard has been its insistence that evangelism is an individual business, so that it is enough to change individuals and then let them change society.

But the evangelization of individuals is never enough. It takes a lifetime to convert even a small group of individuals, after which the process must begin all over again, while the injustices of society are studiously being ignored. What John Bennett has called "social salvation" must go hand in hand with preaching to individuals. To convert a man living in substandard housing, without concern for the appalling conditions under which he must raise his family, is to betray a deficient vision of the concerns of the gospel for that man's life. His "conversion" has not completed the evangelistic task. It has only gotten it properly launched.

It can be argued, in fact, that political action is an integral part of "sharing the good news." An experience recounted by the Rev. George W. Webber illustrates this:

> A colleague of mine was walking down 104th Street when a coal truck, trying to beat the light, knocked an old man down. The old man lay there bleeding in the gutter. This is about as close to the story of the Good Samaritan as you'd ever want to get — for once in your life to be able to do what the Bible says, to pick the man up and take him to a hospital and see that he has good medical care.
>
> And then suddenly you remember that this is against the law. You are not privileged in New York City to touch an injured man lying in the street. All that society permits you to do is to hold the crowd back, make him comfortable, and call an ambulance. So you do this — and you wait there in the street for an hour and thirty-seven minutes for an ambulance to arrive, because this is East Harlem where people don't matter. And on the way to the hospital the old man dies of a cerebral hemorrhage. And you go back and sit down in your office and say, "Something has gone very wrong here. They won't let me be a good Samaritan." [10]

What happened? What happened was that some people tried protesting individually to the mayor and got nowhere. So they got together. They told the local precinct boss that they wanted better ambulance service. They told him they were going to get it or there would be a new precinct boss after the next election. They got better ambulance service.

"Sharing the good news," being an evangelist, meant getting tough with the precinct boss.

People who engage in this kind of evangelism are going to get their hands dirty. No one who engages in politics remains pure. Many Christians resist this fact. The choice appears to them to be the choice of purity versus political effectiveness. But it is fair to ask whether those who choose purity rather than political effectiveness on behalf of their fellow men are really as pure as they imagine themselves to be. Are they not actually proclaiming that their gospel has no relation to the hard realities of contemporary life? Are they not really saying that their own spiritual purity matters more to them than the welfare of their fellow men? Those who make such a choice must realize that harsh words have been uttered concerning it: "I was hungry and you gave me no food, I was thirsty and you gave me no drink, I was a stranger and you did not welcome me, naked and you did not clothe me, sick and in prison and you did not visit me" (Matt. 25:42–43).[11]

The church and "holy worldliness": two examples

None of this means that the church's main task is to become a gigantic lobby in the city, state, and federal legislatures, although it must constantly press its message on legislative assemblies of all sorts. The main task of the church is to carry on its historic mission, which has frequently and correctly been defined as *marturia* (witness to, and proclamation of, the good news), *diakonia* (service to those in need), and *koinonia* (the living expression of fellowship and community). The need today is not to redefine or modify these tasks, but *to perform them in relation to today's world.* The Evangelical Academies, described in Chapter 9, are one attempt to do this. We shall examine two further attempts to build a bridge between the church and the world.

1. Protestantism has been guilty of ignoring a large part of today's world, the part now called *the inner-city*. Protestant churches, being "middle class" churches by and large, have tended to follow the middle class out of the city as soon as the middle class is able to migrate in search of the questionable joys of suburbia. In congested slum areas of the large cities it has been left to Roman Catholicism to minister to the "workers."[12] Recently, however, Protestants have become aware that the inner-city is the missionary frontier of the modern industrial world. If the gospel cannot be heard there, it does not deserve a hearing elsewhere. In Scotland, for example, members of the Iona Community, both ministerial and lay, work side by side during the summer months rebuilding the abbey on the island of Iona, and during the winter months the same people serve in the most neglected parish area of Scotland, the congested inner-city, where they speak and preach and witness to the redemptive power of the gospel in unpromising situations.[13]

In America, the East Harlem Protestant Parish in New York City exemplifies this concern for the inner-city, and it has led to similar experiments in Cleveland, Chicago, and New Haven. Groups of ministers and laymen have moved into inner-city areas and either started new churches or re-activated defunct churches left vacant during the suburban stampede. They have related the good news of Jesus Christ to the ugliness of the contemporary situation in all sorts of ways: fighting for better ambulance service, as we saw above, giving short and long range help to dope addicts, organizing Bible study groups around problems of inner-city life, running country day camps for children, helping people find employment, leading crusades to City Hall against substandard housing, and most important of all, working out a life of worship and discipline that relates to these and other problems.[14]

2. In many cities, large and small, "the church" appears to be no more than a "building," usually empty, that is ignored by most of those who pass by. Can the church wait for the world to beat a path to its door?

It cannot. Since the people will not come to where it is, the church must go out to where the people are, to people whether they are nominal members who never come any more, or non-members who never came at all. *The house church* is an attempt to take the church out into the world around it, to illustrate that there is a fundamental difference between "going" to church and "being" the church.[15]

In the New Testament, "the church" was never "the building." It was such things as

— apostolic teaching
— fellowship
— the breaking of bread
— prayer.

(Acts 2:42)

Canon Southcott, serving in a parish church in Leeds, England, discovered that these things could often be realized with half a dozen people in a house in a way that they could not be realized in a large, empty church, and that when the church is in the house, the church often "comes alive" in a way it does nowhere else.

Members of confirmation classes, for example, meeting in a living-room, discover that when the evening paper is on the same table as the Bible, it is not very long before the relationship between the two of them is being discussed. When the Lord's Supper is celebrated around a kitchen table, with bread from the family larder, it is possible to see in a new way the relation of the gospel to what goes on in the kitchen and in the other rooms of the house. When people who have known each other casually along the block break bread together, they come to know each other profoundly, as brethren in Christ. When people living on the same street gather in a house to pray for one another and for the entire street, it is hard to go out from such a meeting and perpetuate the old animosities. If there have been prayers for the sick next door, the natural outcome of such prayers is an attempt to minister to the sick next door.

None of this is an evangelistic "technique." It is an attempt to build the necessary bridge between the church and the world. The reality of the church's witness (*marturia*), service (*diakonia*), and fellowship (*koinonia*) begin to come alive again in "the church that is in your house."

Holy worldliness. Politics. Evangelism. Witness. Service. Community. They all go together.

The risk of "holy worldliness"

There is a risk in store for those who believe in "holy worldliness." It is the risk of disillusionment. A lifetime of work for peace issues in a new World War. The dope addict goes back to dope. The house-church prayer meeting uncovers new animosities rather than healing old ones.

We have no right to assume that it will be different with us. We must remember that there are no promises of success in the Christian venture. The key word cannot be achievement. But one of the key words can be "obedience" — a recognition that in trying to do the will of God we may fail, and yet that the act of trying is the important thing, since God can use even our failures for the ultimate fulfillment of his purposes.

How, then, do we remain obedient when the results seem so meager? The degree to which we can answer this question will be commensurate with the degree to which we live our lives in the light of another key word, "gratitude." We know that we can make no claims for ourselves, that we can take credit for no achievements. All that we are or do we owe to grace. The thing we cannot do is boast. *The thing we can do is be thankful.* And our thankfulness, our gratitude, will be the real resource for our holy worldliness, far beyond any victories we think we may win, or defeats we hope we may avert, or good works we realize we must do.

"Why must we do good works?" the Heidelberg Catechism asks, and then goes on to answer:

> Because Christ, having redeemed us by his blood, renews us also by his Holy Spirit, after his own image, *that with our whole life we may show ourselves thankful to God for his blessing,* and that he may be glorified through us; then also, that we ourselves may be assured of our faith by the fruits thereof, and by our godly walk may win our neighbors also to Christ.[16]

Where is this found in the Heidelberg Catechism? It is found in the section *On Gratitude.*

17. Living Tensions Within Protestantism

Tensions and conflicts within Protestantism will not disappear. Some of the particular tensions and conflicts may fade away. The supralapsarian-infralapsarian controversy is not the burning issue it once was. But new tensions and conflicts will divide the ranks, and questions yet unasked will be the occasion of future controversies.

To many people this is a deplorable state of affairs. They wish Protestantism would tidy itself up, put its house in order, and provide a proper place for everything. There is nothing, however, that gives less impression of being lived in than a completely tidy house. On that score, at least, Protestantism is not in danger of giving the impression that it has vacated its historic dwellings.

More positively, it can be argued that tensions and conflicts are not signs of sickness and decay but of health and growth. Nothing exhibits less tension than a corpse. And some of the tensions most characteristic of Protestantism, far from being examples of its instability, are really marks of its vitality. The way to deal with these tensions is not to divide them with the preposition "versus," but to join them with the conjunction "and," so that like all other things, they can work together for good to them that love God.

Order and ardor

John Mackay's distinction between order and ardor is a convenient way of describing a basic tension within Protestantism. This tension expresses itself in numerous ways.

It can be stated, for example, as the contrast between *the individual and the church.* The notion of the individual as directly responsible to God is a creative notion. Søren Kierkegaard, the erratic genius of the nineteenth century, said some things that a complacent Christendom has almost forgotten, about the individual who stands before God, naked and alone, as though exposed on the Jutland heath with no place to hide, forced to render up a verdict, and denied the easy alternative of letting it all be done for him by the painless machinery of a state church. As a corrective, this emphasis could not be more important.

But only as a corrective. For it is far from a full-blown Protestant understanding of the matter. In a full-blown Protestant understanding, neither the individual Christian nor the community of Christians can be understood apart from the other.[1] This important fact is recoverable for our day, thanks to a renewed emphasis on the "self" in recent Protestant thinking. Discussion of the "self" could be highly individualistic, but two facts have saved it from going in such an unfortunate direction: (a) the recognition that the self is fully defined only as self-in-community, so that where there is no community there is no true selfhood, and (b) the recognition that "the community" is not built on such foundation stones as a group of doctrines or ecclesiastical procedures, but is the gathering together by God of "living stones" (1 Pet. 2:4f), Jesus Christ being the cornerstone. It is a community of persons before it is a community of ideas. From such a perspective as this, the tension between the church and the individual can be a creative one.

The tension between order and ardor can also be described as a contrast *between freedom and order*. We have already explored some of the Protestant misconceptions of "freedom," which suggest that it means no more than lack of constraint.[2]

Protestants need to remember that in his "Treatise on Christian Liberty" Luther not only said, "The Christian is most free lord of all and subject to no one," (which is where most Protestant appraisals stop) but that he also said, *in the same sentence,* "the Christian is most dutiful servant of all and subject to everyone." This statement helpfully challenges the conventional Protestant notion of "freedom" as permission to do as one pleases, and although it does not deal with the polarities of freedom and order, it must be firmly repeated against those who, in their fear of "domination by the hierarchy" from without or "submission to bureaucracy" from within, offer no more than a kind of spiritual anarchy as an alternative.

Actually, the proper exercise of Christian freedom will be achieved not by rejecting "order" as some evil thing emanating from Rome or from denominational headquarters, but by recognizing that the real task of present-day Protestantism is the achievement of *freedom within order*. We can examine this on the very practical level of denominational "bigness."

Where two or three are gathered together, committees, sessions, and vestries can be cheerfully ignored. But where two or three hundred are gathered together, or two or three hundred thousand, a certain amount of order is the only way to avoid chaos. Order is not antithetical to freedom here, order is a prerequisite for freedom. To be sure, the relationship of the Holy Spirit to the average denominational committee is one of those ultimate mysteries of the faith that defies comprehension. But the necessity of denominational committees is no automatic sign that freedom has been forfeited. It may be a recognition that freedom is being maintained — through order.

On the other hand, in a day of burgeoning denominational executives and top-level ecclesiastical decision-makers, a word of warning is likewise necessary, for committees and executives (even denominational executives) have often demonstrated a well-developed capacity for obstructing the Spirit's working. Perhaps the Spirit will have the healthiest opportunity for creative endeavor if he continually reminds those responsible for order that their powers have been freely given to them and can as freely be withdrawn.

Order can be stagnant, and order can be loveless. But where those things are remembered, let it also be remembered that ardor can be erratic and ardor can be irresponsible.

Sect and denomination

A further example of the tension between order and ardor deserves independent comment. It is provided by the astonishing growth of the sect groups, and the challenge they pose to Protestant denominationalism.[3]

The multiplication of the sect groups today is first of all a judgment on denominational Protestantism. When the children of this age have cried for bread, the denominations have given them stones. The sects have clearly provided bread. Some Protestants will feel that the bread is a bit mouldy. Others will feel, on the contrary, that it has not been fully baked. A few will claim that improper hands have been laid upon it. But it is bread nevertheless, and the bread of life.

There is a degree of concern and a sense of contagion about sectarian Christianity that makes most respectable church Christianity seem pale and insipid. There is a glow in the life of the twice-born sectarian that would embarrass the conventional Protestant, and yet looks suspiciously like the life of the New Testament Christian. There is an assurance in the faith of the sectarian that more sophisticated Protestants, carefully balancing intellectual probabilities, do not even begin to attain. There is a willingness to go to the four corners of the earth and preach the sectarian gospel to every creature, that makes the missionary concern of organized Protestantism look puny in proportion to the vaster resources available to it. Denominational Protestants must be grateful that the sectarians are witnessing to these things.

They must also be chagrined that their own failure to do so has made the sectarian witness so necessary. For we cannot conclude that the answer to Protestant lukewarmness is the exhortation, "Be like the sects!" There are serious limitations in modern sectarianism and these must be acknowledged too. The spirit of these groups is intolerant and often bigoted. They are prone to pronounce damnation on all Christians who do not belong to their particular group, no matter how small the latter may be. They appeal largely to the uneducated, and few will acknowledge even the most elementary facts of historical or Biblical criticism. The personality of the leader is usually the force binding the group together, and his particular interpretation of the faith is accepted unquestioningly. When a questioner finally appears, the end result is a new sect formed around the personality of the dissatisfied questioner, and his particular interpretation of the faith is accepted unquestioningly. When a questioner finally appears, the end result is a new sect . . .

But when all the shortcomings have been catalogued — and the list could be considerably extended — there is one place where Protestant denominations must listen to the sectarian voice with a particularly attentive ear. For the sect groups, over and above all their shortcomings, represent a genuine revival of the power of the Holy Spirit in the life of Christendom. Protestant attentiveness to the Holy Spirit has been conspicuously lacking during much of its history, and if he is to speak with more power in our own day, it will be in large measure because the sect groups have forced denominational Protestantism once again to take his activity seriously.[4]

The one who has been most conscious of the actual and potential sectarian contribution here has been Bishop Lesslie Newbigin of the Church of South India. Bishop Newbigin recognizes that ecumenical discussion has not yet taken the sectarian witness seriously enough. He is aware that many sect groups wage militant and even vicious warfare against ecumenism, but he insists that they have a particular contribution to make to ecumenical Christianity:

> We must therefore acknowledge that we without them cannot be made perfect. We must therefore assure our brethren of our willingness to learn from them in the fellowship of the ecumenical movement, and we must at the same time bear witness to them concerning the things which the Holy Spirit has taught us. We must ask them to recognize the evident tokens of the Spirit's working in the experience of the ecumenical movement, especially in the growth of charity where it had been almost wholly lacking. We must tell them that in order to enter into the ecumenical conversation with us it is not necessary for them to abandon any of their distinctive convictions, but only to recognize us as fellow Christians sharing with them — even though we be in error — the same Spirit. We must ask them to consider whether by denying all fellowship with us, they do not sin against the Holy Spirit who is in them, and whether faithfulness to their Lord and ours does not absolutely require us to seek unity with one another.[5]

Contemporary Protestantism's recovery of the Bible has led to a recovery of the Word. But the Word without the inner testimony of the Holy Spirit is a lifeless Word. From the sects it is possible to learn more of the vivifying power of the Spirit in our midst. Without his presence, Biblical theology will be no more than the study of the dead letter. But if the letter killeth, the Spirit giveth life, and in this hope, we can believe that in the sects the power of God is working, and that the Reformation, even our own reformation, is continuing.

Scripture and tradition

Concern for the Holy Spirit also lies behind the tension between Scripture and tradition.

We attempt to describe the activity of the Spirit in a number of ways, but none of them is ever satisfactory. For our present discussion let us say that the Holy Spirit is *the one who makes the past contemporary for us*. He is the energizing, dynamic activity of the Godhead who assures us that what God did "back then" for someone else, becomes what God is doing "right now" for us. That we are confronted by a living Christ today is only possible because the Holy Spirit is at work making Christ our eternal contemporary.[6]

The question that now concerns us is: by what means does the Spirit do his work in the church? As we saw in Chapter 14, the answer to this question has been a watershed dividing Protestantism and Roman Catholicism.

The conventional Protestant answer has been that Scripture is the channel through which the power of the Holy Spirit flows, and that Roman Catholicism has permitted so many tributaries marked "tradition" to enter the channel that the original springs of living water have become impure and almost unrecognizable. The conventional Roman Catholic answer has been that the Spirit's activity did not cease when the last New Testament book was completed, but that in addition he makes his will known through the traditions of the living organism that is the church.

Both answers, of course, need refinement. Roman Catholics believe, more fervently than Protestants imagine, that Scripture and tradition are complementary rather than antithetical sources of truth. And Protestantism's *sola Scriptura* does not mean that the

Holy Spirit ceased to be active when the New Testament canon was complete, but rather that through the New Testament canon he continues to be radically active in the church, both in judgment and renewal.

However, our present concern is not the "Roman Catholic–Protestant" tension except as it throws light on Protestantism's *inner* tension over the relationship of Scripture and tradition. A study of the evolution of Roman Catholic dogma makes the Protestant understandably wary about what tradition may do to the Biblical faith, but reaction from this has led much of Protestantism to an unrealistic disavowal of tradition. Emphasis on *sola Scriptura* has been the distinctive grandeur of Protestantism, but it has been the source of distinct misery as well. For it has often been based on the faulty assumption that it is possible to "leap-frog," as it were, over 1900 years of Christian history, and read the Bible as though nothing had happened since the documents themselves were composed.

Even if this were desirable (which is debatable), it is impossible. The "leapfrog" is doomed to failure on at least two counts: (a) it ignores the fact that people inevitably read the Bible in the light of a denominational or theological heritage, and (b) it ignores the fact that they read it in the light of their contemporary situation.

a. No one approaches the Bible free of denominational or theological presuppositions. Lutherans tend to read the Bible in the light of the interpretive principle of justification by faith, Presbyterians in terms of the sovereignty of God. The sect groups read it from the perspective of their own practices, which may range from snake handling to speaking in tongues. Liberal Protestants find the Bible a handbook for social justice, while conservatives find it depicting an everlasting hell fire designed for liberals.

b. But our contemporary situation also conditions the way we read the Bible. Americans in East Lansing hear Romans 13 in a different way from Germans in East Berlin. When Mississippi Senators and Afrikaner Nationalists read Paul's speech on Mars Hill, they draw different conclusions about racial discrimination than do natives of Indonesia or Ghana who read the same passage.

No one is trying to be dishonest. Everyone claims to be hearing the Word of God. But the indisputable fact of the matter is that

Lutherans, Presbyterians, sectarians, liberals, conservatives, East Lansingites, East Berliners, southern Americans, southern Afrikaners, Indonesians, and Ghanians, all read the same Scriptures and all hear different things.

Much of this may be due to faulty reading and faulty listening. But it cannot all be explained so simply. It can be explained only by recognizing honestly that Protestants do not rely on *sola Scriptura* in quite the pure way that Reformation Sunday sermons would suggest.[7]

Recognition of this fact will be the beginning of its cure. For once it is acknowledged that our approach to Scripture is conditioned by the tradition and situation in which we stand, then we can listen with new attentiveness to Scripture to see in what ways it may challenge that tradition and situation. In the very risky process of being exposed to Scripture, our own tradition can be made more conformable to it. The mark of Protestant courage is precisely this willingness to subject not simply tradition, but *our own* tradition, to the destructive and healing power of Scripture.

There is another thing we can do, and it too takes courage. We can listen to the interpretations of Scripture that come from traditions other than our own. There is something salutary about the fact that in the ecumenical movement Baptists must now be exposed to Anglican treatments of the New Testament doctrine of the ministry, and that Lutherans must listen while Methodists explain how their social activism is rooted in the Bible. There is no longer any excuse for pockets of Christendom to remain uninformed about the way other Christians interpret Holy Scripture. Denominational exegesis exists to be challenged.

The wider the scope of the church's listening, the better the chances for the corrective power of the Holy Spirit, speaking through Scripture, to break down the barriers men constantly erect so that they will not have to heed his disturbing voice.

Denominationalism and ecumenism

A curious thing is happening in contemporary Protestantism. Alongside an ecumenical concern for the reunion of Christendom is a growing denominational self-consciousness that threatens to perpetuate the ancient divisions. Whether this is creative or destructive has been a topic of considerable debate within Protestantism.

Many Protestants feel that the new emphasis on denominationalism is divisive, and that it jeopardizes ecumenical concern. They argue that denominations spend so much time exploring their own particular tributary of the Christian stream that they never venture as far as the ecumenical river into which their tributary flows. Thus conditions of reunion tend to be denominationally oriented so as to include (a) an acceptance of *our* denominational heritage as normative, (b) an unwillingness to surrender anything that has played a part in *our* past, and (c) a truculence toward those who are so busy inspecting their own backwaters that they cannot see that *our* tributary is the only one flowing directly from the source.

In the face of this many people are dismayed, for fear that the renaissance of denominational self-consciousness will create shoals or rapids that will jeopardize the concurrent sailing of various ecumenical craft down the various tributaries to the main river.[8]

There is particular resistance to denominational emphasis in areas where the "younger churches" have grown up. For it is in missionary situations that the divisiveness of denominational conflict is most apparent and consequently most distressing. Leaders in these areas quite properly plead with the older churches *not* to impose their western patterns of denominational separateness on the mission field. A telling example of what those patterns mean was brought home when the leader of the "untouchables" in India renounced the caste system. He likewise urged his sixty million fellow untouchables to renounce the Hinduism that had been responsible for the caste system. But Christianity had no appeal to the untouchables as a possible alternative to Hinduism. "We are united in Hinduism," they said, "and we shall become divided in Christianity." [9] The argument was unanswerable.

Another group of Protestants feels that denominational self-consciousness is a prerequisite for responsible ecumenical concern. They do not desire to perpetuate the divisions of the past, but to make certain that ecumenical reunion is built upon realistic foundations. They argue that it is unrealistic to ignore four hundred years of denominational history. Denominations do exist, and the vantage point from which every Christian surveys the ecumenical scene is, for better or for worse, a denominational vantage point. In the providence of God denominations have not been merely divisive. They have also conserved things essential to the full ordering of the Christian gospel, and the proclamation of that gospel would have been weakened, if not destroyed, apart from their historic witness. The ecumenical cause will best be served today as each denomination holds up for public inspection, discussion, and possible amendment, its own particular gifts to "the coming great church." In this way, the claims, counter-claims, gifts, and shortcomings can be looked at openly and honestly. Denominationalism is no place to stop, but it is a place to begin — the only place to begin, and a means by which to develop toward unity. The way to unity along this path may be slow, but the unity that is secured will endure.

The hope often seems naïve. The realities of the situation are such that free churches cannot understand why the Anglicans are so stubborn about episcopacy, Lutherans wonder how they can possibly admit Baptists to their communion services, and Methodists cannot see why Congregationalists should be upset by the word "bishop." In the face of such barriers the temptation is to abandon the ecumenical dream and settle for an ecclesiastical equivalent of peaceful co-existence.

But in this situation there is always the possibility — without which the ecumenical movement could not long survive — that God may overrule the divisions of men in ways beyond our knowing, and that the Holy Spirit may be more powerful than all the denominational roadblocks men strew in his pathway. There are even now in contemporary ecumenical discussion signs of the resuscitating power of his breath, and these center around a fresh realization that our task is to move from our outward divisions toward a fuller realization of the oneness *we already possess* in Christ. Professor Albert Outler has written:

> Modern ecumenism begins with *the present fact of our unity in Christ* . . . This beginning point has allowed the positive recognition by the separated churches, of the gifts and fruits of the Holy Spirit in the other churches — even when this recognition may include certain

reservations as to the fullness and validity of the Spirit's work in those other churches . . .

Our only hope for unity-yet-to-be-achieved, lies in the acknowledgement of the unity-already-given by God in Christ. This discovery that the future imperative to unity derives from the present indicative of unity is one of the really crucial impulses of the modern ecumenical movement.[10]

So the new pattern in ecumenical discussion is not that two churches say, "We really ought to be united, therefore let us work out a scheme for becoming united." The new pattern is rather that two churches realize, "We are already united in Christ, therefore let us find a way of manifesting more clearly the unity we already have in him."

On these terms, the apparent divisiveness of denominationalism can be turned to creative use in a day of ecumenical vigor.

Loyalty and criticism

Some people feel that Protestant criticism of Protestantism, particularly if it is publicly expressed, means waning loyalty or growing disloyalty. How firm is the citadel of faith if its innermost precincts are constantly being challenged by those who claim to be its defenders? If the trumpet makes such uncertain sounds, how can soldiers of faith prepare for battle? To change the metaphor, how can outsiders be attracted to the ranks while soiled theological laundry is being aired in ecclesiastical front yards?

A Protestant should be haunted by the impression that the free-wheeling character of Protestant conviction makes on a sensitive Roman Catholic:

On the fundamental question of Christianity — "What think ye of Christ"? — the voices of my Protestant friends, their pastors, and their theologians are raised in a strong but very dissonant chorus. The Protestant theology I read with interest and profit tells me of the "Jesus of history" of Albert Schweitzer, the "Christ of the faith" of liberal Protestantism, the "achievement of authentic selfhood" of Bultmann, or "the man at his best" of some of the more popular preachers.

I cannot enter into personal union, an interchange of knowledge and love, with these partial Christs, nor can I wait until the theologians have arrived at a synthesis. Their art is long but my time is fleeting.[11]

It is true that we raise our voices in a dissonant, and even strident, chorus. There are occasions, indeed, when the chorus seems to be praising another than Jesus Christ, who for us men and our salvation came down from heaven. This threatens the security of many of the singers, as well as discouraging others from listening to the chorus and eventually joining the song.

These are hazards not lightly to be dismissed. But at the same time as we acknowledge their reality, we must assert that they are the risks Protestantism must run. There is no faith without risk. Truth is not won easily, and it is never won fully, but Protestants believe that only through the expression of the dissonances can they come to learn the deeper harmonies into which the dissonances resolve.

One of the most encouraging by-products of the World Council of Churches has been the way in which within it insularities of belief and practice can be challenged, and a deeper understanding of the total faith achieved. When delegates from the western nations, for example, wanted to condemn the depersonalizing effect of technology on modern culture, Bishop Manikam of India wryly asked the delegates if they would postpone the condemnation for about fifty years, so that India could first profit from the benefits of technology.

The Protestants who wrangle so endlessly and so publicly are bound together by a common loyalty. It is a loyalty to Jesus Christ. Each makes his own witness as part of a chorus. The chorus will contain dissonance as long as it sings, for it is an earthly and not a heavenly choir. But each voice contributes, sometimes in unexpected ways. The life of Schweitzer speaks more tellingly than his theology. The books of Bultmann send Protestants scurrying back to their Bibles, not simply to refute him, but to examine the old stories in the light of what he has said, and to learn from them again in ways beyond what they or Bultmann had anticipated.

Because Protestants are loyal, they are critical. Because Jesus Christ is the same yesterday, today, and forever, there must be new attempts to see what he means today. The theologians will not produce a "synthesis," and even if they could a synthesis will never meet our deepest need. But they can point us to one who is greater than all syntheses. They can try to describe him for us, so that we, seeing some things with them, can see other things for ourselves, and share in turn what we have seen, so that every knee may bow and every tongue confess that Jesus Christ is Lord, to the glory of God the Father.

18. Preface: A "Pilgrim People"

A book on the spirit of Protestantism cannot end with a conclusion. It can only end with a preface.

The last word can only be a first word, a recognition that the end of the road has not been reached, that the beginning of the road, in fact, has barely been discovered. For Protestants do not say, "We have arrived," they say, "We are on the way." The Christian life, as Protestants know it, does not have a last chapter. It is a constant succession of new chapters. Its theme is not an arrival, but a series of departures. It is the story of a pilgrimage.[1]

The image of the pilgrimage has been a familiar one ever since Abraham left Ur of the Chaldees "not knowing where he was to go" (Heb. 11:8). It has been the story of Abraham's children, the Israelites. It was the story of the Israelites' Messiah, the Son of Man who had nowhere to lay his head. It is the story of Messiah's children, too.

> These all died in faith, not having received what was promised, but having seen it and greeted it from afar, and having acknowledged that they were strangers and exiles on the earth. For people who speak thus make it clear that they are seeking a homeland . . . They desire a better country, that is, a heavenly one. Therefore God is not ashamed to be called their God, for he has prepared for them a city.
>
> (Heb. 11:13–16)

To see this much is to see a great deal. But there is more yet to be seen, and the pilgrim who sees it is given marching instructions:

> Therefore, since we are surrounded by so great a cloud of witnesses, let us lay aside every weight, and sin which clings so closely, and let us run with perseverance the race that is set before us, looking unto Jesus

the pioneer and perfector of our faith, who for the joy that was set before him endured the cross, despising the shame, and is seated at the right hand of the throne of God.

(Heb. 12:1–2)

How then, as "strangers and exiles on the earth," do we conduct ourselves? Here is one way of putting it: *We are strangers and pilgrims seeking a city, in the company of a band of pilgrims who have been given directions, who have been joined by the builder of the city and who are freed to live as his servants.*

We are strangers and pilgrims seeking a city

Sometimes the atmosphere is so clear that we see the spires of the city.

But sometimes they disappear from sight and we wonder if we will ever see them again. And sometimes we are so busy looking in the wrong direction that we are sure there never was a city. This does not mean — and it is a hard lesson for the pilgrim to learn — that the city no longer exists, or never did exist. It simply means that our eyes are clouded, or that we do not know where to look. The existence of the city does not depend upon the keenness of our vision.

We discover different things at different stages of our journey. At one point, the bells toll out judgment. At another, music of compassion fills the air. At a fresh bend of the road we see the city from a new perspective. We had not expected it to look like that. We are troubled and perplexed, but later we are glad, for we remember that the building of the city has not been left to us.

The pilgrimage continues. We seldom see as much as we would like to see. But the more we learn of the city, the more we realize it was there before we learned of it. The details may still escape us, but that is not a comment on the city. It is a comment only on the dimness of our vision.

We are in the company of a band of pilgrims

We are not alone upon the road. This discovery is both comforting and humiliating, for many fellow pilgrims see the city with more clarity than we. When we fail to discern something of importance, one of them does. Sometimes a whole host of them does. We may not initially assume that they are wrong. We must first of all acknowledge that their vision may be clearer than ours, and that the things they see are really there. We must take the witness of our fellow pilgrims seriously.

It is not easy to do this. For we all want to affirm that what *we* see is what is really there — no more, no less. It is hard to test our vision by the claims of others. But they are there to help us do just that. We are upheld not only by the faith God grants to us, but by their faith as well. When our faith grows dim, we are receiving members of the pilgrim band. We may see nothing, but we walk in company with those who do. They bear the weight of glory for us. When vision is restored to us, and others cannot see, we see for them, and tell them what is there.

This is the good gift the builder of the city gives us — he has not placed us on the road alone, but with a pilgrim band, living a life of exchange, a communion of saints, bearing one another's burdens.

We have been given directions

We are not left to our own resources. We do not make our charts and maps ourselves. We do not vote on what the city shall be like. The builder of the city gives us directions, through certain ones who walked the pilgrim road before our time. These men were keen of vision. Their directions and descriptions can help us on the way. They tell us of the path, the city, and its builder. Sometimes they warn us of wild beasts just off the road not far ahead. Or they tell us the terrain is faulty when we at last had come to feel secure. They speak of woe when things are going well, and just as we despair they tell us that the way is full of hope.

The charts are old, the wording is obscure, the pictures strange. But every time we look for other help, we find our new maps quite unsatisfying. The saints of old saw better than the rest of us, and new light still breaks forth from what they wrote.

We have been joined by the builder of the city

The directions tell us that the builder of the city has become a pilgrim.

And now everything is different. The abstractions can be left behind. For now the builder of the city has a name. We have seen him come out of the city and walk beside us, take the hardships of our journey upon himself, expose himself to all the perils on the way — and join the company. "Though he was in the form of God, [he] did not count equality with God a thing to be grasped, but emptied himself, taking the form of a servant, being born in the likeness of men" (Phil. 2:6–7).

He has taken the long, hard road of becoming man so that we can walk with him the long, hard road to the city. That we continue on a pilgrimage to where he is, is only possible because he came to where we are.

What we know about the city would be very faulty if the builder had not shown us, on the road, what city life was like. If we have to describe how the builder of the city could also be a humble pilgrim, we get a little tongue-tied, and no one explains it very well, for there is nothing else with which we can compare this claim. Builders of other cities have not trod the pilgrim way. But there are many in the pilgrim band who know that when they stumble they are lifted up by one whose name they all affirm, that when they venture off the road they are not left alone. Another goes to guide them back.

We are freed to live as servants

There is a danger in being a pilgrim. It is the danger of watching the distant city so intently that we fail to notice travelers at our side who are in difficulty. In our concern to reach the city all unscathed, we may force others off the road. Those who do this find the city's gates are barred to them. For they have missed the meaning of the pilgrimage.

When the builder of the city joined the band he took the form of servant. In doing so, he defined the nature of the pilgrimage for all the other pilgrims. What does it mean to be a pilgrim? It means to be a servant. Success is not the pilgrim's aim, but service. There is no assurance we will slay the dragons, or have spirits subject unto us, or cross ravines unscathed. We only know the pilgrim is a servant, that we must serve our fellows for Christ's sake — and leave the rest to God.

Notes

Bibliographical suggestions are confined as much as possible to easily accessible works in English. Where references are given to sources in foreign languages it is because the works cited are basic works for which there is no satisfactory English equivalent.

Chapter 1. THE MISUNDERSTANDING OF PROTESTANTISM

1. T. S. Eliot, *Notes Toward the Definition of Culture,* Faber and Faber, p. 75.

2. For a good example of Roman Catholic acknowledgment of the sorry state of things, see Karl Adam, *One and Holy,* Sheed and Ward.

3. Cited in Flew and Davies, eds., *The Catholicity of Protestantism,* Muhlenberg, pp. 13–14. While this book is basically a polemical reply to a polemical Anglo-Catholic pamphlet, *Catholicity,* the reader can discern Protestant rigor and vigor at its best, in the midst of the "Godly polemics."

4. These are far-reaching assertions, treated in more detail in Chapters 2 and 13 below.

5. This point is developed in detail in Chapter 10 below, and in portions of Chapter 4.

6. Howell, *Of Sacraments and Sacrifice,* Liturgical Press, pp. 130–31, italics added.

7. This interpretation of the intent of the Reformers is elaborated in the next chapter.

8. The difficulty with this way of putting it, which appears to overlook the fact that faith itself is a gift of God, is discussed in Chapter 5 below.

9. See the whole of Luther's hymn, "A Mighty Fortress Is Our God."

10. Luther, *A Commentary on St. Paul's Epistle to the Galatians,* James Clarke and Co., Ltd., p. 372.

11. Schaff, *Creeds of Christendom,* Harpers, Vol. I, p. 204. I owe my appreciation of the significance of this quotation to H. T. Kerr, Jr., *Positive Protestantism,* Westminster, Chapter II.

CHAPTER 2. THE CATHOLICITY OF PROTESTANTISM

1. For further examples of such diverse interpretations, see Preserved Smith, *The Age of the Reformation,* Holt, from which the above examples are drawn.

2. Maritain, *Three Reformers,* Sheed and Ward, p. 13.

3. In Lortz, *Die Reformation in Deutschland,* Heider, Freiburg/Breisgau.

4. Karl Adam writes: "The sixteenth century revolt from the Church led inevitably to the revolt from Christ of the eighteenth century, and thence to the revolt from God of the nineteenth." (*The Spirit of Catholicism,* Macmillan, pp. 8–9.)

While Protestants are flattered to be credited with such a decisive influence on the course of history, they must decline sole credit for the disasters attributed to them. History is considerably more complex than the quotation would suggest.

5. It must be clear that although this is the popular view in Roman Catholic polemics, it is by no means the only interpretation. Father Bouyer, for example, in *The Spirit and Forms of Protestantism,* Newman, asserts that at every basic point of theology the Reformers were right, and that only when they tried to incorporate their "spirit" in the new and awkward "forms" of Protestantism did they go astray. I have also heard Roman Catholic theologians assert that in the providence of God the existence of Protestantism must be accepted by them as a judgment on the impurities of their church, and that the continued existence of the Protestant witness is beneficent to the inner health of Roman Catholicism. For further discussion see Chapter 13 below.

6. Nichols, *Primer for Protestants,* Haddam House, pp. 34ff. The word "evangelical" comes from *evangel,* from which the English word "gospel" (meaning "good news") is derived.

7. It is easy to become romantic here, and Wilhelm Pauck issues some helpful warnings against assuming that Luther attempted to copy in the sixteenth century what he had discovered to be the pattern of the first century. See his *The Heritage of the Reformation,* Beacon, esp. pp. 26 and 121.

8. Problems connected with the authority of Scripture are discussed in detail in Chapter 6 below, and more briefly in Chapter 14.

9. Cited in Kerr, *Positive Protestantism,* p. 37, a book to which I am much indebted for the perspective of the present chapter.

10. There is unfortunately no easy way to overcome this difficulty. In the pages that follow, "catholic" is used to express the sense of wholeness, and (except where the context makes it too cumbersome) "Roman Catholic" is used to refer to that portion of Christendom which acknowledges the Pope as the vicar of Christ. See further Chapter 1 above.

11. Cf. J. D. N. Kelly, *Early Christian Creeds,* Longmans, Green,

pp. 385ff. and Kelly, *Early Christian Doctrines,* Adam and Charles Black, p. 190.

12. This statement occurs in the otherwise admirable book by Prestige, *Fathers and Heretics,* S.P.C.K. See the trenchant comments of Whale in *Christian Doctrine,* Cambridge Univ. Press, pp. 146–9.

13. The Roman Catholic Baltimore Catechism, paragraph 160.

14. The best brief survey of the historical currents from the Reformation to the present is Dillenberger and Welch, *Protestant Christianity,* Scribners. Bainton, *The Reformation of the Sixteenth Century,* Beacon, is a readable treatment of the events of the first generation of Reformers. A standard survey from the seventeenth century to the present day is Nichols, *History of Christianity 1650–1950,* Ronald. Further bibliographical suggestions will be found under the various "denominational families" in Chapter 3 below.

CHAPTER 3. THE VARIETIES OF PROTESTANTISM

1. On this point, see Greenslade, *Schism in the Early Church,* S. C. M. Press.

2. The descriptions that follow are obviously minimal. The serious student will need to supplement them by reference to the bibliographical material cited in the appropriate footnotes.

For a single comprehensive treatment of all the bodies of Christendom, with helpful bibliography, see Einar Molland, *Christendom,* Mowbrays. The confessional statements of most of the denominations can be found in Schaff, *The Creeds of Christendom,* Harpers, Vol. III.

Descriptions of their ecclesiastical families by representatives of all the major groups of Christendom are contained in Flew, ed., *The Nature of the Church,* Harpers, a volume produced in preparation for the meetings of the Faith and Order Commission of the World Council of Churches at Lund, Sweden, in 1952.

In his *Varieties of Protestantism,* Westminster, John B. Cobb, Jr., rightly describes his subject matter by other schema than that of denominational boundaries. His book, which appeared too late to be used in the writing of the present work, suggests four main types of Protestantism which in turn are divided into a total of nine sub-types. The book should be used to supplement the material contained in the present chapter. It also has helpful, annotated bibliographical suggestions.

3. The authoritative collection of Lutheran doctrinal statements is *The Book of Concord* (1580). The most up-to-date edition is Tappert, ed., Muhlenberg Press. It includes the Augsburg Confession of 1530 (often called the "Confessio Augustana"), written by Philip Melanchthon, a contemporary of Luther's; Melanchthon's long commentary on the Augsburg Confession, usually called "The Apology"; the Smalcald Articles of 1537, written by Luther; Luther's Shorter and Longer Catechisms (1529); and

the Formula of Concord (1577), a compendium of Lutheran theology written in the light of heretical tendencies in Lutheranism after Luther's death.

Luther's "Shorter Catechism" is probably the best brief introduction to Lutheran faith, and it has always stood in high repute within Lutheranism. The most easily available collection of Luther's writings in English is *Works of Martin Luther,* Muhlenberg, 6 vols. A large definitive English edition of Luther's writings is in process of publication by Concordia, under the editorship of Professor Jaroslav Pelikan.

The chapter on the Lutheran Church in Molland, *op. cit.,* is particularly good. See Gustav Aulen, *The Faith of the Christian Church,* Muhlenberg, for a good statement of twentieth-century, "ecumenical" Lutheran theology.

4. The chief confessional statements of the Reformed tradition can be found in Schaff, *op. cit.,* Vol. III. The most important of these are the Scots Confession (1560), the Heidelberg Catechism (1563), the Second Helvetic Confession (1566), and the Westminster Confession (1647). A number of the Reformed catechisms are freshly translated in T. F. Torrance, *The School of Faith,* Harpers.

The most influential single statement of the Reformed faith, indeed of the entire Reformation, is John Calvin, *The Institutes of the Christian Religion,* 2 vols., Library of Christian Classics, Westminster. For a full history see J. T. McNeill, *The History and Character of Calvinism,* Oxford Univ. Press.

5. Molland, *op. cit.,* Chapter VI, is a helpful brief introduction to Anglicanism, and has been carefully edited by Professor Turner of Durham. See also S. C. Neill, *Anglicanism,* Penguin.

However, the best introduction to the ethos of Anglicanism is surely *The Book of Common Prayer,* which also contains the Thirty-nine Articles, a statement of belief enacted as law in 1571. See further Massey Shepherd, *The Oxford American Prayer Book Commentary,* Oxford Univ. Press, and Bicknell, *A Theological Introduction to the Thirty-nine Articles of the Church of England,* Longmans, Green.

6. On the over-all movements see Horton Davies, *The English Free Churches,* Oxford Univ. Press. Brief articles on the various denominations, with bibliographical suggestions, are found in *A Handbook of Christian Theology,* Living Age.

7. A good treatment of Puritanism is Haller, *The Rise of Puritanism,* Columbia. The most enduring statements of the Puritan ethos are probably the writings of John Bunyan (1628–88); see particularly *Pilgrim's Progress* and *Grace Abounding to the Chief of Sinners,* both of which have gone through many editions.

8. On Congregationalism, see Douglas Horton, *Congregationalism,* Independent Press, and Daniel Jenkins, *Congregationalism: A Restatement,* Harpers. On the Baptists see R. S. Torbet, *A History of the Baptists,* Judson, and E. A. Payne, *The Fellowship of Believers: Baptist Thought and Practice Yesterday and Today,* Kingsgate Press.

9. The best documents for understanding the Quaker testimony are probably the personal narratives of the two leading Quakers, *The Journal of George Fox,* Everyman, Dent, and *The Journal of John Woolman,* Gummere, ed., Macmillan. A readable introduction to Quakerism is Rufus Jones, *The Faith and Practice of the Quakers,* Methuen. The only substantial "theology" produced by Quakerism is the *Apology* of Robert Barclay (1648–90), which shows the Calvinist influence at work in early Quakerism. A brief history is Russell, *The History of Quakerism,* Macmillan.

10. A convenient edition of Wesley's important writings is *The Works of John Wesley,* 14 vols., Zondervan. See also *A Compend of Wesley's Theology,* Burtner and Childs, eds., Abingdon. On Methodism itself see W. K. Anderson, *Methodism,* Methodist Publishing House, H. Carter, *The Methodist Heritage,* Epworth, and H. Bett, *The Spirit of Methodism,* Epworth.

11. See W. E. Garrison and A. T. DeGroot, *The Disciples of Christ,* Christian Board of Publication, and O. R. Whitley, *A Sociological Study of the Disciples of Christ,* Bethany.

12. The definitive historical study of the sect type is F. Littell, *The Anabaptist View of the Church,* Starr King. See also R. Bainton, *The Travail of Religious Liberty,* Westminster; E. Troeltsch, *The Social Teachings of the Christian Churches,* Macmillan; and R. Jones, *Spiritual Reformers of the 16th and 17th Centuries,* Beacon.

On the contemporary sect groups see the writings of Marcus Bach, *They Have Found a Faith, Report to Protestants, Faith of My Friends,* Bobbs-Merrill; Braden, *These Also Believe,* Macmillan; and E. T. Clark, *The Small Sects in America,* Cokesbury.

The description of the main Protestant groups in Flew and Davies, eds., *The Catholicity of Protestantism,* Muhlenberg, has no reference to the sect groups, and in the recent *Handbook of Christian Theology,* the word "sect" is not included. On the other hand, J. S. Whale, in *The Protestant Tradition,* devotes more space to the sects than to Calvinism.

13. Carnell, *The Case for Orthodox Theology,* Westminster, is a good treatment of an "orthodox" faith that disassociates itself from the extremes of fundamentalism. See also his trenchant criticism of "Fundamentalism" in *A Handbook of Christian Theology,* and Carl F. H. Henry, *Evangelical Responsibility in Contemporary Theology,* Eerdmans.

14. A critique of this position is implicit in Chapter 1 above, and also in Chapters 6 and 10 below.

15. A statement of liberalism re-examining itself is Van Dusen and Roberts, eds., *Liberal Theology: An Appraisal,* Scribners. A persuasive contemporary statement is DeWolf, *The Case for Theology in Liberal Perspective,* Westminster. Both DeWolf and Daniel D. Williams, *God's Grace and Man's Hope,* Harpers, take account of the impact of "neo-orthodox" thought in the refashioning of the liberal position. Shifts in the liberal position may be noted by reading the successive volumes of Walter Marshall Horton, one of the most sensitive interpreters of the current scene. The clearest treat-

ment of the theme of the "social gospel" is found in the writings of Walter Rauschenbusch; see *A Theology for the Social Gospel,* Macmillan.

16. Phyllis McGinley, *Times Three,* Viking, pp. 134–5.

17. H. Richard Niebuhr, *The Kingdom of God in America,* Shoe String Press, p. 193.

18. The foremost American exponent of this position is Reinhold Niebuhr. *Beyond Tragedy,* Scribners, is still a good introduction to his thought. His most important theological work is *The Nature and Destiny of Man,* Scribners, but see also, *Faith and History,* Scribners, and *The Self and the Dramas of History,* Scribners.

The most significant Continental representatives of the position are Karl Barth, *Church Dogmatics,* Scribners, 12 "part-volumes" so far, and Emil Brunner, *Dogmatics,* Vols. 1 and 2, Westminster. To group these men together indicates the danger of theological pigeonholes, for each would have differences with the others.

Paul Tillich does not fit into any categorization, being a kind of Protestant theologian *sui generis.* See his *Systematic Theology,* Univ. of Chicago Press, 2 vols., *The Protestant Era,* Univ. of Chicago Press, *Theology of Culture,* Oxford Univ. Press, and an important book of sermons, *The Shaking of the Foundations,* Scribners.

Rudolf Bultmann is a left-wing representative of this position, although he has pushed the implications of Biblical criticism further than most of his contemporaries. See Chapter 6 below, note 14.

19. See D. M. Baillie, *God Was in Christ,* Scribners, pp. 109–10.

20. The best statement of an "ecumenical theology," pointing out both the areas of agreement and the areas of remaining disagreement, is W. M. Horton, *Christian Theology: An Ecumenical Approach,* rev. ed., Harpers, which contains an excellent bibliography. D. D. Williams, *What Present-Day Theologians Are Thinking,* Harpers, rev. ed., is the best survey of the trends discussed in the present chapter. On a less advanced level, W. Hordern, *A Layman's Guide to Protestant Theology,* Macmillan, gives synopses of differing schools of thought within Protestantism.

21. Literature about the ecumenical movement is legion. The definitive history, with a huge bibliography, is Rouse and Neill, *A History of the Ecumenical Movement 1517–1948,* Westminster. The basic primary documents are collected in G. K. A. Bell, *Documents on Christian Unity,* Oxford Univ. Press, 4 vols. J. T. McNeill, *Unitive Protestantism,* Abingdon, relates ecumenical concern to the Reformation, A. C. Outler, *The Christian Tradition and the Unity We Seek,* Oxford Univ. Press, assesses where the ecumenical movement now is and what the next steps must be.

Brief treatments are Bell, *The Kingship of Christ,* Penguin; Neill, *Toward Church Union 1937–1952,* S. C. M. Press; and Van Dusen, *World Christianity,* Abingdon.

Full Roman Catholic appraisals are given in Leeming, *The Churches and the Church,* Newman, and Villain, *Introduction à l'œcuménisme,* Casterman.

22. 't Hooft, "Ecumenism" in *A Handbook of Christian Theology,* p. 90. See also Rouse and Neill, *op. cit.*

23. Morrison, *The Unfinished Reformation,* Harpers, pp. 23–4.

24. The South India experiment is a particularly important one since it united churches possessing all three historic types of polity — episcopal, presbyterial, and congregational. For a full treatment of the issues, see Newbigin, *The Reunion of the Church,* rev. ed., S. C. M. Press.

25. This theme will be pursued more fully in Chapter 17 below.

26. 't Hooft, in *A Handbook of Christian Theology,* p. 95.

CHAPTER 4. THE SPIRIT OF PROTESTANTISM

1. See Oscar Cullmann, *The Earliest Christian Confessions,* Lutterworth.

2. Outler, *The Christian Tradition and the Unity We Seek,* Oxford Univ. Press, p. 141.

3. Cited in Whale, *The Protestant Tradition,* p. 307.

4. Butterfield, *Christianity and History,* Bell, p. 146.

5. See Tillich, *The Protestant Era,* especially Chapter XI, "The Protestant Principle and the Proletarian Situation."

6. *Ibid.,* p. 163.

7. The background of this declaration is described by Karl Barth (who was largely responsible for its composition) in *Church Dogmatics,* II, 1, pp. 172–8. Barth also cites it at the beginning of Vol. IV, 3, first half, as the basis for his treatment of ethics.

8. This seems to be the background of the situation Paul is discussing in 1 Cor. 12:3, when he writes, "Therefore I want you to understand that no one speaking by the Spirit of God ever says 'Jesus be cursed!' and no one can say 'Jesus is Lord' except by the Holy Spirit."

It is unfortunately much easier to denounce false gods than to say in specific terms what it means to follow the true God. H. Richard Niebuhr has some trenchant comments on this problem in *The Kingdom of God in America,* pp. 30–33.

9. See Ferm, ed., *The Protestant Credo,* Philosophical Library, p. 116.

10. In his *Retractiones.* For comments on this problem see 't Hooft, *The Renewal of the Church,* Westminster, one of the most important books on the subject under discussion.

11. On this point see further Chapter 16 below.

12. In Ferm, ed., *op. cit.,* p. 136.

13. Ellul, "Protestantisme français," cited in 't Hooft, *op. cit.,* p. 84.

INTRODUCTORY NOTE TO PART TWO

1. The following "one-volume systematic theologies" give compact statements of Protestant theology: Aulen, *The Faith of the Christian Church,*

Muhlenberg; L. H. DeWolf, *A Theology of the Living Church,* Harpers; G. W. Forell, *The Protestant Faith,* Prentice-Hall; W. M. Horton, *Christian Theology: An Ecumenical Approach,* Harpers; J. M. Shaw, *Christian Doctrine, A One Volume Outline,* Philosophical Library; J. S. Whale, *Christian Doctrine,* Cambridge Univ. Press.

The most important historical statements of Protestant theology have been Calvin, *Institutes of the Christian Religion,* Westminster, and F. D. E. Schleiermacher, *The Christian Faith,* T. & T. Clark. These two treatments represent opposite "poles" in the field of theological forces.

A number of contemporary attempts to restate the Protestant faith are now in progress. See the references to the writings of Barth, Brunner, and Tillich in note 18, Chapter 3 above.

CHAPTER 5.

THE CENTRALITY OF GRACE AND THE LIFE OF FAITH

1. The most helpful over-all work on the doctrine of grace is Whitley, ed., *The Doctrine of Grace,* S. C. M. Press, a symposium of historical and systematic studies. On the Biblical materials see Snaith, *The Distinctive Ideas of the Old Testament,* Westminster, and Moffatt, *Grace in the New Testament,* Hodder & Stoughton. See also Torrance, *The Doctrine of Grace in the Apostolic Fathers,* Oliver and Boyd, and Watson, *The Concept of Grace,* Epworth.

2. See further Moffatt, *Love in the New Testament,* Ray Long and Richard R. Smith, Inc.; Nygren, *Agape and Eros,* Westminster; D'Arcy, *The Mind and Heart of Love,* Holt; De Rougemont, *Love in the Western World,* Harcourt, Brace and Co.; Tillich, *Love, Power, and Justice,* Oxford Univ. Press.

3. See further the discussion in Snaith, *op. cit.,* Chapter 5, "The Covenant Love of God."

4. See the valuable analysis of this verse in Niebuhr, *The Nature and Destiny of Man,* vol. 2, to which the present chapter is much indebted.

5. Outler, *The Christian Tradition and the Unity We Seek,* Oxford Univ. Press, pp. 128–9.

6. On this point Kierkegaard, *Training in Christianity,* Princeton Univ. Press, is exciting reading. Kierkegaard makes the point that only the one who has really gone through the possibility of offense at the notion that "God should become a carpenter's son," can truly accept revelation on the terms in which God offers it.

7. Cited in Lindsay, *History of the Reformation,* Scribners, Vol. 1, pp. 429–45. The full context can be found in the Erlangen edition of *Luther's Works,* xxii, 15, and xv, 540.

8. On the fascinating story of Luther's pilgrimage, see Bainton, *Here I Stand,* Abingdon; Rupp, *Luther's Progress to the Diet of Worms,* S. C. M. Press; and Rupp, *The Righteousness of God,* Hodder & Stoughton.

There is a mistaken notion that "justification by faith" is a peculiarly Lutheran doctrine. In reality, it is part of the conviction of any portion of Christendom that takes the New Testament seriously. See Calvin's treatment in *Institutes,* Book III, Chapter XI, and Article XI of the Anglican Thirty-nine Articles, a portion of which reads:

"We are accounted righteous before God, only for the merit of our Lord and Savior Jesus Christ by Faith, and not for our own works or deservings. Wherefore, that we are justified by faith only is a most wholesome doctrine . . ."

9. Cyprian, an early church father, had put it this way: "God must be appeased by our satisfaction . . . The flame of punishment is quenched by alms and righteous works . . . Whatever defilement we may contract we may wash away with almsgiving." (*de Lapsis, xviii; de Opere et Eleemosynis,* ii, 1; cited in Whale, *The Protestant Tradition,* p. 60.)

10. Such statements obviously imply some sort of doctrine of predestination. See the treatment in Chapter 7 below.

11. The clearest treatment of this "paradox of grace" is contained in D. M. Baillie, *God Was in Christ,* Scribners, pp. 106–18.

12. W. H. Auden, "For the Time Being," in *Collected Poems,* Random House, p. 459.

13. See Bonhoeffer's disturbing essay, "Cheap Grace" in *The Cost of Discipleship,* Macmillan. A full treatment of Bonhoeffer's theology is contained in Godsey, *The Theology of Dietrich Bonhoeffer,* Westminster.

14. Luther, "Treatise on Christian Liberty," *Works of Martin Luther,* Muhlenberg, Vol. 2, p. 331.

15. Luther, Weimarer Ausgabe, Vol. 7, p. 35, 25ff., cited in Nygren, *Agape and Eros,* Part II, Vol. II, p. 509.

16. Augustine, *Serm.* (*de Script. Nov. Test.*) CXLI:IV, 4. See also Przywara, *An Augustine Synthesis,* Harpers, p. 198. The quotation concludes H. Richard Niebuhr's *The Meaning of Revelation,* Macmillan, p. 191, and I am indebted to him for the documentation cited above.

CHAPTER 6. THE AUTHORITY OF SCRIPTURE

1. The problem of the interpretation of Scripture is an area where Protestant pens have always been active. A brief summary, with bibliography, is Grant, *The Bible in the Church,* Macmillan. J. K. S. Reid, *The Authority of Scripture,* Harpers, is a full and well-documented treatment of various Protestant positions since the Reformation, and also has a chapter on Roman Catholic interpretation. The introductory essays in Volume One of *The Interpreter's Bible,* Abingdon, are invaluable. A brief appraisal of a contemporary Protestant attitude to Scripture is given in C. H. Dodd, *The Bible Today,* Cambridge Univ. Press.

Within the present volume, further attention is given to the interpretation and authority of Scripture in Chapters 2, 10, 14, and 17, and the present chapter needs to be supplemented by reference to these chapters.

2. For a summary of the content of the early Christian preaching see C. H. Dodd, *The Apostolic Preaching and Its Development,* Hodder & Stoughton.

3. For examples of "scriptures" that were rejected from the New Testament canon, see M. R. James, *The Apocryphal New Testament,* Oxford Univ. Press. A readable treatment of problems connected with the canon is contained in Filson, *Which Books Belong in the Bible?* Westminster. The Roman Catholic canon is larger than the Protestant canon because it includes books found in the Greek translation of the Old Testament, the Septuagint. These books are usually referred to as "the Apocrypha."

4. See Aquinas, *Summa Theologica,* I, 1, 10.

5. Examples of this tendency are given in Dodd, *The Parables of the Kingdom,* pp. 11–12, who gives a long quotation from Augustine, and in de Lubac, *Catholicism,* Sheed & Ward, pp. 99–100, who gives an almost identical example from Origen.

6. On the relationship of Scripture and tradition see further Chapters 13, 14, and 17 below.

7. Quenstedt, *Theol. did-pol.,* 1:72, cited in Reid, *op. cit.,* p. 85.

8. See the fuller discussion of this point in Chapters 1 and 3 above.

9. The objection can, of course, be stated from other points of view as well, such as the immorality of many of the Old Testament stories. The "scientific" difficulty merely illustrates the problem.

10. It should be clear that for the rest of the chapter we are engaging in an act of radical discrimination, taking account only of those aspects of the Reformers' thought that speak to us today. The venture is justified on the ground that we have already described the *cul de sac* into which some of their less attractive notions led them.

11. *Works of Martin Luther,* Vol. VI, p. 478. Luther could be as rigid as the next man in his use of Scripture, particularly when it suited his polemical needs. But this does not invalidate his principle. It simply validates his humanness.

12. Reid, *op. cit.,* p. 28.

13. de Dietrich, *God's Unfolding Purpose,* Westminster, pp. 21–2. The quotation is also relevant to the discussion of "Scriptural docetism" on p. 71 above.

14. The basic statement of Bultmann's position is contained in his essay in Bartsch, ed., *Kerygma and Myth,* S.P.C.K. A readable and commendably brief statement of his concern is Bultmann, *Jesus Christ and Mythology,* Scribners. A treatment of the implications of Bultmann's position is given in Henderson, *Myth in the New Testament,* Regnery.

15. It is interesting that Biblical criticism, which first seemed to suggest that Scripture was made up of disparate and irreconcilable writings, has in recent years moved in the direction of affirming that there is an underlying unity to the message of the Old and New Testaments.

16. Calvin, *Institutes,* I, vii, iv–v. The full title of the chapter from which the quotation is taken is "The Testimony of the Spirit Necessary to

Confirm the Scripture, in Order to the Complete Establishment of Its Authority."

For vivid examples of how this principle has come alive in recent times, see Gollwitzer, Kuhn, Schneider, eds., *Dying We Live,* Fontana, a collection of letters from Christians condemned to death for their opposition to Hitler.

17. The best way to see this at work is to examine the political and sociological writings of Dr. Niebuhr, in which he brings the insights of Biblical faith to bear on the pressing issues of the moment. See *Christianity and Power Politics,* Scribners; *Christian Realism and Political Problems,* Scribners; *The Structure of Nations and Empires,* Scribners; and *Essays in Applied Christianity,* Meridian.

18. Barth, *Church Dogmatics,* I, 2, Scribners, p. 709, italics added.

19. *Ibid.,* p. 709.

CHAPTER 7.

THE SOVEREIGNTY OF GOD — AND SOME IMPLICATIONS

1. Among the many books dealing with election and predestination, see particularly: Rowley, *The Biblical Doctrine of Election,* Lutterworth, on the Biblical material; Heppe, *Reformed Dogmatics,* Allen & Unwin, on the post-Reformation developments; and Schaff, *Creeds of Christendom,* Vol. III, on the place of the doctrine in Reformation confessions.

Hunter, *The Teaching of Calvin,* Clarke, and Neisel, *The Theology of Calvin,* Westminster, are interpretations of the place of the doctrine in Calvin's teaching, while John Oman, *Grace and Personality,* Cambridge Univ. Press, is an attempt to move beyond the Augustinian notion of "irresistible grace."

Brunner discusses the doctrine in *Dogmatics,* Vol. I, Chapters 22–23, and Barth treats it in *Church Dogmatics,* II, 2, pp. 3–506. Berkouwer, *Divine Election,* Eerdmans, is a conservative treatment.

2. A paraphrase of Psalm 62. See the full text in the *Presbyterian Hymnal,* #86.

3. Kierkegaard has a wonderful treatment of the related fact that the greatest act of omnipotence is the ability to limit itself, in *Journals,* Oxford Univ. Press, pp. 180–81 (¶ 616).

4. See also Kierkegaard's parable of the king and the maiden, in *Philosophical Fragments,* Princeton Univ. Press, pp. 19–27, for an illustration of this point.

5. Arnold Toynbee, *An Historian's View of Religion,* Oxford Univ. Press, takes vigorous exception to the idea of a "chosen people." Religion, he feels, must purge itself of the kind of exclusiveness that assumes that only a tiny minority is favored by God.

6. See for example Aquinas, *Summa Contra Gentiles,* Book III, clxiv.

7. Williams, *The Descent of the Dove,* Faber and Faber, p. 191.

8. The Reformers themselves were quite conscious of the fact that belief in election need not lead to inactivism. Calvin's attitude is typical:

"The eternal decrees of God form no impediment to our providing for ourselves, and disposing all our concerns in subservience to his will. The reason of this is manifest. For he who has fixed the limits of our life, has also intrusted us with the care of it; has furnished us with means and supplies for its preservation; has also made us provident of dangers; and, that they may not oppress us unawares, has furnished us with cautions and remedies. Now, it is evident what is our duty. If God has committed to us the preservation of our life, we should preserve it; if he offers supplies, we should use them; if he furnishes us remedies, we ought not to neglect them." (*Institutes,* I, xvii, iv.)

9. In what follows, readers of Barth's *Church Dogmatics,* II, 2, pp. 3–506, will recognize that I, too, have read those pages. But I am not following them slavishly, nor am I suggesting that they represent the only "right" way to understand the matter. But they surely represent one of the most creative pieces of theological reconstruction on the contemporary scene.

10. Barth points out, *op. cit.,* that Reformed dogmatics has suffered by putting its understanding of predestination in the context of *providence* (i.e. general truths about God's relation to the whole world) rather than in the context of *election* (i.e. the specific, central concern of God with those whom he has called). He argues persuasively that Christian faith always moves from the particular to the general, never the other way around.

11. Modern Protestants are often chary of this kind of talk, because it sounds like a "substitutionary doctrine of the atonement," which in one of its cruder forms they have long since rejected. But there is no way of avoiding the notion that Christ "stands in our place" without avoiding the New Testament. There we discover that God in Christ does not only condemn, but that he takes upon himself the burden of the condemnation.

12. What follows was suggested by an arresting article by Pierre Maury, "Election et foi," in *Foi et vie,* May 1956.

13. For examples of the way this was worked out, see Heppe, *Reformed Dogmatics,* Allen & Unwin, esp. Chapter VII, "The Decrees of God," and Chapter VIII, "Predestination."

14. See Brunner, *The Christian Doctrine of God, Dogmatics,* Vol. I, Westminster, Chapters 22–23, and also Brunner, *Eternal Hope,* Westminster.

15. Brunner, *The Christian Doctrine of God,* p. 337.

16. See Farmer, *God and Man,* Nisbet, pp. 143–51, and *The World and God,* Nisbet, pp. 253–9.

CHAPTER 8. THE PRIESTHOOD OF ALL BELIEVERS

1. The extent to which this belief can be carried is indicated in a pastoral letter from a Roman Catholic bishop:

"[Christ] has set priests in his place so that they may repeat the same sacrifice which he offered. To them he has transferred power over his sacred humanity; to them he has given the same power over his body. The Catholic priest not only can make him present on the altar and enclose him in the Tabernacle — to take him again and dispense him to the faithful; but the priest can also offer him, the incarnate Son of God the Father, as an unbloody sacrifice. Christ, the only-begotten Son of God the Father, through whom heaven and earth were made, who sustains the universe — he is here at the disposal of the Catholic priest." (Johannes Katschtaler, in Mirbst, *Quellen zur Geschichte des Papsttums,* 4th ed., pp. 297–9; cited in Whale, *The Protestant Tradition,* p. 262.)

2. Helpful Protestant treatments of the matter are: T. F. Torrance, *Royal Priesthood,* Oliver & Boyd; T. W. Manson, *Ministry and Priesthood: Christ's and Ours,* John Knox Press; T. W. Manson, *The Church's Ministry,* Westminster; and Norman Pittenger, *The Church, the Ministry and Reunion,* Seabury Press. Come, *Agents of Reconciliation,* Westminster, is one of the most radical (and exciting) attempts to re-think the clergy-laity relationship.

3. On this point, see particularly Torrance, *op. cit.,* Chapter I.

4. Manson, *Ministry and Priesthood,* p. 64.

5. See further concerning this interpretation of "the priesthood of all believers," J. T. McNeill, in Ferm, ed., *The Protestant Credo,* Philosophical Library, p. 111, and Wilhelm Pauck, *The Heritage of the Reformation,* Beacon Press, p. 5. Luther's fullest treatments of the matter are found in the "Treatise on Good Works," and the "Treatise on Christian Liberty," in *Works of Martin Luther,* Muhlenberg, Vols. I and II.

There is a somewhat similar stress in contemporary Roman Catholicism, where fresh attention is being given to the place of the laity in the life of the church. Much of what Roman Catholics mean by "the apostolate of the laity" would correspond to much of what Protestants mean by "the priesthood of all believers." But in Roman Catholic thought, the place of the laity is always set against the background of a cleavage between priest and layman which is more fundamental than anything to be found in Protestantism. See further the encyclical of Pius X, *Vehementer vos.*

6. The best attempts to describe the present Protestant ecumenical concensus on the matter are J. Robert Nelson, *The Realm of Redemption,* Epworth, and Claude Welch, *The Reality of the Church,* Scribners. Varied treatments in contemporary Protestantism are Brunner, *The Misunderstanding of the Church,* Westminster; Newbigin, *The Household of God,* Friendship Press; H. R. Niebuhr, *The Purpose of the Church and Its Ministry,* Harpers; Nygren, *Christ and His Church,* Westminster.

For a Protestant, de Lubac, *The Splendor of the Church,* Sheed & Ward, is one of the best contemporary treatments of a Roman Catholic interpretation.

7. This assertion is important vis-à-vis Roman Catholicism, as will be clear in Chapter 13 below. A Roman Catholic catechism answers the ques-

tion, "Who is the Head of the Catholic Church?" quite unambiguously: "The Head of the Catholic Church is Jesus Christ our Lord." But in Catholic terms to give allegiance to that Lord is also to give allegiance to his vicar on earth, the Bishop of Rome.

The Protestant does not see how one can do both things. To the Protestant it cannot but appear that instead of saying *ubi Christus ibi ecclesia,* Roman Catholicism is saying *ubi Petrus ibi ecclesia,* "where Peter (or one of his successors) is, there is the church."

8. See, for example, the following statements from varying traditions:

Episcopalian: "The visible Church of Christ is a congregation of faithful men, in which the pure Word of God is preached, and the sacraments be duly administered according to Christ's ordinance, in all those things that of necessity are requisite to the same." (Article xix of the Thirty-nine Articles.)

Lutheran: "[The Church is] a congregation of the saints in which the gospel is purely taught and the sacraments rightly administered." (Article 7 of the Augsburg Confession.)

Reformed: "Wherever we find the word of God purely preached *and heard,* and the sacraments administered according to the institution of Christ, there, it is not to be doubted, is a Church of God." (Calvin, *Institutes,* IV, I, ix. Calvin, it will be noted, makes particular place for the congregation, as the italicized words show.)

9. C. C. Morrison, "The Church is a Society of Sinners," *Presbyterian Life,* March 2, 1957, p. 2.

10. The four "marks" are arrived at by conflating the assertions made about the church in the Apostles' and Nicene Creeds. See the illuminating discussion in Pelikan, *The Riddle of Roman Catholicism,* Abingdon, Chapter XII, of Roman Catholic and Protestant agreements and divergences over these "marks."

11. See the further treatment of this theme in Chapter 17 below.

12. The most important contemporary attempt to do this is Jenkins, *The Nature of Catholicity,* Faber and Faber.

13. See the full discussion of this in Kraemer, *The Theology of the Laity,* Westminster, the most important book on the whole problem.

14. See Kraemer, *op. cit.,* esp. pp. 136ff.

15. See Pauck, "The Ministry in the Time of the Continental Reformation," in Williams and Niebuhr, *The Ministry in Historical Perspective,* Harpers. The entire symposium is valuable for anyone grappling with the problem of the ministry in Protestant thought.

16. Cited in Rouse and Neill, *A History of the Ecumenical Movement,* Westminster, p. 478.

17. See the remarkable summary by T. W. Manson, in *The Church's Ministry,* Westminster, pp. 100–101.

18. See further Alexander Miller, *Christian Faith and My Job,* Association Press.

CHAPTER 9. THE CALLING OF THE CHRISTIAN MAN

1. See the elaboration of this image in Whale, *The Protestant Tradition,* p. 103.

2. Cited in Forrester, *Christian Vocation,* Scribners, and in Wolff, *Reformation Writings of Martin Luther,* Lutterworth, p. 276.

3. Cecil Alexander (1823–95), "All things bright and beautiful."

4. See the recent writings describing the plight of the corporation man well up the ladder of success, such as Reisman, *The Lonely Crowd,* Anchor Books; Mills, *Power Elite,* Oxford Univ. Press; Spectorsky, *The Exurbanites,* Lippincott; Whyte, *The Organization Man,* Anchor Books.

5. There is increasing material in this field. A pioneer work was Calhoun, *God and the Common Life,* Scribners. The fullest bibliography is contained in Nelson, ed., *Work and Vocation,* Harpers. A. Miller, *Christian Faith and My Job,* Association Press, is a popular treatment. A. Richardson, *The Biblical Doctrine of Work,* Allenson, presents some of the relevant material from Scripture.

6. In America there have been a few national conferences on vocation, and there are occasional meetings of highly trained leaders, but there has been relatively little concerted effort in this direction across the life of the church. There is an interesting report of a series of meetings between doctors and theologians in Great Britain, in Jenkins, *The Doctor's Profession,* S. C. M. Press.

7. See F. N. Littell, *The German Phoenix,* Doubleday, for an account of the rise of the Evangelical Academies.

8. The quotations are found in W. H. Auden, *Collected Poems,* Random House. An interesting contrast can be found in the works of T. S. Eliot, an Anglo-Catholic. In Eliot's earliest play, *The Family Reunion,* Harry expiates a sense of guilt by following the ascetic path of renunciation. In a later play, *The Cocktail Party,* Eliot presents two alternative ways of coping with the problem. Celia chooses the way of renunciation, goes to Africa as a missionary and is crucified on an anthill by the natives. The Chamberlaynes remain in their humdrum and unspectacular marriage, trying within the situation to work out a tolerable life together. It is not presented in very appealing terms: "making the best of a bad job" is the most they can hope for. The difference between this grudging concession and the affirmative tone of Auden's verse could hardly be greater.

CHAPTER 10. LOVING GOD WITH THE MIND

1. Dorothy Sayers has said all that needs to be said about the presumed dullness of theology in *Creed or Chaos,* Methuen.

2. More and more Protestant books are being directed at laymen. Association Press has issued a great number of "Reflection Books," short paper-

backs on a variety of topics. Under the editorship of Stephen Neill it has also sponsored "World Christian Books," slightly larger works written for use throughout the entire Christian world. Westminster Press has brought out the Layman's Theological Library, a series of 12 books of 96 pages each, designed to present the fullness of Protestant faith in layman's terms. More advanced than any of these is the Christian Faith Series, published by Doubleday under the editorship of Reinhold Niebuhr.

Laymen should not be afraid to turn to the theologians themselves, and the following are good places to begin, though not to end: Niebuhr, *Beyond Tragedy,* and *Discerning the Signs of the Times,* Scribners; Tillich, *The Shaking of the Foundations,* Scribners; Brunner, *Our Faith,* Scribners; Barth, *The Faith of the Church,* Meridian.

3. These are collected in Schaff, *Creeds of Christendom,* Vol. III.

4. This point is emphasized in another connection in Chapter 4 above.

5. There is a fuller development by the author of the implications of Protestant faith for education in "The Reformed Tradition and Higher Education," *The Christian Scholar,* Vol. XII, No. 1, March 1948, pp. 21–40.

6. The relevant documents can be found in Perry Miller, *The American Puritans,* Anchor Books.

7. For a full understanding of the implications of this, the reader is asked to recall the discussion of the authority of the Bible in Chapter 6 above.

8. We are actually talking here about the problem of "natural theology," a problem that the writings of Karl Barth have brought to the forefront of contemporary discussion. A good statement of the first view described above can be found in DeWolf, *The Case for Theology in Liberal Perspective,* Westminster, and also in his *A Theology of the Living Church,* Harpers. The most vigorous exposition of the second view is found in Barth, most fully in *Church Dogmatics,* II, 1, pp. 63–254, and more briefly in *The Knowledge of God and the Service of God,* Scribners, Chapter 1.

The issue has obvious ramifications for an understanding of the relationship of Christianity to other religions; for two extremes, see Hocking, *Living Religions and a World Faith,* Macmillan, and Kraemer, *The Christian Message to the Non-Christian World,* Harpers.

It is also relevant to an understanding of the relationship between Roman Catholic and Protestant theology. The Roman Catholic position, normatively stated by Aquinas, has a generous place for "natural theology" as a prelude to the specific revelation of God in Jesus Christ, as the opening sections of both the *Summa Theologica* and *Summa Contra Gentiles* make clear. The Vatican Council of 1869–70 anathematized those who deny the truth of natural theology (Denzinger, *Enchiridion Symbolorum,* para. 1806; cited in Clarkson, ed., *The Church Teaches,* Herder Book Co., p. 28).

9. Luther, *A Commentary on St. Paul's Epistle to the Galatians,* p. 16.

10. Theology as a "science" is discussed by Protestant theologians otherwise as far apart as Alan Richardson (*Christian Apologetics,* Harpers) and Karl Barth (*Church Dogmatics,* I, 1), though it is not to be assumed

that they mean the same thing. A fuller treatment of the whole question will be available with the publication of Professor Torrance's Hewitt Lectures.

11. Calvin, *Institutes,* IV, i, xii. It should be noted that there are few points over which hyper-Calvinists have been so divided as the very issue which their master here cites as a non-essential one.

12. Even if Calvin's point be conceded, there is still the problem of determining which points of faith are essential, and which non-essential. See further Chapter 14 below.

13. One of the fullest treatments of the problem of doubt is MacGregor, *Christian Doubt,* Longmans. See also the following: Allport, *The Individual and His Religion,* Macmillan, Chapter 5–6; J. Baillie, *Our Knowledge of God,* Scribners, pp. 54ff.; H. H. Farmer, *Towards Belief in God,* Scribners, Chapters 1–3; K. Hamilton, *The Protestant Way,* Essential Books, Chapter 5; and C. Michalson, *Faith for Personal Crises,* Scribners, Chapter IV.

One of the best treatments in classical Protestant theology is in Calvin, *Institutes,* III, ii, xvii–xxi. The way in which the fire of doubt moulds the crucible of faith is sketched with disarming forthrightness by John Bunyan in *Grace Abounding to the Chief of Sinners,* where assurance after assurance is destroyed until finally Bunyan is left trusting in God alone, rather than in himself or his own reasons for believing.

CHAPTER 11. THE WORSHIP OF GOD

1. The influence of Martin Buber (1878–) on Protestant theology has been widespread, particularly among such thinkers as Emil Brunner and Reinhold Niebuhr. A good introduction to Buber's thought is Diamond, *Martin Buber: Jewish Existentialist,* Oxford Univ. Press, which gives special attention to Buber's relationship with Christian thought. See also Herberg, ed., *The Writings of Martin Buber,* Meridian. Buber's most important single work is *I and Thou,* T. &. T. Clark, rev. ed. See also his *Two Types of Faith,* Macmillan, for an account of his own assessment of the relationship of Judaism and Christianity.

2. From the proposed *Directory for Worship,* United Presbyterian Church in the United States of America.

3. In fairness to contemporary Roman Catholicism, which often appears to be under attack when remarks are made about the state of things in medieval Christendom, it should be said that the Liturgical Movement has been attempting to restore to the laity a greater sense of participation in the Mass. This is done not only by efforts to have the Mass said or sung in the vernacular, and by pointing out the inappropriateness of private religious exercises during the celebration, but also by restoring to the people those parts of the liturgy that were originally theirs.

The best organ for keeping abreast of the Liturgical Movement is the monthly magazine *Worship* (formerly *Orate Fratres*), published by The

Liturgical Press, Collegeville, Minnesota. For a Protestant appraisal see Koenker, *The Liturgical Movement in the Roman Catholic Church,* University of Chicago Press.

4. There is a wide literature available on Protestant hymnody. The author has found the writings of Erik Routley especially useful. See particularly his *Hymns and the Faith,* Murray; *Hymns and Human Life,* Murray; *The Music of Christian Hymnody,* Independent Press; *I'll Praise My Maker,* Independent Press; and *Church Music and Theology,* S. C. M. Press. Dr. Routley has the advantage of being both an accomplished musician and a first-rate theologian.

5. Vidler, *Essays in Liberality,* S. C. M. Press, p. 175.

6. Barth-Hamel, *How To Serve God in a Marxist Land,* Association Press, p. 117. After spending a week in Bible study with East Germans in East Berlin, the author can testify that this is in no sense an overstatement.

7. Many readers will feel that this aspect of Protestant life is given less than adequate attention in the present volume. The problem is that to say more than a little is to be called upon to say a very great deal, and that there is no area of Protestant life less susceptible to "description" than the life of individual private prayer.

Those who wish to pursue the matter further are referred to the following: Coburn, *Prayer and Personal Religion,* Westminster, an excellent book with which to start, and to which to return; Buttrick, *Prayer,* Abingdon, one of the fullest treatments; Fosdick, *The Meaning of Prayer,* Association Press, a modern classic. John Baillie, *A Diary of Private Prayer,* Scribners, is a good collection of modern prayers. Coburn, *op. cit.,* has further bibliographical suggestions.

CHAPTER 12.

THE WORSHIP OF GOD (CONTINUED): THE SACRAMENTS

1. On the theology of the sacraments, see Dunkerley and Headlam, eds., *The Ministry and Sacraments,* S. C. M. Press, an ecumenical collection from all the traditions of Christendom. See also the following: O. C. Quick, *The Christian Sacraments,* Scribners (Anglican); D. M. Baillie, *The Theology of the Sacraments,* Scribners (Presbyterian); P. T. Forsyth, *The Church and the Sacraments,* Independent Press (Congregational); R. S. Paul, *The Atonement and the Sacraments,* Abingdon (Congregational). Neville Clark, *Toward a Theology of the Sacraments,* Regnery, is particularly helpful on the Biblical materials.

2. See Calvin, *Institutes,* IV, xvii, xliii–xlvi. An outline of the service is conveniently available in Maxwell, *An Outline of Christian Worship,* Oxford Univ. Press. See also, more fully, Maxwell, *John Knox's Genevan Service Book.*

3. See *The Book of Common Prayer,* pp. 3–20, 67–89; and see Shep-

herd, *The Worship of the Church,* Seabury, on Episcopal worship.

4. Torrance, *Royal Priesthood,* Oliver & Boyd, p. 101.

5. The exception to this statement is the Society of Friends (Quakers), who observe no sacraments at all. Quakers believe that since all places and moments and actions can be holy, no particular ones should be set apart in a way that would deny the holiness possible elsewhere.

6. See, among other references to baptism, "Go ye therefore and make disciples of all nations, baptizing them in the name of the Father and of the Son and of the Holy Spirit . . ." (Matt. 28:19), and with reference to the Lord's Supper, "Do this in remembrance of me" (1 Cor. 11:24).

7. Most Protestants feel that an attempt to increase the number of sacraments beyond the two explicitly ordered by Christ would result in chaos. There would be no limit to the number of experiences in human life that could be "sacramentalized." (At one point in the Middle Ages the number of sacraments had reached twelve.) A Roman Catholic would assert that all seven sacraments have at least implicit warrant in Jesus' teaching, and that the fear is therefore groundless.

Once again, the issue hinges on Biblical interpretation, and Roman Catholic and Protestant exegetes seem hopelessly far apart.

8. This is the element of truth that lies behind the undisciplined charges many Protestants make concerning the affinity of the Roman Catholic sacraments to "magic."

9. This formula is derived from the "great commission" of Christ to the apostles, cited in note 6 above. Scholars differ as to whether or not these words represent the *ipsissima verba* of Jesus himself; at all events, they go back to a very early period in the life of the church.

Those who differ over whether baptism should be administered to infants or only to believers are still agreed that baptism represents the time of active incorporation into the Christian fellowship. The difference is over *when* rather than *whether* this takes place.

The baptism of infants is exceedingly difficult to justify on New Testament grounds, where the evidence overwhelmingly suggests that those who were baptized were "believers." The case for infant baptism must be made, therefore, on theological rather than exegetical grounds.

Karl Barth has created a theological stir by repudiating the idea of infant baptism in *The Teaching of the Church Regarding Baptism,* S. C. M. Press. He has been answered by Oscar Cullmann in *Baptism in the New Testament,* S. C. M. Press. Barth's full-scale treatment of the sacraments will be contained in *Church Dogmatics,* IV, 4, in which the two sacraments will be treated under "ethics," as the beginning and fulfillment of the Christian life.

10. *Liturgie,* Éditions Berger-Levrault, p. 202, my translation.

11. The material that follows has been drawn in part from articles by the author in *Presbyterian Life,* April 3, 1954; *Motive,* April 1956, and one chapter of *The Significance of the Church,* Westminster.

12. It is in terms of what "actually happens" at this moment that some of the greatest divergences of interpretation occur. See Dix, *The Shape of*

the Liturgy, Dacre; Leeming, *Principles of Sacramental Theology,* Newman; Kerr, *The Christian Sacraments,* Westminster; and the references cited in note 1 above for varying interpretations.

13. Calvin, *Institutes,* IV, xvii, 38.

14. This dimension of the communion of saints has been most helpfully communicated by Charles Williams. See *The Descent of the Dove,* and his novels, *Descent into Hell* and *All Hallow's Eve,* all published by Faber and Faber.

CHAPTER 13. PROTESTANTISM AND ROMAN CATHOLICISM

1. The best treatment of the problem by a Protestant is Pelikan, *The Riddle of Roman Catholicism,* Abingdon. From the Roman Catholic side see Tavard, *A Catholic Approach to Protestantism,* Harpers.

Fuller treatments by the author of issues raised in this chapter can be found in Brown and Weigel, *An American Dialogue: A Protestant Looks at Catholicism and a Catholic Looks at Protestantism,* Doubleday, and also in Chapter 3 of Scharper, ed., *American Catholics: A Protestant-Jewish View,* Sheed & Ward, from which much of the material in the present chapter is taken.

2. The best analysis of this problem is Herberg, *Protestant, Catholic, Jew,* Doubleday. A good Roman Catholic appraisal is Ellis, *American Catholicism,* Univ. of Chicago Press. See also the further treatment by the author in Brown and Weigel, *op. cit.,* Chapter 2.

3. For Protestants, the best place to start is surely Adam, *The Spirit of Catholicism,* Macmillan. But see also Martindale, *The Faith of the Catholic Church,* Sheed & Ward, and the illuminating chapter by Charles Donoghue in F. E. Johnson, ed., *Patterns of Faith in America Today,* Harpers. The more "popular" writings of Ronald Knox are also useful to Protestants. See especially *The Mass in Slow Motion,* Sheed & Ward.

4. Some of the best of these are Adam, *One and Holy,* Sheed & Ward; Bouyer, *The Spirit and Forms of Protestantism,* Newman; Tavard, *The Catholic Approach to Protestantism,* Harpers, and *Protestanism,* Hawthorn; and Weigel, *A Catholic Primer on the Ecumenical Movement,* Newman.

5. See Karl Barth's prefatory letter in Küng, *Rechtfertigung,* Johannes Verlag, Einsiedeln, p. 13, where Barth says to Küng, a Catholic, "We are *separated* in the faith . . . but we are separated *in the faith.*"

6. Graham, *Catholicism and the World Today,* McKay, p. 200.

7. See further, Brown and Weigel, *op. cit.,* Chapter 3.

8. Full documentation for such concerns as these is contained in the writings of Paul Blanshard. See particularly his first, and most famous book, *American Freedom and Catholic Power,* Beacon, together with the Catholic rebuttal of O'Neill, *Catholicism and American Freedom,* Harpers.

Unfortunately, the tone of Blanshard's books is so aggressive that many Catholics are willing to dismiss him as a "bigot" without dealing with the substance of his charges. Both Protestants and Roman Catholics should be aware that Blanshard writes from a secularist rather than a Protestant standpoint.

9. There is considerable documentation for this in Nichols, *Democracy and the Churches,* Westminster.

10. Full Protestant documentation of the reality and extent of this debate is provided by Albornoz, *Roman Catholicism and Religious Liberty,* published by the World Council of Churches. This collection and analysis of Roman Catholic materials is indispensable for any full study of the problem. See also the very balanced statement of Protestant hopes and fears about Roman Catholic power in Bennett, *Christians and the State,* Scribners, Chapter 17.

Protestants who still believe that the real intent of Roman Catholicism is to become strong enough to force everyone else to become Roman Catholic, need to ponder the words of Pius XII:

"Though We desire this unceasing prayer to rise to God from the whole Mystical Body in common, that all the straying sheep may hasten to enter the one fold of Jesus Christ, yet We recognize that this must be done of their own free will; for no one believes unless he wills to believe. Hence they are most certainly not genuine Christians who against their will are forced to go into a church, to approach the altar and to receive the Sacraments; for the "faith without which it is impossible to please God" is an entirely free "submission of the intellect and will." Therefore, whenever it happens, despite the constant teaching of this Apostolic See, that anyone is compelled to embrace the Catholic faith against his will, Our sense of duty demands that we condemn the act." (*Mystici Corporis,* para. 101.)

On the Protestant attitude toward religious liberty, see the definitive study by M. Searle Bates, *Religious Liberty: An Enquiry,* Harpers. In a briefer study, Giovanni Miegge lists four minimal conditions for religious liberty: (1) liberty to profess a faith different from that of the majority and to engage in public worship with those who share that faith, (2) assurance that religious profession will not lead to discrimination in other areas of life, (3) full "liberty of witness," i.e. the right to evangelize freely and openly, and (4) a respect by all concerned for the environment in which testimony is to be rendered. (See Miegge, *Religious Liberty,* World Christian Books, Association Press, pp. 90–93.)

11. Documentation for this claim is provided in the next chapter.

12. The following points, and a number of others, are elaborated in the author's contribution to Scharper, ed., *op. cit.,* pp. 112–20.

13. Daniélou, "Holy Scripture: Meeting Place of Christians," *Cross Currents,* Spring 1953, p. 260.

14. Examples of the older treatment are Denifle, *Luther and Lutheranism,* and Grisar, *Luther.* Maritain has unfortunately modeled his treatment of Luther on such research in his *Three Reformers,* Sheed & Ward. The most significant new appraisal, unfortunately not in English, is Lortz, *Die Reformation in Deutschland,* 2 vols. The best example in English of a positive

Roman Catholic appraisal of the Reformation is Bouyer, *The Spirit and Forms of Protestantism,* Newman.

15. Tavard, *The Catholic Approach to Protestantism,* Harpers, describes the gradually changing attitude toward the ecumenical movement in Roman Catholic circles. Leeming, *The Churches and the Church,* Newman, is the fullest Roman Catholic appraisal of Protestant ecumenism. Baum, *That They May Be One,* Newman, is a careful study of all the recent papal pronouncements on Christian unity.

The greatest amount of Roman Catholic ecumenical writing seems to have come out of France. See for example, Aubert, *Problèmes de l'unité chrétienne,* Collection Irenikon; Chavaz, *Catholicisme romain et protestantisme,* Casterman; Thiels, *Histoire doctrinale du mouvement œcuménique,* Louvain, and Villain, *Introduction à l'œcuménisme,* Casterman, and *L'Abbé Paul Couturier,* Casterman, esp. "Troisième Partie," pp. 67–279.

16. Urs von Balthasar, *Karl Barth,* was an early study, and the latest is Henri Bouillard's three-volume exposition and critique, *Karl Barth,* Aubier, Éditions Montaigne. Küng, *op. cit.,* tries to show that Barth's doctrine of justification coincides with what the Council of Trent was *really* trying to say.

17. See Aubert, *La Semaine de prière pour l'unité chrétienne,* Louvain, and both of Villain's books cited above.

18. See Cullmann, *A Message to Catholics and Protestants,* Eerdmans.

19. Niebuhr, "Issues Between Catholics and Protestants at Mid-Century," *Religion in Life,* Spring 1954, p. 202.

CHAPTER 14.

AUTHORITY: THE ACHILLES' HEEL OF PROTESTANTISM

1. See further the treatment of the authority of Scripture in Chapter 6 above.

2. The authoritative collection of primary sources for the study of Roman Catholicism is H. Denzinger, *Enchiridion Symbolorum, Definitionum et Declarationum de Rebus Fidei et Morum,* Herder, Barcione. A convenient translation of important sections of "Denzinger" is J. F. Clarkson and others, *The Church Teaches,* Herder Book Co. For the attitude toward Biblical studies, see the encyclical of Leo XIII, "Providentissimus Deus," Denzinger para. 1941–53 (cited in Clarkson, pp. 48–52), and the encyclical of Benedict XV, "Spiritus Paraclitus," Denzinger para. 2186–8 (cited in Clarkson, pp. 55–7). A more "open" attitude toward Scripture is indicated in the encyclical of Pius XII, "Divino afflante Spiritu," Denzinger para. 2292–4 (cited in Clarkson, pp. 58–64).

3. Tavard, *Holy Writ or Holy Church,* Harpers, p. 3. This book is the most important basic study of a Roman Catholic–Protestant issue to appear for many years.

4. Denzinger, *op. cit.*, para. 783 (cited in Clarkson, p. 45, italics added).

5. *Ibid.*, para. 786 (cited in Clarkson, p. 46).

6. The story of this council has been told from the Protestant side by MacGregor in *The Vatican Revolution*, Beacon, with annotated bibliography. The story is told from the Roman Catholic side by B. C. Butler, *The Vatican Council*, Longmans, Green. Both books should be read.

The decisions of the Vatican Council widen the breach between Roman Catholicism and the rest of Christendom more decisively than any other events since the Reformation.

7. See the further treatment of this claim in Chapter 2.

8. One of the most famous of these is Salmon, *The Infallibility of the Church*, first issued in 1888. It has recently been abridged and revised by H. F. Woodhouse, and published by John Murray. A Roman Catholic reply to the "abridged Salmon" has been written by B. C. Butler, *The Church and Infallibility*, Sheed & Ward. Jalland, *The Church and the Papacy*, S.P.C.K., is an Anglican treatment. See also Scott, *Romanism and the Gospel*, Westminster.

9. Schaff, *The Creeds of Christendom*, Harpers, Vol. I, p. 186, points out that the view that the rock was Peter's confession was upheld by 44 of the early Fathers, while the present Roman Catholic interpretation of the rock as Peter himself was adopted by only 17 of them. This may not prove as much as it intends to prove, but at least it makes clear that the early church was far from united in its exegesis of the passage.

10. Oscar Cullmann, *Peter*, Westminster, argues from a Protestant perspective that the passage refers to Peter himself, but he sees no basis for assuming that it implies anything about Peter's successors.

11. See Denzinger, *op. cit.*, para. 2331–3 (cited in Clarkson, pp. 212–3).

12. This point is developed in more detail in Brown and Weigel, *op. cit.*, Chapter V.

13. The history of mysticism is too extensive to be treated here, but the writings of Evelyn Underhill and Rufus Jones are reliable treatments of this phenomenon by sensitive interpreters. See particularly Underhill, *Mysticism*, Methuen, and Jones, *Studies in Mystical Religion*, Macmillan.

The emphasis in Friedrich Schleiermacher (1768–1834) on "religious consciousness" and "the feeling of absolute dependence" was a contributing factor to nineteenth-century developments, although Schleiermacher must not be held responsible for the conclusions of his followers. See Schleiermacher, *The Christian Faith*, T. & T. Clark, for the full statement of his mature position, and also his early *Speeches on Religion to Its Cultured Despisers*, Harpers.

The most characteristic nineteenth-century statements on the primacy of religious experience over external authority are found in Sabatier, *Religions of Authority and the Religion of the Spirit*, Doran, and Martineau, *The Seat of Authority in Religion*, Longmans, Green.

14. Temple, *Nature, Man and God*, Macmillan, p. 344.

15. There has been surprisingly little full-scale attention given to the

problem of authority. See P. T. Forsyth, *The Principle of Authority,* Independent Press, and Barth, *Church Dogmatics,* I, 2, especially Chapter 3. Johnson, *Authority in Protestant Theology,* Westminster, is a discussion of the problem from the Reformers to the present.

16. The word "witness" is a key word in the rest of the discussion. A "witness" is one who calls attention to something other than himself, who gives testimony, who is called upon to give or to be evidence of something. The Greek word was *marturos,* from which we get the word "martyr." A martyr was a witness; he was not trying to draw attention to himself, but to witness to his trust in the power of God even over death.

17. Luther, Weimarer Ausgabe, Vol. 39, pp. 47, 19; cited in Pauck, *The Heritage of the Reformation,* Beacon, pp. 114, 304.

CHAPTER 15. PROTESTANTISM AND CULTURE

1. See, for example, Scott, *Modern Literature and the Religious Frontier,* Harpers, and Wilder, *Modern Poetry and the Christian Tradition,* Scribners.

2. See the full treatment of "the return to religion" in Herberg, *Protestant, Catholic, Jew,* Doubleday.

3. For a fuller introduction to Williams's thought, see the introductory essay by Anne Ridler in Williams, *The Image of the City,* Oxford Univ. Press, and the author's "Charles Williams: Lay Theologian," *Theology Today,* July 1953, from which the following comments are largely drawn.

4. Williams, *The Figure of Beatrice,* Faber and Faber, p. 9.

5. *Ibid.,* p. 22.

6. *Ibid.,* pp. 9–10, cf. also *The Descent of the Dove,* Faber and Faber, p. 181.

7. The man who has given most leadership in this task (though he must not be held responsible for the pages that follow) is Paul Tillich, one of the few significant emissaries between Protestantism and culture. See *The Protestant Era,* especially the section on "Religion and Culture," and more recently *Theology of Culture,* Oxford Univ. Press. The most important systematic treatment of the problem is H. R. Niebuhr, *Christ and Culture,* Harpers. See also R. Kroner, *Culture and Faith,* Chicago, and Pelikan, *Fools for Christ,* Muhlenberg.

8. Calvin, *Institutes,* II, ii, 15, 16. H. R. Niebuhr makes some relevant remarks about a Protestant approach to science and scientific investigation:

"Any failure of Christians to develop a scientific knowledge of the world is not an indication of their loyalty to the revealed God but of their unbelief. A genuinely disinterested science may be one of the greatest affirmations of faith and all the greater because it is so unconscious of what it is doing in this way. Resistance to new knowledge about our earthly home and the journey of life is never an indication of faith in the revealed God but almost always an indication that our sense of life's worth rests on the uncertain foundations of confidence in our humanity, our society, or some other evanescent idol." (*The Meaning of Revelation,* p. 173.)

9. The most spirited treatment of this whole problem is Hammond, *Liturgy and Architecture,* Barrie and Rockliff. Although the book is oriented toward the British — and Anglican — situation, it is a helpful introduction for American readers as well. It also contains a lengthy annotated bibliography.

CHAPTER 16.

HOLY WORLDLINESS: THE "HIGHEST" AND THE "HIGH ST."

1. See Vidler, "Holy Worldliness," *Essays in Liberality,* S. C. M. Press, pp. 95–112. Needless to say, Canon Vidler is not to be held responsible for the use that has been made below of his striking phrase.

2. One sees the particular difficulty of doing this today in the churches behind the Iron Curtain. Germans, for example, found in the 1930's that they could not fear God and honor Hitler. Some of those same Germans in the 1960's are trying, in the East Zone, to fear God and honor a Marxist "emperor." Their attempts, both successful and unsuccessful, may one day provide material for a new chapter in the attempt of Christians to learn how to be both in the world and against the world. See Barth-Hamel, *How To Serve God in a Marxist Land,* Association Press, and, on the over-all problem, Gollwitzer, *Die christliche Gemeinde in der politischen Welt,* J. C. B. Mohr, Tübingen. The fullest treatment is West, *Communism and the Theologians,* Westminster.

3. On this problem see Nichols, *Democracy and the Churches,* Westminster; Pauck, *The Heritage of the Reformation,* Chapters 13, 14; Bennett, *Christians and the State,* Chapters X and XI.

4. Protestantism has often allied itself with a single segment of economic society as well as a single segment of political society, and the two interests have frequently become conjoined. In the twentieth century, that segment has been the middle class. There are important relationships between the rise of Protestantism and the rise of western capitalism, although these are more complex than early enthusiasts of the thesis recognized. Some of the basic materials dealing with the problem are Tawney, *Religion and the Rise of Capitalism,* Harcourt, Brace; Weber, *The Protestant Ethic and the Spirit of Capitalism,* Allen and Unwin; Fanfani, *Catholicism, Protestantism and Capitalism,* Sheed & Ward; and Demant, *Religion and the Decline of Capitalism,* Scribners.

5. See Calvin, *Institutes,* Book IV, xx, xxxii.

6. Temple, *Christianity and Social Order,* S. C. M. Press, p. 67.

7. Pauck, *The Heritage of the Reformation,* p. 213.

8. R. Niebuhr, *The Children of Light and the Children of Darkness,* Scribners, p. ix.

9. There will be those who will object to the fact that there has been no treatment of "separation of church and state" as one of the cardinal features of Protestantism. W. E. Garrison has said the appropriate word on this matter:

"It cannot be said that separation between church and state is a general characteristic of Protestantism. In view of the existence of established churches in England, Scotland, the Scandinavian countries, and Germany, it is evident that even in the middle of the twentieth century more Protestants are members of state-connected churches than of free churches. The free-church system can be called characteristically Protestant only in the sense that it is thoroughly consistent with Protestant principles, and that all the communions that practice it with wholehearted approval are Protestant." (*A Protestant Manifesto,* Abingdon, p. 196.)

10. From an unpublished lecture. The incident is reported in G. W. Webber, *God's Colony in Man's World,* Abingdon, p. 93–4, in the context of an urgent plea for Christian responsibility in politics.

11. An excellent treatment of the whole problem of the church's evangelistic mission to the modern world is Maury, *Politics and Evangelism,* Doubleday, drawn in considerable measure from the author's experience as a Christian in the French underground resistance movement in World War II.

12. For a time French Roman Catholicism had a very creative way of meeting this problem. Since the workers would not come to the churches, the priests went to the factories, donned working "togs," and joined unions, participated in the strikes and established close relationships with the workers. It is one of the tragedies of modern Roman Catholicism that this "worker-priest" movement has been killed by official action from Rome. Protestants should acquaint themselves with this movement, for out of the Roman Catholic ashes a method of Protestant evangelism might be able to arise. Dansette, *Destin du catholicisme français 1926–1956,* Flammarion, gives much information.

13. See further, T. Ralph Morton, *The Story of the Iona Community,* Iona, and MacLeod, *We Shall Rebuild,* Iona.

14. G. W. Webber, *God's Colony in Man's World,* Abingdon, cited above, is written out of the East Harlem situation. The comments given do not mean that Protestantism should neglect suburbia or even exurbia, or that the job of relating the gospel to those areas may not be every bit as difficult as that of relating it to the inner-city. The point is simply that the inner-city is a *new* area of Protestant evangelism. Protestantism has been working in the suburbs for decades.

15. The best description is in Southcott, *The Parish Comes Alive,* Morehouse-Gorham, in which the author, an Anglican canon, describes his own experiences in making the house church a reality in his parish. J. A. T. Robinson has a theological discussion in "The House Church and the Parish Church," *Theology,* August 1950, pp. 283–9. See also the April 1957

issue of *Laity*, published by the World Council of Churches, which has four articles on the subject and a fairly full bibliography.

16. Schaff, *Creeds of Christendom*, Harpers, Vol. III, p. 338.

CHAPTER 17. LIVING TENSIONS WITHIN PROTESTANTISM

1. See the discussion of this matter in Chapters 1 and 8 above.

2. See particularly Chapter 5 above. The best over-all treatment of the problem is Heimann, *Freedom and Order*, Scribners.

3. The comments about these groups made in Chapter 3 above are presupposed in the discussion that follows.

4. Signs of a new interest in the doctrine of the Holy Spirit in contemporary Protestant theology are contained in Come, *Human Spirit and Holy Spirit*, Westminster; Hendry, *The Holy Spirit in Christian Theology*, Westminster; and Van Dusen, *Spirit, Son and Father*, Scribners. The doctrine of the Holy Spirit has received increasing attention in the later writings of Karl Barth, particularly in *Church Dogmatics*, IV, 1, 2, 3. The most comprehensive treatment is probably H. W. Robinson, *The Christian Experience of the Holy Spirit*, Harpers.

5. Newbigin, *The Household of God*, Friendship Press, pp. 121–2. See the whole of Chapter 4.

6. See further Outler, *The Christian Tradition and the Unity We Seek*, Oxford Univ. Press, p. 54. This and the next section of the present chapter are particularly indebted to Professor Outler's valuable study.

7. For some vivid examples of this see H. R. Niebuhr, *The Meaning of Revelation*, Macmillan, p. 51. See also my "Tradition as a Protestant Problem," *Theology Today*, January 1961.

8. The danger of the aquatic metaphor we have been exploiting is that it may suggest that each church brings a small portion of the truth and that if enough churches participate in the ecumenical venture the sum total may get pretty close to 100 per cent. Oliver Tomkins makes the appropriate rejoinder:

"No church worthy of the name has ever thought of itself as 'embodying a valuable emphasis.' A living Church is one that believes that it offers, not a fragment of the Christ, but the whole Christ. Yet, paradoxically, the renewal of the Church involves each part of the Church acknowledging that, although it should offer the whole Christ, it does not offer a whole Christ to men because men are not offering a *whole* Church to Christ. The whole Christ is latent in every part of a divided Church, but the whole Christ is only patent in a united Church. The whole is not truly present in every part when the Church is divided, for Christ is not divided and where Christ is, there is the Church." (*The Wholeness of the Church*, S. C. M. Press, p. 54.)

9. See Bell, *The Kingship of Christ,* Penguin, p. 140, for the whole story.

10. Outler, *op. cit.,* pp. 24, 146.

11. Philip Scharper, "What a Catholic Believes," *Harpers,* March 1959, p. 48.

CHAPTER 18. PREFACE: A "PILGRIM PEOPLE"

1. There are considerably more significant accounts of the nature of the Christian pilgrimage than the one that follows. The prototype is John Bunyan's *Pilgrim's Progress,* perhaps the greatest devotional classic Protestant piety has created. C. S. Lewis has described the snares that beset a twentieth-century pilgrim in his clever and profound *Pilgrim's Regress,* Bles. Professor Edmund Schlink deals with the subject theologically in "The Pilgrim People of God," in Tomkins, ed., *The Third World Conference on Faith and Order,* S. C. M. Press, pp. 151–61.

Index of Subjects

Index of Persons

Index of Biblical References